The Rise of Public Woman

The Rise of Public Woman

Woman's Power and
Woman's Place
in the United States,
1630–1970

GLENNA MATTHEWS

OXFORD UNIVERSITY PRESS
New York   Oxford

For David Matthews
Karen Matthews
Maria Matthews
and Monica Matthews

Oxford University Press

Oxford   New York   Toronto
Delhi   Bombay   Calcutta   Madras   Karachi
Kuala Lumpur   Singapore   Hong Kong   Tokyo
Nairobi   Dar es Salaam   Cape Town
Melbourne   Auckland   Madrid

and associated companies in
Berlin   Ibadan

First published in 1992 by Oxford University Press, Inc.,
200 Madison Avenue, New York, New York 10016

First issued as an Oxford University Press paperback, 1994

Oxford is a registered trademark of Oxford University Press

Library of Congress Cataloging-in-Publication Data
Matthews, Glenna.
The rise of public woman :
woman's power and woman's place
in the United States, 1630–1970 /
[Glenna Matthews].
p.   cm.   Includes bibliographical references and index.
ISBN 0-19-505460-1
ISBN 0-19-509045-4 (pbk.)
1. Women in public life—United States—History.
2. Women—United States—Social conditions.
3. Feminism—United States—History.
I. Title.   HQ1391.U5M38   1992   305.42'0973—dc20   91-47518

10 9 8 7 6 5 4 3 2 1

Printed in the United States of America

Preface

This book owes its genesis to Berkeley, the university; and its nurturance to Berkeley, the community, and to the community of scholars in the greater Bay Area. Writing a synthetic work would not have been possible without the ability to draw upon the profusion of intellectual resources in such a locale.

The book came about this way. As a historian, I had not focused particular attention on the problem of how women legitimate a public role. Then I gained the opportunity to teach a course on women and politics because of a young woman's network, that is to say, because Elizabeth Greenberg, a friend of my daughter Karen's and a graduate student in political science at Berkeley, convinced her department chair—unbeknownst to me—to consider hiring me for such a purpose. Initially taken aback, I soon came around and prepared a draft syllabus that favorably impressed members of the department. On the first day of class, I asked the students to think of the difference in connotation between "public man" and "public woman," and together we explored the ramifications of that difference. To Elizabeth, to the

Department of Political Science, and to the superb students in PS 109, I owe an enormous debt of gratitude. Looking at the familiar material of women's history from an unusual angle of vision opened my eyes to themes I had not previously thought about, and my students shared my excitement in the discoveries we were making. Never has a teacher been blessed with a more sympathetic audience.

I worked hard on the syllabus for PS 109, and when I showed it to Sheldon Meyer, my editor at Oxford, he told me that he thought he detected a book in the making. With his encouragement, I set to work. The conversation with Sheldon took place in 1986, and I have been reading for this project ever since. Where there existed a secondary literature, I relied heavily, although not exclusively, on the work of others. Where the literature was thin, I conducted, commensurately, more of my own archival research.

I could, perhaps, amend the famous Will Rogers quote about never meeting a man he didn't like to "I never met a study group I didn't like." In any event, I have been fortunate enough to have been able to turn to many different groups for help with references, for research suggestions, and ultimately for people who would read the manuscript. Members of the Bay Area Seminar on Early American History and Culture gave valuable advice about the early chapters, and members of the Bay Area Labor History Workshop responded with dispatch to my queries about the working-class women's literary tradition. I belong to a women's group composed of public women, most of whom have run for office themselves, and they provided a reality check for my generalizations. Hearty thanks to Berkeley city auditor Anna Rabkin, Berkeley city councilmember Ann Chandler, former Boulder deputy mayor and Carter administration official Karen Paget, disabled-rights activist Judy Heumann, and legislative consultant Dion Aroner. Ranging further afield, I am grateful to the members of the teaching women's history workshop at UCLA. This group meets annually, and over the years I have learned a great deal from its members—as they will discover if they check my footnotes.

When I set out to teach in an unfamiliar area, I turned immediately for help to Ruth Mandel and Susan Carroll at the Center for the American Woman and Politics at Rutgers. They responded with generosity and with enthusiasm. I owe a special thanks to Martin Ridge and to the Huntington Library for a fellowship, which I used while researching the library's splendid collection on women and the Civil War. I would also like to thank Patricia King, Barbara Haber, and the staff at the Schlesinger Library. As usual, their welcome made working at their facility even more of a joy than it might otherwise have been. Patricia Hills and Kevin Whitefield were kind enough to provide hospitality in Cambridge.

Fortunately, I had the chance to give talks based on this research in many different venues. The very first presentation I gave, outside of a classroom, was to the Institute for Historical Study in San Francisco. Chapter 4 originated with a paper at the Irvine Seminar on Social History and Theory. Chapter 6 first appeared in the form of a public lecture at the University of Nevada at Las Vegas and a few months later at California State University, Fullerton. I tried out the ideas in Chapter 9 before an audience at the Southwest Labor Studies Conference in Stockton in 1991. Most exciting of all was the experience of giving talks in several European cities, including Berlin, Stuttgart, and Hamburg, where I met a number of German women politicians.

Those friends who responded with alacrity to my pleas for critiques of the work in progress have placed me forever in their debt. Robin Einhorn, Karen Paget, Alice Wexler, Martha Winnacker, and Linda Witt read the entire manuscript. Dee Andrews, Deborah Gardner, Sherry Katz, Jackie Reinier, and Beverly Voloshin read selected chapters. Needless to say, I am solely responsible for any remaining errors.

One of the major influences on this book—my father, Glen Ingles—did not live to see its completion, but his impact is nonetheless present throughout. As I began my research at the Huntington, during which time I stayed with my parents, my father demanded to know if Sojourner Truth would be in my book. He then located a quote from Abigail Adams for me, a quote I subsequently used. Not bad for a man on the verge of turning ninety. His legacy to me and to my children is that he demonstrated the possibility of lifelong engagement with ideas.

As the book neared completion, my daughter-in-law Maria and my son David became the parents of Monica Noel Matthews, my first grandchild. To them; to my mother, Alberta Ingles; to my daughter Karen Matthews; and to the rest of my family and friends, I give thanks for endlessly listening to me and for much emotional support. In particular, I am grateful to Dan Silin for providing many a neighborly cup of tea to keep me going while I was engaged in the arduous task of writing.

Once again, I thank Sheldon Meyer for being an exemplary editor and Stephanie Sakson-Ford for her care as a copy editor. Working with Oxford University Press is a joy, because the entire staff is so helpful to an author. I would also like to thank Richard Katz for his computer wizardry in linking my 1983-vintage machine to a laser printer, thus sparing the eyesight of those who worked on the manuscript.

I have tried to write a synthesis that would do justice to the multicultural nature of American democracy. To the extent that I have succeeded, much of the credit goes to the classes I met while working on this book. To look out and see the wonderful variety among the students at Irvine as well as at Berkeley is to be inspired to try harder to be inclusive. I am proud of my native state for creating so rich, diverse, and stimulating an environment as that in today's University of California. Moreover, I could dilate at some length about how hard my students worked and how much I learned from them in consequence. Suffice it to say that I will never forget them.

Berkeley, Calif.   G. M.
June 1992

Contents

The Rise of Public Woman

Introduction

It requires philosophy and heroism to rise above the opinion of the wise men of all nations and races that to be *unknown* is the highest testimonial woman can have to her virtue, delicacy, and refinement.

ELIZABETH CADY STANTON ET AL.
History of Woman Suffrage

On the night of December 6, 1895, the police of New York City arrested Lizzie Schauer, a young working-class woman, on a charge of disorderly conduct. She had, according to her own account, been looking for the house of her aunt and had stopped to ask directions of two men. This behavior—as well as the fact that an unaccompanied woman was out at night—was presumptive evidence that she was soliciting prostitution in the eyes of the arresting police officers and of the judge who sent her to the work house. They assumed that no "respectable" woman would be unescorted at night, hence that Schauer was a "public woman," or prostitute. Fortunately for Schauer, the *New York World* undertook a successful crusade to secure her release from the work house—but only after a doctor's examination had shown her to be a "good girl."[1]

This episode provides dramatic evidence of the tenuous nature of American womanhood's claim on public space, even in the late nineteenth century and even after decades of political organizing by women. It further demonstrates the link between public female visibility and

sexuality: to be a public woman—in any of several senses of the term—
was to risk the accusation of sexual impropriety, needless to say, a
strong deterrent to such activity on the part of women. Moreover,
from the time of Anne Hutchinson on, there was a handy epithet to
fasten on a would-be public woman. She was a "Jezebel," after the
wife of Ahab, who exercised an undue influence on her husband,
according to the book of Kings in the Old Testament.[2] Because Jezebel had used her sexuality to entice her husband into forsaking Jehovah and then into killing Jehovah's priests, the term became a byword
for a wicked and/or unclean woman whose sexuality constituted a threat
to the well-being of the community.

If we think about the terms "public man" and "public woman,"
we soon realize that the two have had very different connotations in
Western culture. While "public woman" was an epithet for one who
was seen as the dregs of society, vile, unclean, a public man was "one
who acts in and for the universal good."[3] In other words, "public
woman" in a positive sense was literally inconceivable, because there
was no language to describe so anomalous a creature, yet "public man"
represented a highly valued ideal. An emerging feminist political theory deals with the roots of the dichotomy, going back to the Greeks
and their exclusion of women from the polis.[4] It is well known that
women have largely been confined to the private world of home and
family, while men have functioned in the world outside the home.
Even in societies where women have played a role in market activities
outside the home they have been excluded from a role in the polity—
except for the relatively rare instance of an occasional queen. Rare,
also, has been the public space to which men and women have had
access on the same terms. Men have been free to travel where and
when they desired (unless they had the status of serf or slave), while
women frequently risked their reputations if they attempted to do the
same.

Especially serious for women has been the injunction contained
in St. Paul's letter to the Corinthians: "Let your women keep silence
in the churches: for it is not permitted unto them to speak; but *they
are commanded* to be under obedience, as also saith the law. And if

they will learn any thing, let them ask their husbands at home."[5] In the chapters to come, we shall encounter repeated instances of women who felt they had to answer St. Paul before they could speak in public.

In her brilliant work *The Creation of Patriarchy*, Gerda Lerner discusses the artificial division of women into "respectable" and "not respectable" thousands of years ago under Middle Assyrian law—the necessary first step in the process by which "public woman" became either an oxymoron or an epithet. "Class for men was and is based on their relationship to the means of production: those who owned the means of production could dominate those who did not. For women, class is mediated through their sexual ties to a man, who then gives them access to material resources."[6] A "respectable" woman under Middle Assyrian Law sexually served one man, was under his protection, and wore a veil to demonstrate her status and her confinement to the domestic realm. ". . . [W]omen not under one man's protection and sexual control are designated as 'public women,' hence unveiled."[7] Lerner tells us that the law provided savage punishment for a harlot who wore the veil and tried to pass herself off as respectable. Conversely, to go without the veil was to forfeit one's status as a respectable woman.

The separation of women into respectable and not respectable and the subsequent equating of not respectable with public thus has a long history. I have chosen to write about one aspect of that history, the experience of women in the United States from the colonial period to the emergence of modern feminism. Given the invidious cast to the term "public woman," how have American women envisioned themselves as public actors, how legitimated a public role? I would not claim that there is any one period when "public woman" definitively achieved a positive connotation, nor for that matter do I think that at the current time we see real symmetry between public men and public women. What I do think is this: cumulatively, the actions of many courageous pioneers have served to open up new possibilities for public women, both in the real world and in the realm of the imagination.

It must be immediately acknowledged that there is no single

American experience of public womanhood, but rather a multiplicity of experiences based on differences of race, class, region, religion, and ethnicity. The Protestant road to public activity for women, for example, has been different from either the Catholic or Jewish roads. Among Native Americans, women traditionally enjoyed a level of public activity, even political participation, unsurpassed by any other group of American women until recent times.[8] Working-class women have arguably been less constrained by decorous norms of behavior than middle-class women. And so on. Nonetheless, I believe that there are enough commonalities to make possible a synthetic overview; no matter what the group, gender roles have never been fully symmetrical.

Webster's Dictionary defines "public" in this way: "Of or pertaining to the people; relating to, belonging to, or affecting a nation, state, or community at large;—opposed to *private*." When we apply "public" to the roles of women, we can discern at least four possible uses of the word, analytically distinct but often overlapping in the real world: public in the legal, political, spatial, and cultural sense. In each of these areas, American women have suffered from serious liabilities.

In the first sense, the Anglo-American common-law tradition made a married woman legally invisible, her identity subsumed under that of her husband. Only if she obtained "feme sole" status could she control property or dispose of her own income. She could not serve on a jury. Her ability to write a will was severely circumscribed. Thus even if she could be considered a "public woman" owing to her participation in market activities, she lacked the same legal means for protecting her interests as those of a man of an equivalent social station.[9]

In the second sense, the political, we know that women in the United States lacked the guarantee of a fundamental right of democratic citizenship, the franchise, until 1920. Nor could they run for public office. As we shall learn, the lack of these rights did not prevent them from developing a political culture in the nineteenth century. Nonetheless, the disfranchisement of women can be understood as concrete proof of the anomalous status of the concept of public woman. Indeed, evidence exists to link public woman in the political sense with sexual impropriety. For example, Linda Kerber has uncovered a letter from the early Republic in which a woman said that she did not want to be a citizenness, because to be a citizenness meant to be considered as a woman of the town.[10]

In the third sense, the spatial, or social geographic, evidence abounds to demonstrate how restricted women have been in their public access—as witness, the case of Lizzie Schauer. Much public space has been either proscribed to women, at least to respectable women, or sexually segregated. In the ensuing chapters, I shall examine the topic of the social geography of gender with some care. When could a woman alone employ public transportation with impunity? When could women work side by side with men in offices without scandal? These are important breakthroughs. (For that matter, it is still the case that an unescorted woman risks being the target of sexual epithets.) For now, a single example will suffice to illustrate the dilemma created for a woman, in this instance a middle-class woman unlike Lizzie Schauer, by the lack of access. In June 1907 the noted feminist Harriet Stanton Blatch was refused service at a New York restaurant because she was unescorted by a man. The manager explained to her that the policy had been instituted to protect "respectable" women.[11]

Finally, there is the issue of public access in a cultural sense— which often has a geographical dimension. One can enumerate many manifestations of limited female access in this realm. There were no women on the English-speaking stage at all until 1660, for example, and it would be well into the nineteenth century before an actress could be received in polite female society in the United States, in other words, could expect to be treated as a respectable woman.[12] It was virtually unheard-of for women outside the Quaker community to give public speeches until the antebellum period, and then only the bravest attempted this feat. Indeed, the taboo was so strong that a man chaired the famous meeting at Seneca Falls in 1848.[13] When women began to publish, they frequently hid behind a pseudonym, sometimes a male one, so that they would not render themselves vulnerable to charges of immodesty or impropriety. They had reason to be cautious. In 1830, for example, Nathaniel Hawthorne denounced contemporary women writers for exposing their "naked minds" to public scrutiny.[14] Finally, as Mary Ryan has shown in her recent book *Women in Public*, women played little role in public civic rituals until the late nineteenth century.[15]

Thus the struggle by American women for political rights, for full integration into political life, must be seen as part of a larger process of gaining public access more generally. Moreover, the process of gaining public access, while anchored to changing material conditions, as will be argued subsequently, is inexplicable apart from its cultural dimension. This assertion rests on the fact that women began their demands for public access and political rights *before* they enjoyed economic independence and controlled property in their own names. Indeed, as Nancy Cott points out in *The Grounding of Modern Feminism*, the achievement of woman suffrage was a "conceptual anomaly" because traditional explanations had "predicated the vote on having an independent stake in society"—which the law did not fully grant married women even as late as 1920.[16] Therefore, only full attention to such topics as the means by which women gained a public voice with which to combat traditionally patriarchal political discourse—indeed, to change the terms of the discourse—can make possible an understanding of the rise of public woman.

What makes the case of women so striking, moreover, is the fact that they are the only group which has had to struggle for political rights in a context which not only denied them the franchise but also denied them the right publicly to advocate for it. For example, in the antebellum North, Frederick Douglass, ex-slave, became a forceful abolitionist orator. While the substance of his speeches might be controversial, no one said that as a black or a former slave he had no right to stand in front of an audience. Yet his exact contemporary Angelina Grimké met this type of charge when she began publicly to oppose slavery and, after criticism of her temerity, to advocate women's rights.

It is time to sketch briefly the compass and the argument of the book to come. I shall begin in the seventeenth century by examining the public role of women in several different traditions. The major focus of attention, however, will fall on two groups whose legacy was especially consequential for white and black American women: the Puritans and the Quakers.

It is my contention that these two religious traditions helped create and valorize a plane of subjectivity upon which men and women could meet as equals. Contemporaneous with the growth of these denominations were the spread of literacy and the diffusion of books, both of which encouraged privacy and introspection. I will argue that, paradoxically, the valorization of private life was a necessary step before women could begin to define their own identities, hence conceive of themselves as public actors, in defiance of societal taboos, and develop the self-confidence to seek and obtain a public voice.

I will then go on to explore a variety of changes in the eighteenth century that were conducive of greater female autonomy, such as new patterns of land tenure, the emergence of new norms of family life, and the possibility for independent female choice in the realm of religion that had been opened up by the Great Awakening. Because the American Revolution was so consequential for women, as demonstrated by the work of Linda Kerber and Mary Beth Norton,[17] I will devote a chapter to the subject of women and republicanism. Another important development of these years was the dawning public activity of black women, beginning in the 1770s with the published work of Phillis Wheatley—thereby beginning the articulation of what Hazel Carby calls a discourse of black womanhood[18]—and the creation of the first black women's voluntary organizations in the 1790s.[19] Finally a chapter on the emergence of the novel will explore the ways in which women were able to use the power of the word to legitimate a public role.

When we reach the nineteenth century, we will encounter a full-blown women's politics, as well as marked changes in the social geography of gender, and the beginnings of reform in married women's property laws. For the first two-thirds of the century, the flowering of public womanhood was both grounded in and constrained by domesticity, as has been demonstrated by the pioneering work of Nancy Cott,

Kathryn Kish Sklar, and others.[20] I will devote a chapter to the period in which this domestically based politics enjoyed perhaps its fullest expression—the Civil War years.

I will argue that the late nineteenth century then constituted a watershed, because by this time there began to be a substantial number of women who were gainfully employed outside the home. Not only that, but there was also a growing number of women who earned enough to live outside the confines of a family, if only by scraping together their resources as best they could.[21] Therefore, for the first time a woman's politics could be predicated on a basis other than domesticity. And where earlier in the century middle-class white women had usually, if not invariably, been the most outspoken public advocates of change, in the Gilded Age, working-class women began to come into their own, as, for example, the career of Emma Goldman will attest.

Goldman is a pivotal figure, because she was a public woman in every positive sense of the term, speaking, writing, and acting in the world, while showing herself little bound by conventional norms of appropriate female behavior. Where earlier women reformers had almost invariably been careful to protect their reputations from any charge of sexual misconduct, Goldman lived her life as she chose and paid little heed to such considerations.[22] Thus her life and career constitute a benchmark in establishing the possibilities for public women, in divorcing a woman's sexual conduct from her public influence.

Chapters dealing with the twentieth century will address such topics as the role of women in unions, the vast contribution of black women to the civil rights movement as well as the activities of other women of color, and the emergence of modern feminism. I will conclude with the Women's Strike for Equality on August 26, 1970, the fiftieth anniversary of suffrage. On that day there took place the largest demonstration by women in American history, thereby launching a new epoch in the history of public women.[23]

I want to make clear at the outset that I do not define every instance of public outspokenness by women as proto-feminist. As is well known, there is a long history of women organizing *against* feminist goals, from the women's anti-suffrage leagues of the early twentieth century to Phyllis Schlafly's Stop-ERA of the recent past. I would entirely concur with the definition of feminism offered by Linda Gordon: "Feminism is a critique of male supremacy, formed and offered in the light of a will to change it, which in turn assumes a conviction that it is changeable." Quoting this, Nancy Cott goes on to say that she likes this definition, because "[i]t does not posit that what women do of a public or civic character is in itself feminist unless a challenge to male domination is present."[24] Again, I would concur. But feminism could never have been formulated until a wide array of women had felt some security in staking out their claims to a variety of public roles. An actress's ability to be received in polite society does not have the same weight in the history of feminism as the Seneca Falls conference, but the two are surely related.

I earlier wrote a book, *"Just a Housewife": The Rise and Fall of Domesticity in the United States,* based on the conviction that history has something important to teach us about the means by which women can liberate themselves into fuller and more gratifying lives without sacrificing the very real benefits of nurturant homes.[25] In other words, I was wrestling with the relationship between the home and the world and the way history illuminates this topic. I continue to be fascinated by it. In my opinion, as valuable as public access for women is, such access is only part of the solution to a better and more just world for all people. If we lack adequate provision for a nonexploitative private sphere, we will still fall short. As I did the research for this book, I became increasingly convinced that we still lack not only the practical means for reconciling justice for women and provision for the private sphere—as witness the failure of American public policy to deal with family leave, for example—but also a vision, a political theory, that gives more than superficial attention to the maintenance of private life. Thus, while this is a book about women and politics, it is also about the relationship between private and public, the personal and the political, the home and the world. I would like to contribute to what I deem to be an essential discourse.

Woman's Power and Woman's Place in Seventeenth-Century America

To consider the role of women among the indigenous peoples of North America is to be reminded that history does not move in only one direction. An account of public women in the United States that begins with the experience of Native Americans is about losses as well as gains. Before the coming of the European invaders, native peoples in what would become the United States constituted twelve major language groups as well as an estimated two thousand smaller groupings. Because it is clearly impossible in a general study to explore the variety of gender roles among so great a number of discrete tribes, the strategy will be to single out two tribes whose gender roles have been well studied, the Iroquois and the Cherokees. As it happens, the women of both tribes enjoyed public roles and a public influence that exceeded anything that would be seen among the Anglo-Americans for centuries to come.

The Iroquois, the most powerful tribal group in the Northeast, granted political power to women in two different ways. In the first place, "[p]olitical authority in the villages derived from the *ohwa-*

13

chiras at whose heads were senior women of the community. It was these women who named the men representing the clans at village and tribal councils and who named the forty-nine sachems or chiefs who met periodically at Onondaga as the the ruling council for the confederated Five Nations."[1] Moreover, when individual clans met, the women caucused separately and had a kind of veto power over decisions. They also possessed a de facto veto of military expeditions, because they could decide to withhold such necessary military supplies as moccasins and food.[2]

An observer in the early eighteenth century, a Jesuit priest, had this to say about the Iroquois women:

> Nothing, however, is more real than this superiority of the women. It is of them that the nation really consists; and it is through them that the nobility of the blood, the genealogical tree and the families are perpetuated. All real authority is vested in them. The land, the fields and their harvest all belong to them. They are the souls of the councils, the arbiters of peace and of war.[3]

As the Iroquois lost their territory and their capacity to maintain their cultural integrity, such customs were lost, too.

Among the Cherokees, who were located in the Southeast, an especially striking trait was the sexual freedom enjoyed by married women. An eighteenth-century observer wrote, "The Cherokees are an exception to all civilized or savage nations in having no laws against adultery; they have been a considerable while under a petticoat government, and allow their women full liberty to plant their brows with horns as oft as they please, without fear of punishment."[4] Thus the link between sexual impropriety and public influence, ubiquitous in European culture, could not be forged, inasmuch as women were not separated into the categories of respectable and not respectable in the same way. An article by Theda Perdue elaborates some of the consequences of this situation: "Traditionally, women had a voice in Cherokee government. They spoke freely in council, and the War Woman (or Beloved Woman) decided the fate of captives. As late as 1787, a

Cherokee woman wrote Benjamin Franklin that she had delivered an address to her people urging them to maintain peace with the new American nation."[5] Over time, Cherokee women lost their influence, because male tribal leaders thought—wrongly—they could protect the tribe's interests by assimilating to white customs. Only in the 1980s with the election of Wilma Mankiller as the chief of the Cherokees has there been a reassertion of the traditional power of women among this group.

It is important to begin with these Amerindian alternatives to Western culture because they are reminders of the extent to which the exclusion of women from public influence among Europeans—which seemed both natural and God-given to the invaders—was, in fact, socially constructed. Moreover, we must realize that the first chapter in the history of public woman in the United States was a story of declension.

As the English arrived in the New World in the first half of the seventeenth century, they brought with them family forms and religious beliefs from the Old World, both of which soon began to change under the impact of new demographic and economic circumstances. Among the Puritans of New England, patterns of land tenure, the relatively long life spans of first-generation males, and their religious tenets all served to create an especially patriarchal pattern of authority in which women played virtually no public role. Moreover, the common-law doctrine of coverture for married women operated with particular vigor in this region.[6]

The father was the unquestioned head of the Puritan household, to whom both his wife and children owed obedience; toward his wife he had the reciprocal, if not symmetrical, obligation to show consideration. Fond marriages there undoubtedly were among the Puritans—as the love poetry of Anne Bradstreet will attest—but they were based on a subordinate-superordinate relationship between wife and husband, rather than the companionate norms that would come into being in a later period. Moreover, as Edmund Morgan showed in his pioneering book on the Puritan family fifty years ago, living outside the boundary of family life would have been impossible for a good

Puritan.[7] Everyone, including apprentices and household help, was under the authority of the father of the particular household. And the polity was made up of households, not individuals.[8]

At first glance, Puritan religious beliefs seem to be quite inhospitable to the claims of women. The Puritans of New England, who sought to redeem the established church in England by building their holy City on a Hill in the New World, were among the most rigorous Calvinists in human history, and Calvinists were especially likely to depict God the Father as a figure of stern authority. As the Protestant Reformation downgraded the importance of human effort and good works in favor of faith and God's grace relative to Catholic theology, so then did Calvinism go even further in this direction than had Martin Luther or the founders of the Anglican Church. John Calvin contended that God had foreordained a few to be saved and the rest to be eternally damned. There was nothing that a sinning human could do to change this awful fate. All he or she could do was to pray for the grace to live life as a "visible saint." Should the sinner be enabled so to live, there might be the hope of redemption and the terrible anxiety attendant on this system of belief might be somewhat allayed—but not permanently relieved. There was little room for a "female principle" embodying tenderness or mercy in Calvinism—except insofar as grace visited the elect. Such had been banished along with the female saints of Roman Catholicism. God was a stern and fair Being—Puritans believed that they could rely on grace because He had actually granted mankind a covenant of grace—whose earthly authority was represented by the authority of an all-male clergy and by the father of each household.[9]

In terms of church governance, too, women played little or no role except on rare and anomalous occasions. Puritanism evolved into Congregationalism, an established religion in most of New England until the nineteenth century. Women played no public role at either the level of the congregation, where such weighty matters as choosing a minister took place, or at higher levels.

The law reinforced these patterns. "Patriarchal authority in the Puritan family ultimately rested on the father's control of landed property or craft skills," [10] a control fully supported by statute and custom. Moreover, Puritan fathers were permitted wide discretion in how they could will property—in other words, the law provided for partible inheritance—and this meant that his heirs had strong incentives to heed the father's wishes.

Marylynn Salmon, the leading scholar of colonial women and the law, asserts unequivocally: "New Englanders gave male heads of household more control over family property, including what wives inherited or earned, than was common elsewhere." [11] There were several reasons for this, the most important being the Puritans' Utopian aspirations. Ideologues, they were consequently willing to be innovators and to revise English common law to conform more closely to their patriarchal ideals. For example, the law in Connecticut and Massachusetts assumed that families would be loving, so it reduced a wife's chances of protecting her own individual interests by eliminating the requirement that she must express public approval of a conveyance of property before such a conveyance could take place. [12] When we recall the propensity for men to live to old age, we can see that the necessary ingredients to create a powerful patriarch were in place in New England.

In certain circumstances, such as the absence or prolonged illness of her husband, a wife could act as his deputy with a fair amount of autonomy. Surviving records tell of wives who supervised complicated business transactions, who oversaw the planting of crops, who acted as attorneys for absent husbands. But ultimately they were accountable to those absent husbands for their decisions, and thus the overall system of coverture remained intact. [13]

The work of Carol Karlsen is telling about the penalties which could be visited on those women who "stood in the way of the orderly transmission of property from one generation of males to another." [14] Her research suggests that the most important single risk factor for a woman in accusations of witchcraft in late seventeenth-century New England was to be a widow without sons or brothers. Should such an individual go to court to protect her property interests, she took the chance of being accused of consorting with the Evil One. Indeed,

Karlsen contends that it was "the fear of independent women that lay at the heart of New England's nightmare."[15] And yet, as we shall be learning, it was in this seemingly inhospitable soil that seeds took root that would grow into a woman's movement.

That the Quakers who settled Pennsylvania in the late seventeenth century would also provide many woman's movement leaders is more immediately comprehensible. Their creed placed so much emphasis on the "Inner Light"—which might be cultivated in both men and women—as the vehicle for truth and salvation that it gave women a kind of authority both in the family and even in the outside world. Indeed, a recent scholar of the Quaker family argues that the Friends' very survival in the absence of a church hierarchy depended on empowering women.[16]

As an instance in point, we have a remarkable account of a Quaker marriage, a document that provides evidence of at least one Quaker husband's profound respect for his wife's judgment. John Bevan was born in England in 1646 and married Barbara Awbray in 1665. Converting to Quakerism earlier than his wife, he argued unsuccessfully with her about religion until an episode involving her Anglican minister precipitated her conversion to Quakerism. One day in church the minister denounced her husband for his apostasy. "She went to the priest and spoke somewhat home to him, and that she thought she deserved more civility," John later recalled.[17] After her conversion, she became so ardent a believer that she talked her husband, initially resistant to the idea, into following Penn to the New World, where they stayed for more than thirty years. She believed this move would benefit their children. Says Margaret Bacon, a scholar of Quaker women: "The Bevans' story illustrates the central position the early Friends gave both to childraising and to the role of women in family decision-making."[18]

Barbara Awbray Bevan, a woman who had the courage to speak "somewhat home" to her Anglican minister and the forcefulness of personality to talk her husband into a transatlantic relocation, was the mother of Barbara Bevan, who became a minister at the age of sixteen, one of many woman preachers among the Quakers. Thus Quaker women comprised the first sizable group of public women in what would become the United States—other than the women of certain tribes like the Iroquois and the Cherokees. Quaker women spoke at meetings and, what is more, they traveled extensively as preachers, sometimes in the company of other women and sometimes with men not their husbands. Along the way they encountered difficulties, and even death, with fortitude. So important was this activity in the eyes of the Friends that the Society raised money to support both male and female itinerants.

From the earliest decades of the Society of Friends in England in the mid-seventeenth century, women had played a remarkable role. When they were touched by revelation, by the Divine Light, they were empowered to "speak truth to kings," as well as priests. Known as "Mothers of Israel," such women became legendary for their courage and for the range of their activities. Consider, for example, Elizabeth Hooton. "Elizabeth Hooton was active buying and selling property, distributing charity, and advocating prison reform, during the same period that she was admonishing the English king and the magistrates of Boston and (aged at least sixty) was stripped to the waist, tied to a cart, and whipped out of town and into the wilderness at least three different times because she kept coming back to preach."[19] Of the first 59 "publishers of the truth" who came to America between 1656 and 1663, 26 were women.[20] As we shall be learning, Quaker women maintained their preaching into the nineteenth century (and beyond) when they would provide some of the most important women's movement leaders such as Lucretia Mott and Susan B. Anthony.

In addition to the role of women preachers, the Society of Friends provided another forum for the blossoming of public womanhood: women held separate meetings. Mary Maples Dunn has discovered records documenting "vigorous decision-making" in these meetings virtually from their beginnings in 1681.[21] Moreover, in the New World—unlike England—women had more or less the same space for their meetings as did men, another indication of the importance granted them.

Yet even among Quakers, a married woman had little legal pro-

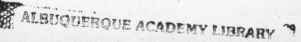

tection for the right to be an independent actor, in part because the Quakers, like the Puritans, had such high expectations of their ability to create loving and united families. For example, as in New England, Pennsylvania law did not require that a wife be separately questioned about the conveyance of property, a departure from English common law.[22] There were, however, some areas in which Pennsylvania wives were better off than those in New England, such as in the law governing feme sole trading. In 1718 the General Assembly of Pennsylvania gave wives of mariners or deserted wives the right to operate businesses in their own names,[23] a provision considerably more liberal than any in New England for some time to come. Thus, more flexible gender norms among Quakers evidently had a certain impact on the omnipresent system of legal coverture as it functioned in Pennsylvania—although it may be conceded that this reform could well have been motivated by the desire to avoid providing poor relief for destitute wives.

The Chesapeake and the area further south saw the development of a third set of regional gender norms, less patriarchal than those in New England—at first men did not live long enough to be effective patriarchs—but not so egalitarian as those influenced by the Quakers. Many scholars have documented the extent to which disease and early death rendered seventeenth-century family life in the Chesapeake chaotic. Indeed, Edmund Morgan suggests that for the first several decades an individual's chances of surviving five years after arrival—no matter what his or her age might be—were only fifty-fifty.[24] This extraordinary death rate made "the orderly transmission of property from one generation of males to another" difficult if not impossible to achieve. In short, as in the case of war, tragedy opened up opportunities for women.

In her pioneering study of women in the colonial South, Julia Cherry Spruill discussed a number of women who played prominent public roles in the area. For example, at the time of Bacon's Rebellion in Virginia in the 1670s Sarah Drummond gave "fiery speeches" on behalf of the rebels, denouncing Governor Berkeley and urging strong action.[25] She was not alone as other women took public action on both sides of the controversy. But the best-known woman in the colonial South was Margaret Brent of Maryland, a single woman who became one of the leading personages in the colony in the seventeenth century. Arriving from England in the New World in 1638 with her brothers and sister, she soon began to take vigorous legal action to protect the family's substantial landed property. Indeed, Spruill found that her name appeared 134 times in court records between 1642 and 1650, because she was often prosecuting her debtors. So successful was she in handling her own and her family's affairs that she frequently received the power of attorney for others. The culmination of her career as a public woman came in 1647 when Governor Calvert died, having appointed her to be his executrix, and she claimed the right to vote in the assembly—unsuccessfully it should be noted.[26]

If Spruill found a relatively substantial number of prominent upper-class women in the colonial South, the context for this discovery is illuminated by Salmon's work on colonial property law. High death rates undermined patriarchal property dispositions, and southern law perforce took recognition of this phenomenon; with husbands subject to such harsh demographic circumstances, it was impossible that wives be excluded from the transfer of property to the extent that they were in New England. Moreover, southern law was not based on the same high ideals of unified family life as obtained further north. In consequence, "[t]raditional safeguards against male coercion found strong support in the South."[27] When men started living longer, patriarchal patterns became stronger, peaking in the early eighteenth century.[28]

The dominant religion in the southern colonies, except for Catholic Maryland, was the Church of England, less stern than the Calvinism of New England but no more propitious to public activity by women. Governed by an all-male hierarchy of English bishops under the ultimate authority of the Archbishop of Canterbury and the monarch, the Anglican Church thus reproduced the most negative aspect of Roman Catholicism—insofar as women were concerned—the elaborate male hierarchy, but without such mitigating features as female saints or an elevated status for the Virgin Mary. In the early eighteenth century an observer noted that the gentlemen entered a particular Anglican church in Virginia in a body and left the same way, with the women and lower-status men waiting for this exit to occur before they made their own departure.[29] In other words, the rules governing conduct in church reflected upper-class male privilege even in seemingly trivial matters.

Despite regional differences, there were many commonalities of gendered behavior among the colonies, especially in the realm of social geography. The population was overwhelmingly rural, and that dictated that men and women work in close proximity, even if they were working at different tasks. Laurel Thatcher Ulrich reminds us that coverture was a legal fiction, not a social fact, because "in the small communities of seventeenth- and eighteenth-century America, women were everywhere, in gardens and fields, kitchens and taverns, on horseback and in canoes, in stagecoaches and at ferry crossings, in church pews and at the front lines of armies."[30] In other words, there was relatively little public space from which women were formally excluded as there would be after industrialization moved most male work to a separate sphere.

Yet before we see the transition away from rural life exclusively in terms of a loss of freedom for women, we should remind ourselves of the circumstances by which women moved through public space in the colonial period: except for Quaker women, they were inevitably under direct male authority. Rather than acting on behalf of their own interests, they were acting to advance the interests of their families. Thus in a sense, they, too, were "wearing a veil" that protected them from charges of impropriety; occupying public space, they were rarely autonomous public actors.

Another commonality lay in the exclusion of women from a role in the polity throughout the American colonies. Much has been written about the broadening of the franchise among men in the New World owing to the larger percentage of them who owned property here. At the same time, representative government grew and flourished in the colonial legislatures—until such time as those legislatures saw fit to challenge the authority of Parliament. Many New England men also participated in political decision-making through their attendance at the famous town meetings. In all of this Americans were forging a new concept, "democratic citizen" rather than "monarchical subject," but the concept did not apply to women.[31]

There was one method of exerting social power that was everywhere available to women, however, and that was the power of the word, or gossip. As obnoxious as the division of women into the categories "respectable" and "not respectable" may be to modern sensibilities, it is incontestably true that in the past women themselves enforced this standard, and that their capacity to rule on other women's sexual reputations gave them power. (Indeed, generations of historians contended that Martin Van Buren owed his elevation to the role of Andrew Jackson's chosen successor to the Peggy Eaton affair. Wives of Cabinet members and Mrs. John C. Calhoun, wife of the vice president, thought that Mrs. Eaton, wife of Secretary of War John Eaton and special favorite of the President, was no better than she should be. They refused to entertain her, and the bachelor Van Buren emerged victorious, according to this interpretation.)[32]

Mary Beth Norton has studied a sample of two thousand civil cases in seventeenth-century Maryland and has discovered that women, only one-fourth to one-third of the population at the time, appeared in slightly more than half of the defamation cases. She explains this phenomenon as follows: "For men, gossip was an available option; for women it was an essential tool, perhaps the most valuable and reliable means of advancing or protecting their own interests."[33] Women's prominence in these cases is especially noteworthy because, under the usual English legal practice of the day, married women were not supposed to appear by and for themselves in court. Yet in Maryland they did, publicly attacking one another's sexual behavior and publicly defending themselves from such charges. Norton makes the further point that a woman's sexual behavior was virtually the only area of conduct in which she could be held personally responsible, so thoroughgoing was the legal assumption of dependence on husbands in every other aspect of life.[34]

Gossip—words as power: this points us toward understanding the means by which women outside the Quaker community began to legitimate public, and eventually political, roles. Feminist theory has elaborated the concept of patriarchal discourse: words used to reinforce the status quo, words used to denigrate the subjectivity of the powerless female Other, words used in such a way as to foreclose the possibility of imagining alternative social arrangements. When women gained the capacity to explore, define, and ultimately to validate their own subjectivity, they were on their way toward undermining patriarchal discourse, because they were gaining the power of self-representation. And for all its sternness, it was Calvinism that provided the best opening for this, because it so promoted introspection and so privileged subjectivity. Moreover, when women began to give public accounts of their conversion experiences, as they were allowed to do, this created an unprecedented link between private female experience and the public world.

Let us examine how the valorization of female subjectivity operated in New England. Two aspects of seventeenth-century Calvinism must receive special attention as we try to understand how so patriarchal a belief system gave birth to so many remarkable public women from Anne Hutchinson to Mercy Otis Warren to Harriet Beecher Stowe. In the first place, the importance placed on God's grace meant that the Puritans soon developed what has been called a "morphology of grace." Inasmuch as no one could ever know with certainty whether he or she was among the elect, Puritans learned to scrutinize themselves and to analyze their experiences minutely, looking for hopeful indications that grace had been granted to them. For many years church membership, which carried with it status and worldly privilege as well as spiritual benefit, was limited to those who could give a convincing account of conversion and of the seeming accession of grace. Thus, Puritans had every reason to look inside themselves and to become fluent at self-analysis. Fortunately for scholars, in some instances, written accounts of their conversion experiences have survived.

Patricia Caldwell examined 51 such narratives, 22 clearly belonging to women, recorded by the minister Thomas Shepard in Cambridge between 1637 and 1645. She explains that she wanted "to locate some of the first faint murmurings of a truly American voice, emerging from little-known, ordinary people in community who, during a few decades in our history, tried to act on the idea that their lives were worth writing—or talking—about. Their minds saturated with the Bible, [they struggled] to express in an unfamiliar public arena their most vital and private religious concerns. . . ."[35] Worth noting is the fact that the Cambridge Platform of 1648 described these narratives as "personall and publick," making the very linkage that would prove to be so consequential for women.

For our purposes the most striking aspect of the narratives is the fact that—despite the misgivings of certain ministers—those women who gave their testimony to the whole congregation were in effect defying the Pauline injunction against women speaking in church. And Caldwell found solid evidence that this, indeed, happened in several churches. At other times, elders of the church would read the narratives of those, especially women, who felt timid about doing it on their own behalf.[36]

Given to self-scrutiny, confident that the results of such scrutiny were of profound interest and importance to other members of the community, Puritan women and men were constructing what can be called a plane of subjectivity that was a new phenomenon in Western culture. In the classical period public and private life had been highly differentiated, but the public sphere was accorded all the prestige. In medieval Europe private and public had been less sharply differentiated, so private life lacked much of a distinctive character. What is more, most people did not have the material resources to cultivate a rich private life. Not until the early modern period did material realities and value systems such as Quakerism or Calvinism coalesce in such a way as to permit the flowering of private life.[37] At this stage, new possibilities for dignity emerged among creatures who were largely assigned to the private sphere, that is, women.

The second way in which Puritanism valorized subjectivity, and hence proved beneficial to women, lay in its promotion of reading and, consequently, of literacy. In his *Worlds of Wonder* David Hall contends that reading the Bible was so highly valued that the ability to read was nearly universal among seventeenth-century Puritans, men and women both—although writing would not be similarly universal for another one hundred years.[38] Moreover, the act of reading was not supposed to be passive; the clergy counseled their flocks to ruminate as they read. "The import of this advice was always to transform reading into action."[39] In consequence, although these dwellers in a wilderness were unable to read widely, they read deeply, not only the Bible but also the lives of holy men and women, thereby schooling themselves to speak fluently about their own spiritual experiences. In other words, reading gave people the language for the new discourse of subjectivity. And in a society where the physical arrangements for privacy were difficult or impossible to achieve owing to small houses and large households, reading was perhaps the only means of achieving it.

Especially noteworthy is the fact that some evidence suggests that mothers in the household were the ones who taught children of both sexes to read. Making this point, Hall quotes John Paine, who, in 1704, wrote in his journal after his mother died:

> Careful mother eke She was
> unto her Children all
> teaching them gods word to read
> when as they were but Small.[40]

The empowering of women through the valorization of subjectivity was not merely a tendency with long-term consequences but also a phenomenon which produced two extraordinary public women in the first generation of settlement in Massachusetts—Anne Hutchinson and Anne Bradstreet. Both married to men of substance, both mothers of large families, the two women had very different fates, one banished into the wilderness, the other living out her life as a respected member of her community. For our purposes their most important commonality was a willingness to transcend the conventional definition of a woman's role: they entered the public arena to advance their own ideas and not merely to serve as deputy husbands.

Anne Hutchinson was born in England about 1590, the daughter of a Lincolnshire clergyman and his wife. She arrived in Boston with her merchant husband in 1634, joined the church, and almost immediately began to attract attention by holding meetings for the women of the church at which she criticized most of the clergy for subscribing to a covenant of works rather than one based on grace. Her religious stance was predicated on a kind of radical subjectivity, which exalted the indwelling of the Holy Spirit in every believer and consequently downgraded the role of the clergy in leading the faithful to an understanding of God's truth. Not surprisingly, her ideas proved controversial, especially when men as well as women began to listen to her in "promiscuous" meetings. Her many partisans, men and women both and some quite prominent, were as devoted as her even more numerous critics were disapproving. Soon the dispute, known to history as the Antinomian controversy after the name of Hutchinson's heresy, had become the leading public issue of the day, affecting such disparate matters as the levy of troops to fight the Pequots and the distribution of town lots. Remarkably, a woman precipitated the first political crisis of the new colony within less than ten years of its founding in 1630.

Despite the mounting air of crisis, Hutchinson persisted in her activities. At one point when the minister who was the particular object of her disapproval, John Wilson, rose to preach, she walked out of church, followed by many other women.[41] Both the clergy who opposed her and the magistrates found this behavior to be intolerable, and they proceeded against her. Subject to two trials, one civil and one religious, she was eventually both excommunicated and exiled (along with her family and a group of supporters), and she died in what is now upstate New York in 1643 as the result of an attack by Indians.

When one examines the transcript of her trials, it becomes clear that the issue of "public womanhood" was at the heart of the dispute. The court accused her of behaving inappropriately by conducting public meetings. She replied that others had earlier done so, hence she had felt entitled to do the same. "There were private meetings indeed, and are still in many places, of some few neighbors, but not so publick

and frequent as yours . . . ," was the response. Asked for her scrip-
tural warrant, given the Pauline proscription, she replied with Titus
2:3–5, which says that elder women should teach the younger. Teaching was permissible, the court maintained, but not "teaching in publick." Hutchinson thought otherwise. "I do not conceive but that it
[Titus 2] is meant for some publick times."[42]

Her defiant insistence on her right to have a public voice horrified many, who evidently felt especially anxious about trying to maintain order in a frontier setting. Thomas Shepard, for example, focused
on her alarming fluency with language:

> But seeinge the Flewentness of her Tonge and her Willingness to open
> herselfe and to divulge her Opinions and to sowe her seed in us that
> are but highway side and Strayngers to her and therefore would doe
> much more to her owne . . . I account her a verye dayngerous Woman
> to sowe her corrupt opinions to the infection of many and therefore the
> more neede you have to look to her.[43]

His own language is revealing. The words "corrupt" and "infec-
tion" suggest the way in which this middle-aged mother of fifteen children, faithful to her husband so far as subsequent historians know,
came to symbolize uncontrolled female sexuality—after she insisted
on playing a public role. In fact, soon after her emergence as a public
figure, rumors had begun to circulate about her sexual conduct, and
then, when she had a miscarriage, they accelerated. She had given
birth to thirty monsters, according to Governor John Winthrop: "And
see how the wisdom of God fitted this judgement to her sinne every
way, for looke as she had vented mishapen opinions, so she must
bring forth deformed monsters; and as about 30. Opinions in number,
so many monsters; and as those were publike, and not in a corner
mentioned, so this is now come to be knowne and famous over all
these Churches, and a great part of the world."[44]

For at least 200 years, New England conservatives adverted to the
horrible example of Mistress Hutchinson, the American Jezebel, when
they wanted to discredit contemporary female activism. She had trans-

gressed by claiming a public voice, had threatened the community with social chaos, had been reputedly tainted with sexual crime, and any woman who sought to play a similar role was seen as her off-spring. For example, during the Great Awakening an opponent of the New Lights, among whom were many women, likened them to Hutchinson and the Antinomians, a terrible insult in his view.[45] In the 1830s the young Nathaniel Hawthorne wrote a piece on Hutch-inson, linking her to the "ink-stained Amazons" of his own day, who were so immodest as to publish what they wrote. They were all "pub-lic women" in Hawthorne's eyes, and this was a term of oppro-brium.[46]

Given the vulnerability to attack from which women writers suf-fered as late as the 1830s, the career of Anne Bradstreet, about twenty years younger than Hutchinson, seems all the more remarkable. She wrote poetry, she published, and she thrived—although she does tell us that, in so doing, she was "obnoxious to each carping tongue/ Who says my hand a needle better fits." Moreover, America's first poet wrote on an extraordinary range of topics from the domestic to the world-historical.

Anne Dudley was born in England in 1612 or 1613, the daughter of an elite family. Her father was the steward of the Earl of Lincoln and, in consequence, his daughter had access to a fine library while she was growing up. Marrying Simon Bradstreet in 1628, she came to Massachusetts with her husband on the *Arbella* in 1630. Her biogra-pher suggests that it was a combination of her exposure to literature as a child in addition to the emotional resonance of the Puritans' "errand into the wilderness"—before which she initially quailed—that led her to begin writing poetry in 1632. Certainly, the writing of poetry was an unusual avocation for a serious-minded Puritan—let alone a Puri-tan woman who would eventually give birth to eight children.[47]

At first she wrote, on an epic scale, poems about Christian his-tory, about the English Civil War, and one in honor of Queen Eliz-abeth I. She circulated these among her acquaintance, where they met with the approval of many of her male relatives. Apparently un-beknownst to her, her brother-in-law John Woolridge took a collection of her writings to London, and they were published in 1650 as *The Tenth Muse, Lately Sprung Up in America*, the first book of poetry to emanate from the New World and a substantial publishing success. Although it appeared anomymously, the book's authorship was no great mystery because the title page contained a dedication to her father, along with his name. Explaining that the author was a member of the "inferior sex," her brother-in-law made it clear in a preface that the poems had been written in time "curtailed from sleep" and not at the expense of her family.

Although the first edition appeared without her knowledge, she evidently prepared a revised second edition for publication, writing a poem to express her ambivalence about becoming a "public woman":

The Author to Her Book

> Thou ill-formed offspring of my feeble brain,
> Who after birth didst by my side remain,
> Till snatched from thence by friends, less wise than true,
> Who thee abroad, exposed to public view . . .

Calling the book her "rambling brat," she expressed the desire to spruce it up: "In better dress to trim thee was my mind,/ But nought save homespun cloth i'th' house I find."[48] In other words, she used homely metaphors to express her authorial anxiety.

After 1650 her poems were more explicitly addressed to her family, including ardent love poems to her husband, among the first by a woman in the English language. Subsequent criticism has seen these as her strongest work. Nonetheless, it is important to take note of the earlier epics, because they demonstrate the breadth of her ambition. Ambivalent though she may have been about publishing, she seemingly had confidence in her ability to say something worthwhile about large public events—although it must be noted that in some instances she displays considerable diffidence: for example, at one point in "The Four Monarchies" she apologizes, "My tyred brain leaves to some better pen/ This task befits not women like to men. . . ."[49]

A latent feminism was best expressed in the poem to Queen Elizabeth I, "In Honour of that High and Mighty Princess Queen Elizabeth of Happy Memory." Bradstreet exulted in the great monarch's achievements: "The world's the theatre where she did act." So excellent was Elizabeth's conduct that "She hath wiped off the aspersion of her sex/ That women wisdom lack to play the rex." [50] That her father Thomas Dudley had been a soldier for the queen may explain some of the fervor. Nonetheless, it is hard to avoid the conclusion that Bradstreet was angry about her society's devaluation of women and chose to make a counterattack on behalf of a woman who, as the defender of Protestantism against the Spanish Armada, was unassailable.

All in all, both Bradstreet's achievement and her temerity are astonishing. Many of her poems are deeply felt and beautiful, giving us an unparalleled window on the life and emotions of a Puritan woman. To write them at all required courage. To publish them was more than courageous. In the very year, 1650, in which *The Tenth Muse* appeared, the Puritan Thomas Parker wrote this of his sister, who had published a book: "Your printing of a Book beyond the custom of your Sex, doth rankly smell." [51]

Quaker preachers, Margaret Brent, Anne Hutchinson, Anne Bradstreet—these were white America's first public women. In a society which granted them no political rights and few legal rights, they contrived to be influential. Not surprisingly, none came from humble origins. Except for Brent, their primary means of exerting influence lay in words—words which could be deployed in new and more effective ways because of the discourse of subjectivity to which Quakerism and Calvinism were giving birth. The law everywhere gave patriarchs the preponderance of power, but it could not stop the flow of women's words, and ultimately these words would make it possible for women to articulate an alternative vision of their lives. In the next century, moreover, material conditions fostered new patterns of land tenure and new forms of family life that began to erode the basis for patriarchy. To that subject we now turn.

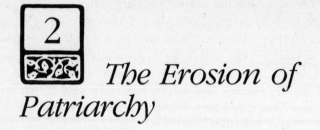

2

The Erosion of Patriarchy

The eighteenth century saw a thoroughgoing transformation of colonial life, a transformation that has been described in book titles as "From Puritan to Yankee" and as "The American Revolution against Patriarchal Authority."[1] Each of these titles gives us insight into the nature of the change, which encompassed the economic foundations of life, the social patterns, the religious tenets and practices, and ultimately the nature of the polity.

During the first stages of colonial growth in the seventeenth century and given the initial paucity of commercial development, land was the primary form of wealth. Access to land was, in consequence, crucial to most men's ability to make a living, and he who controlled that access—usually one's father—was a figure of towering importance. Young people of both sexes were unlikely to make such major life decisions as, for example, whom and when to marry on their own. This meant, in turn, that the inmost nature of the families launched by the second generation received the imprint of paternal decisions made by the first. In essence, as long as fathers controlled the ownership of land—and such ownership was the only game in town, so to speak—fathers would be able to enjoy extraordinary dominion over others.

Economic growth and commercial development soon began to undermine this arrangement. Such growth was disruptive of paternal control in a number of ways. In the first place, as growth occurred, wealth became less evenly distributed than in the earliest stages. There were more poor people, and poor fathers had less clout because they had less property to will to their heirs.[2] In the second place, as growth occurred, young men enjoyed a greater range of options about the future. While fathers still had a substantial impact on such matters as access to higher education, the acquisition of a craft, or the ability to go into business, the process of growing up and setting up a household became less rigidly determined than in the seventeenth century. Finally, the increasing importance of personal, as opposed to landed, wealth meant that marriage was less likely to be part of a long-term family property strategy and more likely to be up to the individuals involved than in the seventeenth century.

In a work aptly entitled "Loosening the Bonds," Joan Jensen has written about an eighteenth-century Quaker community undergoing these changes. She contends that, despite patriarchal legal restrictions placed on the Pennsylvania farm women in her study, their "gender-based commodity production" of butter and eggs laid the foundation for much vigorous activity outside the home by which they ultimately freed themselves from hegemonic male control.[3] In other words, economic activity had the potential for "loosening the bonds" of patriarchy, even among women. And in the eighteenth century growing prosperity gave more women access to such activity.

This process was going on throughout the colonies, though obviously at differing rates depending on the nature of a particular regional economy. And almost everywhere, economic change was precipitating new demographic patterns as well as changes in the internal dynamics of family life. What is more, because these changes were so widespread, albeit going on at differential rates, it is likely that the regional differences in family life were becoming less pronounced.[4] It is possible, therefore, to summarize those changes with the most impact on women.

Happily, a generation of scholarship has now documented the eighteenth-century revolution in the family on both sides of the Atlantic, a revolution that would ultimately make the family more democratic. Simply stated, a woman began to be able to make choices about her life, including the identity of the man she would marry, clearly the most important single choice of all in a society where divorce was rare and "careers" unheard of. Further, the evidence suggests that marriage was becoming a more affectionate and more companionable institution. Both these changes were necessary, if not sufficient, before public womanhood could flourish; a creature subordinate to either father or husband was unlikely to move into vigorous public action.

How did these changes come about? Lawrence Stone, a pioneer in writing about the eighteenth-century family, in his case, in England, called the eighteenth century the age of "affective individualism" because he found evidence of a new importance placed on the quality of emotional life in this period and more interest in nuances of feeling than had obtained previously.[5] Subsequent research by historians of the American experience has extended these generalizations to the New World. Toward the end of the eighteenth century, family life in the American colonies was becoming more openly affectionate, more intimate, more emotionally intense, and less formal.[6]

With the new value placed on the quality of emotional life—for reasons which are still subject to debate[7]—fathers wanted to be loved rather than feared. (As we have learned, they were losing their ability to control their children's destiny in any event.) In consequence, children began to receive attention as individuals rather than as pawns in a chess game of family property enhancement. Moreover, the tyrannical father who forced a child into an unwanted marriage began to be a stock figure of disapproval. Written in England, but read widely on both sides of the Atlantic, novels such as *Clarissa* by Samuel Richardson or *Cecilia* by Fanny Burney made this type of father a byword for injustice and oppression.[8]

If mid- to late-eighteenth-century fathers felt impelled to be warmer and less authoritarian to their children than their own fathers had been to them, then in their capacity as husbands—husbands who might well have chosen their wives on the basis of personal liking rather than paternal directive—they felt similarly inclined. This was all the more true as, toward the end of the century, romantic love began to be an increasingly important factor in marriage.[9] As an instance in point, in a book about late-eighteenth-century Virginia, Jan Lewis provides this account of Thomas Jefferson's reaction to the death of his beloved wife in 1782: "In his love for his wife and his near collapse after her death, Jefferson had much in common with his descendants of the nineteenth century. But in his fierce determination to gallop over his grief and obliterate its traces, he was a child of the eighteenth."[10] In other words, the late eighteenth century was a watershed.

This emerges with particular clarity in a study of divorce conducted by Nancy Cott. Reviewing divorce petitions in eighteenth-century Massachusetts—because divorce was so rare it was possible to read the entire population of 229 petitions and not just a sample thereof—Cott found that petitioners never mentioned "loss of conjugal affection" before 1765. Afterward, this complaint was voiced rather often. Moreover, divorce became more common toward the end of the century, and more women were the initiators of the process. She concludes that "[t]he apparent severing of parents' control over adult married children's lives, the inchoate influence of romantic love in marriage, and the improvement in women's status suggested by their more frequent petitions for divorce and their greater success in obtaining it, point to modern conceptions of family life."[11]

In sum, economic change began to erode the material base of patriarchy, and new value systems also emerged to foster a more affectionate family. These changes, in turn, cleared the way for more public access for women, because they began to make possible a certain level of female autonomy. At the same time, the Great Awakening at mid-century provided a spark that lit the fuse of public womanhood in New England, a development affecting far more women than the handful of outspoken women in the seventeenth century. Religious ferment mobilized women other than Quakers to organize outside the home for the first time in American history—and women would never again be without extra-domestic networks of some fashion. As we shall learn, women agonized about their faith during this time, made painful and remarkably independent choices, and, in so doing, further enhanced their own autonomy. Selfhood and sisterhood—both themes emerge strongly as one reads women's writings from the Great Awakening. And both undergirded the rise of public woman.

Although revivals took place throughout the colonies, nowhere did the Great Awakening have a stronger impact than in New England, where it permanently altered—and fragmented—what had been a strikingly unitary religious order. To understand this development in the mid-eighteenth century and its impact on New England women, we need to return to the subject of Puritanism in its seventeenth-century manifestation.

From the first decade of settlement with its Antinomian controversy, tensions within Puritanism had been apparent. Orthodox Puritans downgraded works in favor of grace; that is, human effort was seen as ineffectual as a means of achieving salvation. Yet when Anne Hutchinson began to propound her ideas, the dangers inherent in undervaluing the importance of behavior were soon made manifest. Hutchinson and her adherents even further exalted the covenant of grace over works than did the orthodox. In effect, each Christian became his or her own source of authority on earthly behavior. Such a view was not likely to sit well with those who had the responsibility for maintaining the social order. In addition to banishing Hutchinson, over time in the seventeenth century, Puritan clergy began to suggest that, while human effort would not guarantee salvation, it was nonetheless important to behave in as godly and orderly a manner as possible so as to be in a state of "preparation for salvation." [12] Over even more time and into the eighteenth century, Congregationalist divines began to propound a doctrine of salvation that rested so much on rational argument and on human exertion that it would surely have been deemed a heresy in the preceding century. Out of this tension between works and grace came some of the seeds for the Great Awakening.

Another source of instability within Puritanism lay in the treatment of the self. So much introspection and so much self-analysis led people inevitably to a certain self-absorption—which led more or less equally inevitably to feelings of guilt on the part of the sinner who was brooding on the state of his or her soul. Morbid self-abasement in the midst of morbid self-concern—this phenomenon emerges as the leitmotif of more than one diary. When, in addition, we consider the increasing prosperity enjoyed by some, with the attendant guilt about worldly success, we can understand more about the dynamics of the religious ferment of the mid-eighteenth century.[13] In short, Puritanism contained within itself built-in sources of guilt as well as anxiety.

The Great Awakening began with the exhortations of Jonathan Edwards to his parishioners in Northampton, Massachusetts, in the 1730s to cast off the modern emphasis on good works and human effort and to return to what he deemed to be the original Calvinist vision, the omnipotence of God and the utter depravity of humanity. A similar message came from the young British evangelist George Whitefield, who traveled up and down the Atlantic seaboard in the early 1740s holding revivals and winning adherents. In the ensuing decades preachers held revivals, congregations split into Old Lights and New Lights as the latter withdrew under the impetus of revivals, and adherents of each founded new institutions. The result was an unprecedented pluralism, not only in religion but also in other types of institutions such as colleges. Perhaps the most unusual aspect of the Awakening lay in the direct challenge to clerical authority mounted by radical New Lights. For example, surviving records describe Old Light sermons interrupted by parishioners who called out, "carnal, carnal," because they believed their minister to be under the covenant of works and overly rational.[14]

What does all this have to do with women? In the first place, more than one scholar has suggested that the challenge to the authority of the father in the family and the minister in the church were related phenomena. Says James Henretta: "The inability of the traditional holders of power during the 1740's to control the lives of their children or to regulate the religious activities of the New Lights testi-

fied to the inroads made by the process of social and economic evolution on the patriarchal and authoritarian system inherited from the
seventeenth century. . . ."[15]

In the second place, the emerging pluralism among churches and
the chance to choose between Old Light and New Light congregations
gave women, beginning to acquire the right to pick a marriage partner
for themselves, their first consequential choice in the public realm.
Female subjectivity, the dignity of which had earlier been enhanced
as we have seen, could now struggle, even if painfully, with profoundly important options. In effect, women were becoming their own
authority figures. In some cases, they were also turning to other women
for advice.

Finally, despite the intentions of New Light preachers like Edwards to return to the spirit of seventeenth-century Calvinism, in fact,
their powerfully emotional appeals engendered a new type of religious
"enthusiasm," a pejorative term used by Old Lights. This had the net
impact of privileging the realm of emotion—no doubt one reason for
the horror felt by the much more rationally inclined Old Lights. Edwards himself wrote about religious affections and their role in direct-
ing the soul to Christ. For women, these developments meant that
they had all the more validation for analyzing their feelings, all the
more impetus to write about those feelings.[16]

Happily, the historian of eighteenth-century New England women
during the Great Awakening has the benefit of more evidence from
women themselves than for the seventeenth century, where except for
Bradstreet's poetry and a handful of conversion narratives, most of the
evidence regarding female consciousness has been mediated through
male eyes and is therefore highly inferential. By the mid-eighteenth
century, women had begun to keep journals about their religious
struggles. Moreover, they had also begun to cultivate close women
friends to whom they wrote letters about similar matters. Those journals and letters as well as surviving conversion narratives provide us
with vivid accounts of a process which can perhaps be described as an
awakening to self-conscious selfhood.

The "earliest ongoing record of a woman's daily life in the colonial United States" was the journal of Esther Edwards Burr, the daughter of Jonathan Edwards and his wife, Sarah. She, living in New Jersey, and her best friend Sarah Prince, living in Massachusetts, decided to write regular accounts of their religious lives, which they would share with one another. Burr used this as an occasion for recording not only her spiritual growth but also certain more mundane matters like the comings and goings of her clergyman husband, Aaron Burr—they were the parents of Aaron Burr, the third vice president of the United States—and the political events that were agitating her fellow New Jerseyites. She and Prince then mailed packets of these journals to one another, although only Burr's journal has survived.

Born in 1732, a child when her father began to preach the sermons that helped ignite the firestorm of religious enthusiasm, Burr grew up in the kind of household and region which could be expected to produce a woman who took religion seriously. Marrying in 1752, she moved from her native Massachusetts to Princeton, New Jersey, where her husband was president of the College of New Jersey, recently founded by New Lights. Her journal begins in 1754 and ends in 1757, shortly before her death in 1758. In it she recorded for herself and her best friend Sarah, whom she called "Fidelia," her struggles to submit herself to God's will and yet to preserve her own identity. There are many passages of interest to historians of women. Moreover, the correspondence/journal, whose very existence had been animated by religious fervor, constitutes one of the first pieces of literary evidence for that special female friendship that would reach its fullest flowering in the nineteenth century.[17]

Indeed, Prince's friendship meant so much to Burr that one of the most vivid passages has to do with the latter's counterattack against a man who had spoken slightingly of female friendship. It is worth quoting at some length:

April 12, 1757

I have had a smart combat with Mr. Ewing about our sex—he is a man of good parts and Lerning but has mean thoughts of Women—he began the dispute in this Manner. Speaking of Miss Boudanot I said she was

> a sociable friendly creture. A Gentleman seting by joined with me, but Mr. Ewing says—*she and the Stocktons are full of talk about Friendship and society and such stuff—and made up a Mouth as if much disgusted*—I asked what he would have 'em talk about—whether he chose they should talk about fashions and dress—*he said things that they understood. He did not think women knew what Friendship was. They were hardly capable of anything so cool and rational as friendship*—(My Tongue, you know, hangs prety loose, thoughts Crouded in—so I sputtered away for dear life.)[18]

Burr goes on to proclaim that she "talked him quite silent" after a dispute lasting an hour. She and Prince considered themselves literally to be soulmates as they shared their spiritual quests with one another. Knowing the depth of this mutual feeling, Burr had the courage to conduct a lengthy public argument with a man, an unusual act on her part according to her testimony in other parts of the journal.[19]

On another occasion, Burr confided her concern about the conduct of the French and Indian War to her friend: "I wish I could help troubling you with my troubles that can do neither you nor me any good, but I am perplexed about our publick affairs. The Men say (tho' not Mr. Burr he is not one of that sort) that women have no business to concern themselves about em but trust to those that know better and be content to be destroyed because they did all for the best."[20] Thus the journal, originally inspired by religious feeling, also became a vehicle for discussing public events. We know from Bradstreet's poetry that female interest in public events was by no means a new phenomenon. What was new in the eighteenth century was the way in which the expression of religious and political opinion was intertwined with the fervent expression of sisterhood.[21]

Although Prince's journal, the companion piece to Burr's, has not survived, we do have her private journal of religious meditations, from the 1740s and the period 1756–64.[22] Like Burr the daughter of a prominent minister, Prince wrote about her spiritual condition with what can be described only as anguish. Born in 1728, she saw herself as having been thoroughly carnal until 1740 when she heard White-field. She mentions several sermons that had an influence on her, including one by Edwards—"I heard dear Mr. Edwards"—but casti-gates herself for being still too "vain and airy." In an entry for Novem ber 4, 1743, she describes reading the Gospel of John, which gave her momentary comfort because of the extent to which Jesus is depicted as co-equal with God the Father. Nonetheless, when the journal re-sumes in 1756, she is still going through torment: "O my Leaness my Sensuality and Stupidity—I feel guilty and confounded at what a low very low rake do I live" (February 21, 1756). "I see my bent to vanity I feel a reluctance to Holiness. My heart is often rising up in secret dissatisfaction with the Providence of God. O my heart is hard—my will is stubborn . . ." (September 12, 1756). "O methinks I am the vilest stubbornest of all Flesh Never did any make so little progress in sanctification as I. I loathe and abhor myself I desire to be broken to peices" (January 21 and 22, 1757). What seems to be excessive self-loathing to a modern reader was far from an atypical attitude.[23] For our purposes the important point is that out of this kind of suffering were born religious choices which could propel women into public visibility and even public action.

The life of Sarah Osborn demonstrates how this could come about. Born in 1714, Osborn lived until 1796, spending most of her life in Newport, Rhode Island. So exemplary was her life that in 1799 the noted clergyman Samuel Hopkins wrote a biography of her. As pub-lished in a book over 300 pages in length, Hopkins's biography is sup-plemented by a brief autobiographical fragment and by extracts from Osborn's journal. The resulting volume provides a splendid opportu-nity to follow a woman's spiritual odyssey over the course of a long life.[24]

In the autobiographical fragment, which she begins by expressing the hope that in writing it she will not be doing anything to "puff up" self, Osborn relates her struggles before she finally joined the church in 1737. Satan had been assaulting her with doubt as to whether so confirmed a sinner as herself *could* be saved. She saw herself as an "heir of hell, by practice a rebel against God, a resister of his grace, a piercer of the lovely Jesus, unworthy of the crumbs that fall; yet, through free grace, compelled to come and partake of children's bread. . . ." [25] This religious zeal never slackened. During the first stages of the Great Awakening, she was instrumental in forming a women's society that continued to meet at her house for another fifty years. This activity was in addition to her schoolteaching, the latter being necessary to supplement the income brought in by her second husband Henry Osborn, to whom she was married for 36 years.

Besides founding a women's group, Sarah Osborn can be seen as a public woman in several other ways. She corresponded with a number of ministers, says Hopkins. Because of this and her well-regarded school, "her name and character was spread abroad." [26] In fact, in achieving this type of fame, however innocuous, a woman ran the risk of being seen as notorious (à la Anne Hutchinson) and tainted with sexual scandal. That Osborn became famous for her piety without becoming infamous is an indication of how much change had taken place since the 1630s.

Nonetheless, she was cautious about playing too visible a role. For example, she wrote a letter to a woman friend in Boston about religious matters. The letter came to the attention of the Reverend Mr. Prince, who asked her permission to publish it. She assented— on the condition that her name not be used—and the letter went into three editions. Her diary entry for April 22, 1755, reads: "I heard that day, also, that my poor performance was printed. This gave me a sense of my vileness, and earnest longings that God might be glorified thereby." [27]

Osborn's most noteworthy achievement as a public woman came with her leadership during a revival in the mid-1760s. People, especially African-Americans, sought her out because of her reputation for piety. Hopkins relates that when she saw all those who were resorting to her house, "she trembled with fear that if she encouraged their meeting at her house, it would be going beyond her sphere." Receiving encouragement from her clerical friends, she persevered, but "when she had opportunity she would invite some Christian man to pray with them," thereby making a gesture of deference to male authority. Eventually there were several hundred people who came to her house on a regular basis.[28]

Sarah Osborn was clearly exceptional in the extent of her public visibility and leadership. There were, however, many other women who were exercising independent judgment in unprecedented ways as they responded to the religious ferment. A surviving cache of conversion narratives from the Reverend Mr. John Cleaveland's parish of Chebacco in Ipswich, 37 of which were dictated by women, provides the opportunity to understand more about their decision-making.[29]

Especially striking is the absence of non-clerical male authority figures in these accounts. Only one woman talks about her husband and one other about her father. Otherwise, the decisions seem to have come out of either solitary reflection or discussions with a peer group. Mary Tarring, for example, provides the following explanation of her conversion: "I was bro't under conviction last winter, when I came over here, hearing what some young people that had been wro't upon say; but by going in airy company I seemed to lose it all again. . . ." At this point she heard Mr. Cleaveland preach, and "the fire was enkindled in my heart." Sarah Butler was brought under concern by seeing "friends and acquaintances pressing into Christ." She was afraid that they would go to heaven without her.

Esther Williams's narrative is more specific than most, both about the nature of her sin—so many young women referred to themselves as "vile" that the reader perforce wonders what the reason for that self-perception may have been—and about her doubts. She already knew that she was guilty of telling lies, Sabbath-breaking, and disobedience to her parents. Then one of her friends drowned, and she began to be concerned about being left behind as more of her friends converted. She had a hard time, though, understanding why it was just to damn her for the sins of Adam and Eve. ". . . [A]t length I was brot to see it was just with God to damn me for that."

Several women mentioned the earthquake of 1755 as having first brought them under concern. Susanna Low explained that she had worried about heaven and hell since childhood. She had tried to live a righteous life, but she realized that her own righteousness was a "sandy foundation" after the earthquake.

To sum up, the Great Awakening further validated female subjectivity by providing so much incentive to introspection, however painful on occasion. True this had been the case in the seventeenth century, too. What was new in the eighteenth century was the choice available after the introspection had taken place. Says Sarah Juster of women in a slightly later period, "The experience of grace thus implicitly strengthened women's sense of personal autonomy and moral agency. The sense of empowerment that grace brought to women is suggested in this account of Mrs. Prudence Stille: . . . When engaged in the publick exercises of religion, her spirit was on the wing.' " Juster provides another telling quotation. A minister wrote of a new woman convert, " 'Her liberated tongue now broke out in unknown strains.' "[30] Again, we encounter the link between the strengthening of selfhood and the power of the word.

What is certain is that conservative Old Light clergymen, already disposed unfavorably toward revivals, or "enthusiastic religion" in their words, were especially horrified by the public release of female energy at this time. For example, in a sermon written in 1742 Charles Chauncy recalled with distaste the sight of a Quaker woman preacher in his youth. Now he was forced to confront public women on a regular basis:

> And it deserves particular consideration whether the suffering much more the encouraging women, yea GIRLS to speak in the assemblies for religious worship is not a plain breach of that commandment of the Lord wherein it's said, "Let your women keep silence in the churches; for it is not permitted to them to speak—It is a shame for women to speak in the church." After such an express constitution designedly made to restrain women from speaking in the church, with what face can such a practice be pleaded for. . . . 'Tis a plain case, these female exhorters are condemned by the apostle.[31]

As for Quaker public women, the eighteenth century saw a con-
tinuation, in some instances an extension, of the practices of the preceding century, rather than the innovations taking place in New England. Yet because the phenomenon of traveling women ministers had
been so powerful an example of public womanhood and so unparalleled a departure from traditional practices, Quakers remained the most
advanced group in colonial society with respect to this issue. In their
daily lives, traveling women ministers constituted a living reproof to
those who would invoke Paul to silence women. Joan Jensen tells of
forty-seven-year-old Ann Moore, for example, a minister for nineteen
years, who had a spirited exchange with a Presbyterian minister as they
were dining in a tavern. He undertook to prove to her that what she
was doing violated the Pauline injunction. She responded by citing
other scripture that could be interpreted as giving women more of a
chance to speak than did Paul in his letter to the Corinthians.[32]

In addition to the role of traveling ministers, Quaker women also
exercised leadership in the eighteenth century within the women's
meetings. Jean Soderlund has studied the minutes of such meetings
and has concluded that older women "kept watch over the female
flock and called to task the young women who married outside the
fold or engaged in premarital sex. . . ."[33] Moreover, in the 1750s the
entire denomination instituted reforms aimed at the very issues of most
concern to women as revealed in the minutes, issues such as marriage
within the faith or "worldly" behavior. Finally, Soderlund found evidence within the men's meetings of "an acute regard for [the] participation of women at all levels of the Society."[34]

After the American Revolution, Quaker women instituted the first
charity in the United States organized by and for women. In 1795 a
young single woman named Ann Parrish launched a committee called
the Female Society of Philadelphia for the Relief and Employment of
the Poor.[35] In the ensuing decades such activities would expand greatly
as Quaker women pioneered what subsequent historians have called
the "benevolent empire" of women's voluntarism and became a "public moral force."[36]

Finally, it should be noted that Quaker women began to be great

writers of journals. In so doing, they were validating the strength of
their already strong women's culture and laying down the foundation
for the activism to come. Moreover, on some occasions they were
allowing these journals to be disseminated to the larger community,
another advance into the public sphere.[37]

As we move further south to the Chesapeake and beyond, we see
an erosion in the position of women, at least in the early part of the
eighteenth century, compared with the seventeenth century.[38] This
owed to the strengthening of patriarchal family patterns as a result of
a more favorable set of demographic circumstances. Julia Cherry Spruill
compared women's petitions to colonial governments from the two
periods and found a deterioration in this area, too: "The women of
the later period appear disinclined to admit any interest in public
policy and anxious lest their private requests be mistaken for an un-
womanly meddling in politics."[39] Above all, women in the southern
colonies lacked the kind of intense religion—at least until the Awakening—that provided a springboard into public action for New England women and for Quakers.

Yet there are scattered accounts of southern women, principally
of the upper class, taking an interest in public affairs in the eighteenth
century and even participating in the boisterous electioneering. For
example, Elkanah Watson visited Warrenton, North Carolina, on
election day in 1786. Eager to see the sights he went with an Irish-
man, who wanted to show him an especially noteworthy spectacle.
"We pressed through the mob, intermixed with some respectable
planters, and a few females. 'There,' says he, 'did you ever look upon
the like?' pointing to the most obese woman I ever had seen; and,
what was more striking, she appeared to be an active leader at the
polls." Thunderstruck by this, Watson pointed her out to a local
gentleman, who then engaged him in conversation and invited him to
dinner. To Watson's considerable surprise, the fat woman was the
hostess on that occasion, the mother of the local gentleman. "And I
was assured that she had more political influence, and exerted it with
greater effect, than any man in the county."[40]

After the Revolution, the Virginia legislature granted women the right to petition. In her book about Petersburg, Suzanne Lebsock writes of discovering several taxpaying widows who used this right, particularly Eliza Spencer, the proprietor of a tobacco warehouse, who took vigorous action to protect her interests.[41] As we shall be learning, however, such anomalous women had few successors in the antebellum South, where public women were very little in evidence. In short, we must note the existence of the stout woman politician of Warrenton, but not inflate her significance.

There was one other form of public activity available to eighteenth-century women, a form that was important in the cities where so-called mobs took action. Women of the "lower sort" regularly took part in such activity and, in some cases, led it. For example, in November 1783, as British forces were evacuating New York City, a mob led by women sought to drag to the jail a man who had been the jailer during the British occupation. Convinced that the mob meant to hang their victim, George Washington intervened to save the man's life.[42] Public activism by women engaged in collective protest would continue into the nineteenth century when women would participate in such massive outbursts of public violence as the New York City draft riots.[43] But after the birth of an industrial proletariat in the early nineteenth century, as Paul Gilje argues in his splendid book on crowds in New York City, crowds were seen by the rest of the community as far less legitimate than they had been in the eighteenth century. Perhaps as a consequence, when working-class women began to play influential public roles in the modern period—the subject of Chapter 9—they would employ the power of the word to dignify working-class female subjectivity as well as draw upon older traditions of collective protest.

That the American Revolution itself changed the nature of the relationship between public and private life with vast consequences for women is now becoming increasingly well understood, thanks to important books by Linda Kerber and Mary Beth Norton.[44] The next chapter will be devoted to an exploration of the topic of women and republicanism, with special attention given to Mercy Otis Warren, pioneer woman historian, and to Elizabeth Freeman, a slave in Massachusetts who sued for her freedom.

Indeed, in the decades following the Revolution, public women began to emerge in a variety of social settings, from white actresses on the stage in Charleston in the 1790s[45] to black and white women in northern cities, under the prompting of both democratic and evangelical impulses, organizing voluntary associations for the relief of those less fortunate than themselves—of which more later.[46]

Two women who used the power of the word to create new discourses, each in its own way challenging traditional discourse, furnish the coda to a discussion of the erosion of patriarchy in the eighteenth century and the consequent possibilities for public womanhood. In her Pulitzer Prize-winning book on Martha Ballard, a Maine midwife whose practice flourished between 1785 and her death in 1812, Laurel Thatcher Ulrich has performed the valuable service of providing excerpts from a diary that Ballard kept for the 27 years of her practice.[47] In this diary, Ballard recorded, baldly and one may even say clinically, information about the 814 deliveries she attended in the course of the 27 years. Especially remarkable are her descriptions of autopsies she attended, for which she provides anatomical detail about the deceased, in so doing asserting her own authority as a medical practitioner. On other occasions, she indicates that she took a dim view of the male doctors who were her rivals. Thus the diary is not merely the record of one engaged in the traditional female undertaking of midwife, but also the record of a woman with a proto-scientific awareness who took herself seriously enough as a practitioner to want to write down her observations.

Moreover, as Ulrich points out, "Outside her own diary Martha Ballard has no history."[48] That is, her husband's name, as with countless other couples, is the one that appears in public records. But Martha had the sense of self not only to value her own opinions but also to leave a record of them, thereby allowing herself the possibility of becoming known to history. One may say that she inaugurated an American discourse of the woman scientist.

At more or less the same time Martha Ballard began writing her diary, Phillis Wheatley, the first American black woman poet, was meeting her untimely end. Dying at approximately the age of thirty-one—her exact date of birth is unknown—Wheatley had been in every sense of the word a public woman, because she wrote both religious and patriotic poetry, published it, and enjoyed notoriety, if not the genuine success her talents might have brought her had she been male and/or white.

Wheatley's story is extraordinary. Brought to Boston as a slave in 1761 at seven or eight years of age, she had the good fortune to be purchased by a woman, Susanna Wheatley, who soon realized that her slave was a person of unusual talents and who therefore dedicated herself to providing her young protégée with an education and with creature comforts. John Wheatley, Susanna's husband, wrote:

> Without any Assistance from School Education and by only what she was taught in the Family, she, in sixteen Months Time from her Arrival, attained the English Language, to which she was an utter Stranger before, to such a Degree, as to read any, the most difficult Part of the Sacred Writing, to the great astonishment of all who heard her. . . . She has a great Inclination to learn the Latin Tongue, and has made some Progress in it. . . .[49]

A prodigy, young Phillis was writing poetry with Alexander Pope as a model while still in her early teens. Her mistress subsequently invested considerable effort in seeing that her work would be published.[50]

What captured Wheatley's most intense interest was her passionate Christianity, to which she converted soon after her arrival in Massachusetts. The Boston of the 1760s was still very much under the influence of religious enthusiasm, and young Phillis, like so many others, was captivated by the preaching of George Whitefield. Indeed, one of her earliest poems, published in 1770, was an elegy on his death.

Thus as white women first found a voice in articulating their religious feelings, so too, unsurprisingly, did the first American black

woman to publish find her voice on this subject. Moreover, her evi-
dent piety won her influential friends. Because the idea that so young
a woman, recently arrived from Africa, would be writing poetry using
an ornate vocabulary seemed on the face of it very unlikely, Mrs.
Wheatley enlisted the support of a number of clergymen who bore
witness to the fact that Phillis was indeed the poet. In other words,
her religious fervor both inspired Phillis Wheatley and made it more
likely that her poetry would be published.

It should be noted that in her patriotic poetry Wheatley dealt with
the subject of freedom in a way that no white woman could have. In
a poem addressed to "His Majesty's Principal Secretary of State for
North America," she wrote the following lines:

> Should you, my lord, while you peruse my song,
> Wonder from whence my love of Freedom sprung,
> Whence flow these wishes for the common good,
> By feeling hearts alone best understood,
> I, young in life, by seeming cruel fate,
> Was snatched from Afric's fancied happy seat:
> What pangs excruciating must molest,
> What sorrows labour in my parents' breast?
> Steeled was that soul and by no misery moved
> That from a father seized his babe beloved:
> Such, such my case. And Can I then but pray
> Others may never feel tyrannic sway? [51]

In this and other poems she pioneered the written expression of the
black experience in the United States.

Thus even before the outbreak of the American Revolution itself,
the eighteenth century had seen changes of so great a magnitude that,
for their impact on women, they may be deemed revolutionary in
themselves. In particular, the family had become less patriarchal—
although by no means fully democratic—and the groundswell of powerful religious sentiment had afforded women the chance to make
choices of a public nature, to join together with other like-minded
women, and, in a few instances, to play a leadership role. In all cases,

the net impact was a strengthening of female autonomy and a digni-
fying of female subjectivity. By the end of the century, women from
unlikely social settings like Martha Ballard, a rural midwife, and Phillis Wheatley, a slave, were taking pains to make sure that their experiences would be part of the historical record—as opposed to being
buried in the obscurity of the private sphere along with the experiences
of so many of their talented sisters who had had no chance whatsoever
to become public women.

3

Women and Republicanism

The concept of "republicanism" has been much used in American historical writing of late, as we have had a number of important books either dealing with the subject directly or else using it as a major component of a larger argument.[1] Indeed, some have suggested that the concept has been so much used as to have lost its specificity of meaning. It is, nonetheless, impossible to write about the rise of public woman without paying careful heed to republicanism. This is because this political ideology, born in ancient Rome and reinvented in the Renaissance as civic humanism, had evolved by the time of the American Revolution in such a way as to create a link between private virtue and public life, making possible a new, if not necessarily coequal, political role for women.[2] Before the advent of the age of reason and the articulation of liberalism, much Western political thought— and practice—had assumed a pattern of authority in which God, king, and the father of the family were joined in what one might call a divine right of fatherhood.[3] The link between state and family, hence between public and private life, was through the father. Moreover, neither with absolutism in a monarchy nor with patriarchy in a family did consent of the governed enter in; the governed were subjects in both cases. Under this dispensation, it was rare, indeed, for a woman to play an independent public role.

The first modern expression of a republican ideal that would constitute an alternative to absolutism came in Renaissance Florence, most particularly in the writings of Machiavelli and Guicciardini. In a magisterial work published in the mid-seventies, J. G. A. Pocock first explicated what he called "The Machiavellian Moment" in Florence itself and then examined the impact of the Florentines on both English and American republicans. Pocock contends that the Machiavellian moment in its first manifestation came when an increasingly prosperous Florence began to identify itself with past republics rather than with a timeless Christian providence. At this juncture, citizens began to cultivate a vision of civic loyalty to the public good. As Pocock explains the civic humanists' outlook: "Particular men and the particular values they pursued met in citizenship to pursue and enjoy the universal value of acting for the common good. . . ."[4] If one citizen exhibited traits of dependency, however, this negatively affected the whole, because others might be tempted to take advantage of him, which would lead to corruption. In articulating his political beliefs, Machiavelli (according to Pocock), placed a high value both on *virtu*, in the sense of prowess, and on virtue in the sense of devotion to the common good. *Virtu* was needed to tame *fortuna*, or contingent circumstance, so as to make virtue possible and ensure that each citizen would work toward the common good.

This brief summary of Pocock's argument with respect to Florence and to Machiavelli makes it clear how male-oriented Florentine republicanism was. Women were not public actors and were not deemed capable of cultivating virtue in the politicized sense of the word.[5] Legally dependent on men, they were incapable of being citizens of the republic for that reason alone. Yet Hanna Pitkin reminds us in her *Fortune Is a Woman* that Machiavelli did forge a new type of link between public purposes and private life:

Machiavelli at his best summons us to heroism rightly understood: to public action for higher goals that nevertheless serve our natural private needs, action that recognizes both our vulnerability and our capacity as creators and judges. He strives for, and sometimes achieves, a synthesis of the traditionally "masculine" and "feminine" views of heroism. But insofar as he excludes or encourages his readers to exclude the women and things feminine from the vision, the synthesis is bound to be lost.[6]

The Machiavellian moment, while far from proto-feminist, posed an alternative connection between civic life and private life than through the male *qua* father of the family. As such, it had possibilities for women. Principally this was because virtue as a political trait, while male in its Machiavellian definition, was not *necessarily* male as fatherhood undoubtedly was.

Moving forward in time, a truly important political thinker in establishing a new link between public and private was John Locke.[7] Setting forth a theory of the human mind as a *tabula rasa*, Locke was of necessity arguing for the malleability of human nature. Childhood thus assumed a new importance, as did the education of the child. Education could best be accomplished in an atmosphere free from coercion, one that would encourage filial esteem. In effect, Locke's psychology led to the redefinition of both political authority and family authority and provided an intellectual justification for the increasingly affectionate family.[8]

It should be noted that in a recent book on the Quakers, Barry Levy argues that the Friends had made the affectionate family the centerpiece of their system of governance in the late seventeenth century, in other words, at about the same time that Locke was writing. Absent a formal set of institutions—the denomination possessed meeting houses and committees rather than churches and a hierarchy—and adrift in a hostile Church of England sea in the Old World, the founding father George Fox—and, significantly, founding mother Margaret Fell—early understood the value of a new style of family life in providing social cohesion for the Friends. Affection would be the cement, fathers would surrender some of their power and authority to mothers, and both parents would strive to be loved rather than feared.[9] In other words, the Quakers pioneered the modern family, replete with political ramifications having to do with authority and consent. That Quaker women were the first Anglo-American public women demonstrates the powerful impact that this kind of linkage between public purposes and private life would immediately create.

What, then, was American republicanism? Aside from the obvious opposition to absolute monarchy, most fundamentally, the American variant was a world view whereby ideas generated by a group of radical Whigs in the mother country, the so-called country party or Commonwealthmen, about the need for a vigorous, vigilant, and virtuous citizenry to stand guard against ministerial corruption were given a specifically colonial spin. Deeply read in both classical literature and the writings of the radical Whigs, American republicans feared the concentration of power and associated it with corruption and the addiction to luxury and bloated tastes. When Parliament began to try to obtain more revenue from the colonies in 1763, colonists thought they could discern the lineaments of the monster—corruption—they had been reading about. The people must spring into action at such a juncture, they held. Yet clearly there was a need for social cohesion as well as for an embattled citizenry. Gordon Wood explains the way they solved this dilemma: "Public liberty was thus the combining of each man's individual liberty into a collective governmental authority, the institutionalization of the people's personal liberty, making public or political liberty equivalent to democracy or government by the people themselves."[10] In such an undertaking, virtue was the guarantee that each individual would be public-spirited enough to surrender some of his or her liberty so as to make a government possible.[11] The cultivation of virtue thus became an essential political task.[12]

The religious fervor of the Great Awakening, so consequential for women, as we learned in the last chapter, also played a major role in shaping the new political outlook by reinforcing the moral fervor of republicanism. As Ruth Bloch contends in her book *Visionary Republic*, the Awakening, with its visionary and even millennial qualities, was "the first mass movement in American history." As such it served to enhance the expectations of social perfection already present in radical Whig ideology, thus giving virtue all the more importance.[13]

This brief overview of the ideology suggests the ways in which public and private were connecting in the realm of ideas. In the realm of political action, a similar connection was taking place from the earliest stages of the Revolution on, because the consumer boycott proved to be the single most valuable tool, short of war, that the patriots possessed—and no boycott of consumer goods could take place without enlisting the cooperation of women. The women themselves documented their participation in the boycotts, which entailed the mundane act of not buying such products as tea, as a significant public act. One woman wrote:

> Let the Daughters of Liberty, nobly arise
> And tho' we've no Voice, but a negative One,
> The use of the Taxables, let us forebear,
> (Then Merchants import till yr. Stores are all full
> May the Buyers be few and yr. Traffick be dull.)
> Stand firmly resolved and bid Grenville to see
> That rather than Freedom, we'll part with our Tea
> And well as we love the dear Draught when adry,
> As American Patriots,—our Taste we deny.[14]

Women occasionally made agreements among themselves to boycott goods, and they also circulated petitions addressing the issue of nonimportation.[15] In other words, the boycott provided a bridge between the private world of the household and the public world of resistance to what was deemed British aggression, and many women marched across that bridge, leaving a history of public activity and employing a newly politicized language.

These events were antecedent to the actual outbreak of hostilities, at which time women participated in many public ways. Both Linda Kerber and Mary Beth Norton enumerate a range of actions by women such as the campaign by the women patriots of Philadelphia to raise money for Washington's troops.[16] As another instance in point, Phillis

Wheatley wrote a deeply patriotic poem in honor of George Washington when he was chosen to head the Continental Army, sent it to him, and received a courteous reply.

> Anon Britannia droops the pensive head,
> While round increase the rising hills of dead
> Ah, cruel blindness to Columbia's state!
> Lament thy thirst of boundless power too late.
> Proceed, great Chief, with virtue on thy side,
> Thy every action let the goddess guide.
> A crown, a mansion, and a throne that shine,
> With gold unfading, Washington! be thine.[17]

No doubt feeling somewhat abashed about the mention of a crown, Washington nonetheless complimented her on her poetic talents.[18]

Yet as several scholars, most notably Linda Kerber, have demonstrated, even given female political activity, visibility, and contributions of some magnitude, there were ways in which the older traditions of coverture persisted. Married women were seen as automatically partaking in their husbands' political choices, for example, rather than being capable of independent choice. While the new state governments in general held women capable of committing treason, thus granting them wills of their own in this regard, even patriots who were ardent revolutionaries shrank from suggesting that women married to loyalists should rebel against the will of their husbands and join the revolutionary cause.[19] Single women, on the other hand, were seen as capable of making political choices. For example, vigilantes tarred and feathered one unmarried female Tory as an object lesson to the community.[20]

What all this means is that the revolutionary period was a time in which changing circumstances for women clashed with older traditions of woman's invisibility, incapacity as a public actor, and exclusion from the *polis*. Would she be a citizen or not? Only New Jersey gave propertied women the franchise—till 1807 and not beyond. Only Virginia explicitly made women into citizens.[21] Kerber reminds us that to the extent that republicanism had seeds in classical Rome, it partook of the legacy of an arms-bearing citizenry, a legacy from which women were excluded.[22] At the end of the war, woman's status as a citizen, a necessary step toward the emergence of public woman in the political sense, was opaque at best.

Yet there were exciting transatlantic currents of discussion about women's role in this period, and women in other countries were beginning to stake out new terrain for action. These developments were indicative of profound changes taking place throughout the Western world in family life and political attitudes both. Thus the halfway—or less—nature of the American Revolution itself where women were concerned was likely to be challenged before too much longer.

Let us turn to France, where the legacy of the Enlightenment for women was mixed, but where women revolutionaries were soon to create a remarkable legacy of their own. One of the fathers of liberal political theory and a man whose ideas were of utmost interest to the creators of the American nation was Montesquieu, who wrote in addition to *The Spirit of the Laws*, analyzing the English government, *The Persian Letters*, in which the position of women in harems received sympathetic attention as a metaphor for discussing human freedom and unfreedom more generally. An epistolary novel, *The Persian Letters* contains the observations of Usbek and Rica, two Persians traveling in France, as well as letters to and from the harem. It ends with a letter from Roxana, Usbek's favorite, explaining to him how, although she has been enslaved, she has always been spiritually free, because "I reformed your laws by those of nature, and my spirit has always held to its independence."[23] There are other passages in his writings, too, in which Montesquieu shows interest in the social position of women. But in the end, his imagination failed him where it came to thinking of a political solution to woman's plight. Moreover, he made it clear that he thought there was a "natural subordination" of wife to husband in marriage.[24]

Another major Enlightenment figure, Jean-Jacques Rousseau, emphasized, as had Locke, the role of education in creating the good society. Even more explicitly than Locke, he wrote about the value of female virtue for such a society: "Could I forget that precious half of the Republic which makes the happiness of the other and whose sweetness and wisdom maintain peace and good morals. . . . 'Tis happy when your chaste power, exerted only in the conjugal union, devotes itself to the glory of the state and to public happiness."[25] In this passage we see both what was positive for women in Rousseau's body of work and what was negative: he took private life seriously, he saw female virtue as essential to his scheme of things, but he also saw women as instruments for promoting male happiness with their charming ways rather than as subjects in their own right. Moreover, he thought a wife should be under "the absolute law" of her husband.[26]

The most unequivocal feminist among the major male figures of the Enlightenment was the Marquis de Condorcet, who argued that the only significant factor in producing differential intellectual capacities between men and women was the latter's inferior education. In consequence and as a matter of justice, women should be integrated into public life. In his celebrated essay on the rights of women, published in 1790, Condorcet brought up the example of the British historian Catharine Macaulay to underline his point about female capacities. Was she not better thought of in France than most Britons?[27]

As for French women, during the Revolution they engaged in vigorous activity in many sectors of society. In October 1789, for example, Paris street women marched to Versailles and captured the king and royal family, returning them to Paris, where the people could keep better track of them. This was merely the most significant of many collective protests during the period. Women wrote some of the "Cahiers de Doléance," in which, during the early stages of the Revolution, the French articulated their political grievances. Women formed clubs such as the Society for Revolutionary Women—clubs which were shut down in 1793. And finally there were brilliant and accomplished women who wrote about their views of a more just society. The best-known advocate of women's rights was Olympe de Gouges, author of the "Declaration of the Rights of Woman and Citizen."[28]

England did not have the benefit of a revolution to liberate its women into unprecedented social roles, but it did have, in the person of Mary Wollstonecraft, a pioneering feminist writer and a woman with the daring to lead an unconventional life by the standards of her day. For our purposes what is important is that she published her *Vindication of the Rights of Women* in 1792, animated in large part by anger at Rousseau for his relegating women to the "empire of softness." Conceding that men may have been "designed by Providence to attain a greater degree of virtue,"[29] she nonetheless advanced a natural rights argument to convince her readers that women should receive a better education and should be treated as rational beings rather than as men's playthings. Stopping short of advocating symmetrical public roles for men and women, she thought that women should be introduced to political discourse: "But these *littlenesses* would not degrade their character if women were led to respect themselves, if political and moral subjects were opened to them; and, I will venture to affirm, that this is the only way to make them properly attentive to their domestic duties."[30] In this way, Wollstonecraft connected public and private and sought to promote the spread of morality.

Americans, too, were dealing with such issues in the late eighteenth century, both because of the new currents of opinion and because women's role in the polity was engaging the attention of certain men and women with a large view of democratic possibilities. For example, Charles Brockden Brown, a Quaker who became the leading American writer of the early national period, published his first work in 1797, *Alcuin: A Dialogue on the Rights of Women*. A short piece featuring a dialogue between Alcuin and Mrs. Carter, hostess of a salon where lively conversations take place, *Alcuin* constitutes a remarkable document demonstrating that some people were taking the possibility of public women seriously.

Alcuin begins by asking Mrs. Carter: "Pray Madam, are you a federalist?"—that is, a supporter of the new frame of government. She replies with some surprise because she is unused to being asked for her political opinions, but soon warms to the topic. He, on the other hand, merely meant to be polite and quickly resorts to patronizing her. She will not allow this to happen and asserts: "Of all the forms of injustice, that is the most egregious which makes the circumstance of sex a reason for excluding one half of mankind from all those paths which lead to usefulness and honour."[31] She laments women's absence from the liberal professions and their legal disabilities in marriage. He replies that she is exaggerating, and that women could do more on their own behalf if they so desired. In short, Mrs. Carter gives a proto-feminist critique of the status quo, while Alcuin represents the male who sees himself as sympathetic to women's claims, but is in reality blind to the extent of the injustice from which they suffer.

When Alcuin repeats his original question, Mrs. Carter develops a critique of the constitution that is the heart of the dialogue: "What have I as a woman to do with politics? Even the government of our country, which is said to be the freest in the world, passes over women as if they were not. We are excluded from all political rights without the least ceremony."[32] Going on, Mrs. Carter says that she is a federalist insofar as she prefers union to war and disunion, but that the constitution is "unjust and absurd" in its treatment of women. She asserts, therefore, "No I am no federalist." In the end, Alcuin has the last word, first bringing up the lack of independence that is the lot of married women, then adverting to the preposterousness of seeing a woman speaking on a weighty topic, and finally delivering a fulsome tribute to the superiority of women. Having raised such significant questions, *Alcuin* ends on a note of ambiguity.

On the one hand, women's legal and political status changed little during—and in the immediate aftermath of—the Revolution. On the other hand, the most revolutionary aspect of republicanism where women were concerned, the linkage between public purpose and private virtue, fostered the new discourse about women and the family, of which *Alcuin* was a notable example. In particular, many writers focused on the role of affection in providing social cohesion for the young Republic—as had the Quakers one hundred years earlier. In this enterprise, the ideas of the Scottish Enlightenment, with their emphasis on the cultivation of the moral sense, proved invaluable.[33]

Writing about the impact of republicanism on ideas about child-rearing in Philadelphia, for example, Jacqueline Reinier puts it this way:

> The American republic would have to become a union of affection. Young Americans educated together in their own country would form bonds of "mutual benevolence" that were especially essential in a pluralistic society like that of Pennsylvania. . . .[34]

The new discourse in the context of the developments in the nature of the family and the economy about which we read in the last chapter inevitably began to create social change. This social change, most particularly better educational opportunities for women, may have stopped short of political rights per se, but would prove extraordinarily beneficial for women nonetheless. Benjamin Rush is perhaps the best-known advocate of educational reform for young women:

> I beg pardon for having delayed so long to say any thing of the separate and peculiar mode of education proper for women in a republic. I am sensible that they must concur in all our plans of education for young men . . . they should not only be instructed in the usual branches of female education, but they should also be taught the principles of liberty and government; and the obligations of patriotism should be inculcated upon them.[35]

Rush may have been the best-known but he was merely one of many who not only were making speeches and writing about the necessity to provide young women with a good education but were also building schools.[36]

Even more important, the new Republic, whose very survival according to its leading spokespeople depended on a virtuous citizenry trained in just and affectionate families, in essence lent female subjectivity a kind of political weight, a new phenomenon in Western culture. This was because public-minded women were supposed to be the guarantors of their husbands' and children's attachment to the new frame of government.[37]

The significance of this development is clear. Before the valorization of private life and female subjectivity that took place in the early modern period, women had had little opportunity for public influence except by accident of aristocratic birth or as a member of a crowd. Coverture rendered them legally invisible. In the American colonies both Puritanism and Quakerism had played a major role in beginning to reverse this situation because both placed so much emphasis on introspection and both created a plane of subjectivity where men and women could meet as equals. Now republicanism gave female subjectivity even more dignity. With this kind of encouragement and even without the franchise, women were soon organizing for benevolent purposes on a variety of fronts, hence moving out of the home and into the public sphere.[38]

What is more, the identification of women with political virtue, visible in both the iconography[39] and the imaginative literature, as we shall discover in the next chapter, represented a stunning reversal of traditional stereotypes of woman as temptress or Jezebel. This is all the more remarkable inasmuch as earlier in the century a key epithet hurled by radical Whigs at their opponents had been "effeminate," meaning luxury-loving or dissolute. Now, the valence of "woman" or "feminine" in political discourse was far more likely to be positive.

Ruth Bloch has attributed the feminization of the concept of virtue to three factors. In the first place, there was the heightened value placed on emotions after the Great Awakening. In the second place, she mentions the psychological theories of Locke and of the Scottish Common Sense school. And finally, literary sentimentalism—novels such as *Pamela* and *Clarissa*, for example—altered gender symbolism.[40] Since the association of public womanhood with sexual impropriety had been at the heart of the proscription of public activity to women, the feminization of virtue was of the utmost significance.

As Anne Hutchinson, Anne Bradstreet, and a group of influential Quaker women had taken immediate advantage of changing religious ideologies to march into the public sphere in the seventeenth century, so, too, did a number of remarkable public women emerge in the late eighteenth century, under the influence of republican ideas. Some of them made what we would now call explicitly feminist demands; others did not. What they had in common was a sense of the legitimacy of their entering into political discourse. Earlier public women had derived empowerment from their religion, and a few had made political comments along the way. Now, with republican ideas having gained so much currency, politics per se was the dynamic for entry into new roles.

For example, in 1793 Priscilla Mason gave the salutatorian's address to the Young Ladies Academy of Philadelphia and made a bold statement on behalf of public womanhood: "A female, young, and inexperienced, addressing a promiscuous assembly, is a novelty which requires an apology, as some may suppose. I, therefore, with submission, beg leave to offer a few thoughts in vindication of female eloquence." She then went on to argue that if women have the talents of the orator, they should use them. Moreover, she anticipated many of "Mrs. Carter's" criticisms of the status quo. But her most radical ideas had to do with the Pauline injunction against women speaking in church. "But Paul forbids it! Contemptible little Body! The girls laughed at the deformed creature. To be revenged, he declares war against the whole sex; advises men not to marry them; and has the insolence to order them to keep silence in the church. . . ."[41] One wonders what her audience thought of such outspokenness. Heretofore, the typical response to Paul by women who sought larger public roles had been to counter him with other scripture. Ridicule was a new—and probably ineffective—tactic. The wave of piety engendered by the Second Great Awakening would soon make such attacks even more unlikely. In fact, not until Elizabeth Cady Stanton's *Woman's Bible* of the late nineteenth century did an American feminist tackle scripture head on—and then Stanton's own organization disavowed the effort.[42]

From an outspoken schoolgirl to the new nation's second first lady, heady political developments engendered innovative ideas. One approaches Abigail Adams with trepidation because so much has been

written about her and because her famous injunction to her husband
John to "remember the ladies" has received so much attention.[43] Yet
in many ways she was the quintessential republican woman, in her
ideas and in her behavior, in her accomplishments and in her—by
modern standards—limitations.

The daughter of a clergyman, Abigail Smith married John Adams
in 1764, just before she turned twenty. John soon began to involve
himself in the activities that would place him at the center of the
efforts to build a new nation, and Abigail, perforce, learned to be
more self-reliant than most American women because her husband
was gone so often. Happily for her, she had servants to lighten the
load. Owing to this, she could be a devoted mother to her four children while still finding the time to read extensively to make up for her
lack of formal education. Well-read as she was, her other favored activity was writing letters, and, in consequence, more than two thousand of them have survived. There are letters of family gossip to her
sisters, countless letters to her frequently absent husband, and many
about public issues to other statesmen such as Thomas Jefferson. What
is more, Abigail was never shy about expressing her opinions, pun-
gently, forcefully, and wittily.[44] This one woman wrote more letters
than have survived from all American women put together in the seventeenth century.

Although it would be pushing the argument too far to claim that
Abigail Adams was a proto-feminist—the injunction to remember the
ladies in the new frame of government referred specifically to the tyranny that husbands enjoyed in marriage and not to women's rights
more generally—nonetheless she made an eloquent statement about
female patriotism to her husband, a statement that perfectly captures
what republicans thought female virtue could bring to public life:

> Patriotism in the female Sex is the most disinterested of all virtues.
> Excluded from honours and from offices, we cannot attach ourselves to
> the State or Government from having held a place of eminence. Even
> in the freest country our property is subject to the controls and disposal
> of our partners, to whom the Laws have given a sovereign Authority.

Deprived of a voice in Legislation, obliged to submit to those Laws which are imposed upon us, is it not sufficient to make us indifferent to the publick Welfare? Yet all History and every Age exhibit Instances of patriotical virtue in the female Sex, which considering our situation equals the most Heroick of yours.[45]

If interest led men down the road to corruption, then disinterested women could make a political contribution of great value.

Abigail Adams read, thought, and wrote about public issues, but did not attempt to publish her views. Her close friend Mercy Otis Warren, on the other hand, published extensively—albeit anonymously until 1790—in so doing attempting mightily to have an impact on actual policy outcomes. Indeed, she even referred to herself as a "politician," writing to her son about the Quasi-War, for example, "I dread it as a Woman, I fear it as a friend to my country; yet think (as a politician) I see it pending over this land."[46]

Like Abigail Adams, Mercy Otis Warren (1728–1814), was an upper-class woman, sister of one man deeply involved in patriot affairs and wife of another. Like Abigail, too, she was a letter-writer par excellence, writing in an ornate eighteenth-century prose. On one occasion, for example, she opined to a correspondent, "Happy indeed should we all feel had we no self upbraidings but what arise from such slight causes as a deficiency in the etiquette of an epistolary intercourse."[47] Mother of four sons, Warren, again like Abigail, did not see her maternal role as foreclosing a profound interest in the public life of her beloved country. In addition to the voluminous correspondence, she was the author of plays, pamphlets, and a three-volume history of the American Revolution, all of which were politically inspired.

Mercy Otis Warren was fortunate enough to have a role model, Catharine Macaulay, British historian and radical Whig who supported the American Revolution and who wrote a reply to Edmund Burke's animadversions on the French Revolution. The two women corresponded for eighteen years—until Macaulay's death in 1791—discussing ideas, military engagements during the war, the character of George Washington, and the fate of the young nation. We know that Macaulay was important to the younger woman because she said as much: "You see madam I disregard the opinion that women make but indifferent politicians. It may be true in general but the present age has given us an example at least to the contrary." [48]

Having met Abigail Adams in 1773, Warren was soon on terms of friendship, epistolary and otherwise, with both Adamses. Husband and wife both had a high opinion of Warren's judgment and intelligence. In consequence, over the ensuing months of crisis, with Parliament trying to tame the colonies and patriots beginning to assemble in the Continental Congress, John Adams asked Warren what she thought the form of government should be, once the people had shaken off "the fetters of monarchic and aristocratic tyranny." She wrote him a long and eloquent letter in favor of a republic. [49] She never swerved from her devotion to the republican ideal and actually had a falling-out with the Adamses that lasted for some years, after both of them had become more conservative than they had been during the full ardor of the revolutionary moment.

Correspondent of patriots, if not personally present at their deliberations, Mercy Otis Warren became even more active during the 1780s. Although she deplored Shays' Rebellion—which scared more than one former revolutionary into supporting a concentration of power at the national level—she failed to see the need for so powerful a central government as the Constitution provided. She therefore became an anti-Federalist, confiding her anxieties at this juncture to Catharine Macaulay: "You will doubtless be surprized when I tell you that republicanism, the Idol of some men, and independence the glory of all, are nearly dwindled into theory. The ideas of the first are defaced by a spirit of anarchy and the latter almost annihilated by the views of private ambition and a rage for the accumulation of wealth, by a kind of public gambling, instead of private industry." [50]

In 1788 she published, pseudonymously, an anti-Federalist pamphlet, setting forth eighteen principal reasons for opposing the Constitution. They ranged from the lack of a Bill of Rights to what she saw as too much power concentrated in the hands of the judiciary to the possibility of a standing army. The pamphlet testifies both to her close study of political theory—she cites Machiavelli at one point and at another she expresses the opinion that a republic should not be too large, a favorite argument of Montesquieu's—and to her fervent fear of the concentration of power. [51]

But her most noteworthy feat, as a public woman was her authorship of a three-volume history of the American Revolution, published in her own name in 1805, the year she turned seventy-seven. She explained in the preface that the crisis "stimulated to observation a mind that had not yielded to the assertion that all political attentions lay out of the road of female life." Knowing that men were usually the historians, because of their greater experience with military affairs, she nonetheless recollected "that every domestic enjoyment depends on the unimpaired possession of civil and religious liberty, that a concern for the welfare of society ought equally to glow in every human breast, [and] the work was not relinquished."

This is not the place to analyze what was the first substantial work of history by an American woman. Subject of two insightful articles by Lester Cohen, Warren has yet to receive the full-scale biographical treatment she so clearly deserves. Nor has her monumental history been adequately noticed. The grumbling judgment of John Adams can perhaps explain this state of affairs. Unhappy that she had criticized him, he complained to Elbridge Gerry: "History is not the Province of the Ladies." [52]

That she thought otherwise—and acted on her beliefs—has everything to do with republicanism. As strongly committed to her ideals as any man, she drew from those ideals the validation for public activity by a woman. At times her need to justify so marked a departure from the norm even led her a few steps down the path of what we would now call a feminist ideology—especially where education was concerned. As we have seen, the eagerness for improved education for young women was the hallmark of the republican position on women. [53]

Human freedom as an ideal—this was the subject of discussion in taverns and homes during the period, as well as in letters among friends, the Adamses and Warren included. Women clearly overheard these conversations, even if they did not themselves participate. Local tradition in Berkshire County, Massachusetts, has it that Elizabeth Freeman, affectionately known as Mumbet, overheard such a conversation and decided to sue for her freedom from enslavement. [54] While this can never be conclusively proven, what we know with certainty is this: *Brom and Bett v. Ashley* in 1781 was one of two cases that ended slavery in Massachusetts.

Freeman was a slave in the household of Colonel John Ashley and Mrs. Ashley, members of the local elite in Sheffield. A patriot, Colonel Ashley regularly played host on occasions during which he and his guests discussed the principles of the Revolution and the Declaration of Independence. According to Catharine Sedgwick, the nineteenth-century novelist in whose family a free Elizabeth Freeman became a servant, the enslaved woman heard a reading of the Declaration: "Action was the law of her nature, and conscious of superiority to all around her, she felt servitude to be intolerable." [55] Both Sedgwick and local tradition agree that Mrs. Ashley was a "termagant" and that this circumstance reinforced Freeman's decision to sue for her freedom.

These are the facts that can be fully documented: Brom, a male slave about whom little is known, and Bett were joined in a suit for freedom; the attorneys for the plaintiffs were Theodore Sedgwick and Tapping Reeve, both prominent men; the suit was successful; and Colonel Ashley dropped his appeal, thus providing "formal recognition of the abolition of slavery in Massachusetts." [56] We also know that Elizabeth Freeman was a beloved member of the Sedgwick household after she obtained her freedom. Two Sedgwicks wrote about her, one painted her portrait, and she is buried in the family plot.

If we go beyond the realm of what can be conclusively proven to that of folklore, we shall find the case to be especially suggestive about the public access of women in the late eighteenth century. Local tradition says that Bett was the one who took the initiative to obtain her freedom, but that, as a woman, she could not be the sole plaintiff, hence the addition of Brom to the case. Local tradition also says that

Mrs. Ashley was bitterly opposed to her slave being freed but that, as a woman, she was unable to go into the court to defend her own interest. Indeed, Sedgwick (no doubt the source for much of the local tradition) comments: "Happily for the servile household, those were the days of the fixed supremacy of man."

It seems incontrovertibly true that Freeman must, at some point in her life, have been inspired by the Declaration—whether or not her memory was fully reliable about the role it played in her suit.[57] That is, we can legitimately infer that Sedgwick's recollection was not made up out of whole cloth. Furthermore, Freeman must have had a formidable sense of self to have so impressed various Sedgwicks. As with Abigail Adams and Mercy Otis Warren, that self had been politicized—was connecting with public issues—and thus represented the new, republican-inspired style of female subjectivity.[58]

It is appropriate to end this chapter with Elizabeth Freeman, because her case captures the gains republicanism produced for public womanhood and those it did not—inasmuch as neither of the female principals went to court to defend her own interests. Moreover, it demonstrates that in the quest for public access, there could be antagonistic interests among women themselves.

By the late eighteenth century the discourse about women had begun to change, and women themselves were participating in the discourse about public issues to an unprecedented extent. Married women still could not control property in their own names, women still could not vote, but some at least were beginning to receive an education to equip them for intelligent participation in their society.

The most serious liability of republicanism, in the eyes of certain scholars, is the fact that in the body of writing of Mercy Otis Warren, as a prime example, virtue received so much emphasis and power so little. Lester Cohen argues that women became too good for this world whereas male anti-Federalists began to enter the government and make the compromises necessary to carry on a practical political life.[59]

Even acknowledging the force of this insight, it must still be recognized how much republicanism, with its perhaps undue emphasis on virtue insofar as integration into the rough-and-tumble world of politics was concerned, contributed toward countering the older, invidious connotation of public woman, a connotation with a very long life span, as we are discovering. That the link between public woman and sexual impropriety was still alive and well in the early Republic is borne out by an argument made by Thomas Jefferson: "Were our state a pure democracy in which all the inhabitants should meet together to transact their business, there would yet be excluded from their deliberations 1) infants . . . 2) women, who to prevent depravation of morals, and ambiguity of issue, could not mix promiscuously in the public meetings of men; [and] 3) slaves. . . ."[60] Republican women, as carriers of virtue, had the language and the intellectual tools to challenge this stereotype. And in the antebellum United States, many of them, or their daughters, would do just that.

4

The Power of the Word

Thus, towards the end of the eighteenth century a change came about which, if I were rewriting history, I should describe more fully and think of greater importance than the Crusades or the Wars of the Roses. The middle-class woman began to write.

VIRGINIA WOOLF

Between the novel and America there are peculiar and intimate connections.

LESLIE FIEDLER

American women had been reading from the time of the earliest colonial settlement, principally the Bible, and, as we have seen, a few of them had also been writing. Not surprisingly, the changes of the eighteenth century in family life, in religion, in the economy, and in the polity turned more of them into writers. Then in the late eighteenth century the appearance of the novel as a genre and its burgeoning popularity in the New World created a new set of publishing possibilities for literary woman, hence new possibilities for public woman. Indeed, one can go so far as to state that the novel symbolized the eighteenth-century changes in the status of female selfhood as it also ratified and extended them.

Virginia Woolf understood that the novel has been crucial to the advancement of women. In *A Room of One's Own* Woolf asserted that when middle-class women in England began to write, this was an historical event of the first magnitude. Yet surprisingly, until quite recently, feminist scholars have not explored the implications of this assertion.[1] Nonetheless, the rise of public woman in the United States is incomprehensible without a full understanding of the role played by the novel, because this genre provided an essential link between purely private expression and the public world. Moreover, it gave women, authors and readers both, a voice for the self-representation which had been made possible by the valorizing of female subjectivity. Further, if republicanism in its American manifestation relied in part on female virtue for its success, the novel spread the word of that development. Finally, the novel gave women authors a means for taking powerful public action in a polity where they lacked the franchise.

The novel was well suited to be the vehicle by which women "publicized" their subjectivity. Indeed, in many ways the novel resembles a higher form of gossip, hence is akin to the discourse by which women have been able to exert power even under the most inauspicious of circumstances. Like gossip, novels tell stories about human behavior, probe motives, and frequently deal with sexuality. Moreover, in the words of Margaret Drabble: "Much fiction operates in the spirit of inspired gossip. . . . It speculates on little evidence, inventing elaborate and artistic explanations of little incidents and overheard remarks that often leave the evidence far behind."[2] For all these reasons—at bottom, because the novel was a published version of familiar discourse—women writers have been novelists from the eighteenth century on, and other women have avidly read what they have written.

Perhaps the most crucial element for our purposes in the resemblance between gossip and the novel is the fact that both occupy a liminal position between private and public realms. Gossip often deals with the most private and intimate of subjects, yet can have consequential ramifications in the public sphere. A novel is published and may be reviewed and, if the author is fortunate, widely discussed, but is read in private and deals with the stuff of emotional intimacy.[3]

That the novel appeared when it did, in the midst of the profound changes in the family on both sides of the Atlantic in the mid-eighteenth century, was far from coincidental. According to Ian Watt in his classic study, *The Rise of the Novel*, "The rise of the novel, then, would seem to be connected with the much greater freedom of women in modern society, a freedom which, especially as regards marriage, was achieved earlier and more completely in England than elsewhere."[4] Who a woman would choose—and be chosen by—as a marriage partner furnished the subject for Samuel Richardson in *Pamela* and *Clarissa*, two pioneering novels,[5] as it did for Fanny Burney and Jane Austen, the first great female artists of the genre in England.

Moreover, the rise of the novel was closely related to the increasing value placed on private life in the early modern period. Real-life memoirs before the advent of the novel had seldom probed emotional states, focusing rather on the (male) author's recollection of public events in which he had played a part.[6] As Puritan conversion narratives were pathbreaking in their sustained introspection, so too was the novel in its delineation of psychological states. The eighteenth-century encyclopedist Denis Diderot exclaimed that Richardson had taken a lantern into the cavern that is the human heart and illuminated the darkest recesses thereof. He also commented about the experience of reading *Clarissa* that he felt alone after he finished the book, alone because the characters had become like personal friends.[7]

Suffice it to say, then, that changes in the material world and in the world of ideas created the preconditions both for the novel's emergence and for a new type of family which permitted more privacy, more opportunity for reading, and a growing female autonomy. Given this congruence, it is not surprising that the first real novel—as opposed to adventure tale—in the English language, Samuel Richardson's *Pamela; or, Virtue Rewarded*, which appeared in 1740, focused on a female protagonist and a female subject, the struggles of a servant woman to protect her virtue and to improve her lot in life. The eponymous heroine successfully defends herself against numerous attempts at seduction carried out by her master—who eventually marries her. Cast in letters, *Pamela* permits the reader to enter into its heroine's every nuance of thought. Richardson prided himself on how close he was to the feminine point of view, and he went out of his way to include not only minute descriptions of Squire B.'s conduct as seen by Pamela but also domestic details and information about clothes.[8]

In effect, *Pamela* established a breach in patriarchal discourse by valorizing the realm of feelings. Squire B., Pamela's would-be seducer, could have ravished her and been done with it—in fact he nearly does this. But instead Pamela succeeds in fascinating him with her mind and spirit and thereby hangs the tale. He wants to enjoy these as well as her body, and this desire of his gives Pamela the leverage she needs to become Mrs. B. She thus exercises a new kind of power. Says Nancy Armstrong: "Power operates by reconstituting the subject out of words."[9] Specifically, Pamela gains the power of self-representation, essential for a woman to possess before she can imagine new social arrangements and assert a claim to the public realm.

Women needed to discuss *Pamela* and the issues it raised. For example, those dear friends and frequent correspondents Esther Edwards Burr and Sarah Prince both read *Pamela*, as many other Americans did in the mid-eighteenth century.[10] Burr wrote to Prince: "Pray my dear how could Pamela forgive Mr. B. all his Devilish conduct so as to consent to marry him."[11] They both preferred *Clarissa*, which has a tragic ending, to the happy ending of *Pamela*, which requires the heroine to forgive a man who had done his best to ruin her by the standards of the day.

Pamela and *Clarissa* soon had numerous progeny, many written by women themselves.[12] The names of Fanny Burney, Ann Radcliffe, and—supremely—Jane Austen come immediately to mind. It is important not to overstate the argument and claim that these pioneering women novelists were proto-feminist in their orientation. Few among them approached the type of analysis offered by their contemporary Wollstonecraft, for example. Nonetheless, if they could not completely escape the framework of the traditional patriarchal discourse with which they had grown up, neither were they completely bound by it.[13] Burney's *Cecilia* (1782), for example, offers a harsh critique of patriarchal patterns of inheritance. Thus the novel in its first decades already had begun to display its capacity to articulate female concerns and to attack male privilege.

On the American side of the Atlantic, women were the beneficiaries of two significant developments in finding a novelistic voice: the large-scale changes in the Anglo-American world that precipitated a female literary tradition and the changes specific to this country that brought women into the political community, albeit in a limited fashion, as we learned in the last chapter. In fact, both *Charlotte Temple* and *The Coquette*, the first two novels by American women, show a woman writer finding a voice about an issue—seduction—with political implications in the new nation.

Written by the British-born Susanna Rowson, *Charlotte Temple* appeared in 1794, after first having been published in England, and enjoyed the status of the leading best-seller in this country until the publication of *Uncle Tom's Cabin*.[14] Hence, when we deal with this book, we are dealing with a document that was central to the culture. So loved was *Charlotte Temple* that readers tinted the illustrations of the heroine and treated the book itself like a precious object. Says Cathy Davidson in her *Revolution and the Word*: "*Charlotte Temple* enjoyed the longest popularity of any American novel and was the first fiction in America to signal the novel's rise to cultural prominence. . . ."[15] Like *Pamela, Charlotte Temple* is about a woman's struggle, in this case unsuccessful, to defend her virtue. The young heroine is a schoolgirl in England who listens to the blandishments of a soldier and runs away with him to the New World, only to face abandonment and early death. It should be noted, too, that the seducer is aided in his efforts by a corrupt Frenchwoman, a teacher at the school.

Because many Americans had begun to see female virtue and female innocence as metaphors for the national virtue they were so eager to protect, seduction was an especially compelling theme in the new nation. Thus, *Charlotte Temple*, a tale of the seduction of a young girl, can be read as being about the perils facing virtue in a corrupt world, a quintessentially republican theme, as well as being about chastity per se.[16]

For our purposes, one of the most striking qualities the book possesses is its emphatic rhetoric: no mere asides to the reader grace its pages, but rather page-long admonitions to the "dear girls" who are its presumed readers. A typical passage is the following:

> Oh my dear girls—for to such only am I writing—listen not to the voice of love, unless sanctioned by paternal approbation . . . pray for forti-

tude to resist the impulse of inclination when it runs counter to the precepts of religion and virtue.[17]

The modern reader is struck not only by the invoking of *paternal* approbation as a touchstone for proper conduct, surely a bow to the potency of patriarchy, but more importantly by Rowson's declared reason for picking up her pen to write. Concerned about the tragedy awaiting a young woman who might fall from virtue, she undertook the highly public act of writing a book, a book that would constitute a powerful warning about the consequences of such a fall. Yet she also displays considerable sympathy for her young heroine.

Changes in the role of women and a new concern about virtue in every sense of the word combined to furnish a topic that brought Rowson into the public sphere as author. A few years later she was joined by Hannah Foster, whose epistolary novel *The Coquette* (1797) is also about seduction. But in this case, the heroine is not a naïve schoolgirl, but rather a woman in her thirties.

Eliza Wharton, the coquette, has two suitors, neither of whom is entirely satisfactory. One is a rake, and the other is a self-righteous prig. She tries to buy time for herself, in a sense to increase her options in life, by playing them off against one another. This strategy fails when they both marry other women. Her reaction is to engage in an affair with the rake—which results in her dying in childbirth at a roadside inn. The novel was based on the real-life story of Elizabeth Whitman, a story used by several writers for purely moralistic purposes. In Foster's rendering, however, the tale gains a new dimension because implicitly she criticizes the limited options open to a woman at the time. And her heroine is clearly motivated by the desire for an egalitarian marriage.

Akin to the themes of *Alcuin* is this remarkable passage. A male correspondent reports to another man that one of Eliza's friends has made a lively speech on her own and on Eliza's behalf.

> Miss Wharton and I, said Mrs. Richman, must beg leave to differ from you, madam. We think ourselves interested in the welfare and prosperity of our country; and, consequently, claim the right of inquiring into

those affairs, which may conduce to, or interfere with the common weal. We shall not be called to the senate or the field to assert its privileges, and defend its right, but we shall feel for the honor and safety of our friends and connections, who are thus employed. If the community flourish and enjoy health and freedom, shall we not share in the happy effects? If it be oppressed and disturbed, shall we not endure our proportion of the evil? Why then should the love of our country be a masculine passion only? Why should government, which involves the peace and order of the society, of which we are a part, be wholly excluded from our observation? Mrs. Laurence made some slight reply and waved the subject. The gentlemen applauded Mrs. Richman's sentiments as truly Roman; and what was more, they said, truly republican.[18]

Thus in the first decade of the nation's existence, within less than ten years from the date of the appearance of the first American novel, *The Power of Sympathy*, which came out in 1789, two women assumed the public role of author. They wrote books that enjoyed a wide audience and that connected with important political concerns. What makes this especially remarkable is the fact that the novel as a genre was still regularly the target of moralistic attack, a phenomenon that enhanced the possibility that a female novelist might come in for her share of particularly snide comment.[19] Worth noting is the fact that despite the novel's morally ambiguous reputation, women regularly met for joint performance of such tasks as sewing or quilting while one member of the group read aloud from a novel. As Cathy Davidson puts it: "The discourse of fiction was itself made contiguous with or incorporated into their discourse."[20]

Moving forward in time to the antebellum period, we find that certain American women were pioneering a new type of fiction, which has been called the "domestic" novel. Beginning in the 1820s and continuing till the genre played out around 1870, women authors wrote enormously popular novels featuring, in addition to themes of romance and seduction, intimate details of the daily life of ordinary women. Frequently didactic and almost invariably sentimental, these novels had heroines whose dilemmas involved not only the choice of a marriage partner but also how they would support themselves and how they would learn to be proficient at housewifery, a particularly nasty problem inasmuch as the prototypical heroine of a domestic novel was an orphan. Moreover, like male characters in other genres, the heroines struggled with fate—and also sometimes with cruel circumstances created by men themselves.

In order to situate the domestic novel in its social context, we need to understand the profound changes occurring for American women at the time, especially for women in the settled areas of the Northeast. Many of the products that they had laboriously made by hand, such as soap and textiles, were now commercially available. A generation of attention to female education had given them better access to schooling. Finally, the birth rate was beginning its long decline. All of these changes meant that hundreds of thousands of women had both a better background for reading and more time in which to enjoy it. Moreover, domesticity itself enjoyed a status that has rarely been equaled in human history, providing the linchpin for a powerful woman's culture.[21]

The first important American woman novelist in the nineteenth century was Catharine Maria Sedgwick, whom we earlier encountered as the memorialist of Elizabeth Freeman, or "Mumbet." Author of a number of works ranging from historical novels to didactic tracts about the benefits of home, Sedgwick was both very popular and highly respected in her own day. Her third novel, *Hope Leslie*, is especially indicative of the proto-feminist potential inherent in the genre. Set in colonial Massachusetts, *Hope Leslie* features a young heroine—an orphan—who sees the dictates of her own conscience as having greater authority than the rulings of the local magistrates. Courageous and determined, Hope rescues two different Indian women, who have been, in her opinion, wrongly accused. In the course of the narrative, Sedgwick provides her own history of the interaction between the Puritans and the indigenous peoples of the area—highly sympathetic to the plight of the natives—to counter the then standard narratives of these events.[22] Written in 1827, *Hope Leslie* in effect rewrote important parts of American history from a woman's point of view, in addition to elevating a woman's conscience over constituted male authority.

Happily, we now have a substantial literature about the domestic

novel, to which both literary scholars and historians have contributed.
Dismissed by male guardians of the canon for much of the twentieth
century, these novels first received respectful attention from Helen Papashvily in her *All the Happy Endings*, published in 1956.[23] Although
current scholarship would take issue with many of Papashvily's arguments, such as the notion that the domestic novelists were somehow
"warped," it is important to acknowledge that she recognized these
novels as powerful political documents. That is, she understood that
the authors were often picking up their pens in anger to mount frontal
assaults on male privilege—as well as seeking to entertain their readers.

Like Papashvily, the literary scholar Ann Douglas in *The Feminization of American Culture*, published in 1977, also reads the domestic novels as political documents.[24] But more than any other recent writer, she is deeply critical of them for their sentimentalism,
indicting authors and their books both for sapping the supposed virility
of American culture, a virility she sees embodied in, for example, the
austere and tragic vision of the human condition to be found in Calvinism.

Since the late 1970s, there has been a plethora of writing about
these novels, almost all of which is insightful and some of which is
brilliant. In *Private Woman, Public Stage*, Mary Kelley analyzed the
lives and writings of twelve of the literary domestics, as she calls them.[25]
The great strength of her work, especially for the purposes of understanding the rise of public woman, is that she is sensitive to the dilemmas experienced by her subjects as they made the transition from being
a private person to   public figure, sometimes a public figure
surrounded by the trappings of celebrity. Nina Baym provides a valuable overview of the whole field and intelligent readings of a vast number of the novels in *Woman's Fiction*.[26] Two key texts, Susan War-
ner's *The Wide, Wide World* and Harriet Beecher Stowe's *Uncle Tom's
Cabin*, are the focus of attention in *Sensational Designs* by Jane
Tompkins.[27] Of the latter, Tompkins says, ". . . Stowe relocates the
center of power in American life, placing it not in the government,
nor in the courts of law, nor in the factories, nor in the marketplace,

but in the kitchen. And that means that the new society will not be controlled by men, but by women."[28] In short, Tompkins reads Stowe as a profoundly political writer. Another recent entry is Susan K. Harris's *19th-Century American Women's Novels: Interpretative Strategies*. Of the novels of the mid-century she writes: "The exploratory novel of the mid-nineteenth century . . . created a literary history that valorized women's experience, encouraged readers to consider alternative possibilities, and ultimately altered the social framework within which women's ambition could be contained."[29] Finally, in *Declarations of Independence* Barbara Bardes and Suzanne Gossett conclude: "Nineteenth-century novels make clear that the debate within the political culture over the role of women was indeed a struggle over power. In a series of 'declarations of independence,' " from *Hope Leslie* through *The Crux*, novelists proposed ways in which women might gain and exercise power over themselves, over their communities, and over the men in their lives."[30]

A close reading of both the secondary literature and of many of the novels themselves suggests the following ways in which these novels not only created a new discourse but also had an impact on the real world. In the first place, as Puritanism, Quakerism, and the American version of republicanism all dignified female subjectivity in their various ways, so, too, did the domestic novel carry this process even further. Many, such as *The Wide, Wide World* and *St. Elmo*, were female *bildungsromans*, in which details of the education of and early influences on a middle-class girl were given loving attention, the assumption being—and this was a new and startling assumption—that there could be as much narrative interest adhering to such a topic as with a male protagonist.[31] Moreover, what was especially innovative about these novels was that the reader could enter into the consciousness of a wide range of female characters and not merely that of a genteel young woman as she pondered whom to marry.[32]

In the second place, many of the novels are proto-feminist in their anger about property arrangements, divorce laws, and other elements of male privilege in a society whose laws still reflected patriarchal imperatives. Indeed, some, such as E. D. E. N. Southworth's

The Deserted Wife and Fanny Fern's (Sara Parton) *Ruth Hall* seem to have been written with pens steeped in acid, so angry do their authors appear to have been. Writes Mary Kelley about the struggles of the widowed Ruth Hall—which closely paralleled those of the book's author—"[t]hroughout, little aid and no comfort are offered by hostile parents-in-law, an unbeloved father, and a nasty brother. The only comfort comes from the memory of a beloved but dead mother."[33] If women even today can be crippled by the denial of justifiable anger— as the volume of best-sellers dealing with this theme would suggest— then how valuable it was that literary domestics taught women in the mid-nineteenth century that it was legitimate to be angry at the men who might be making their lives difficult.

Third, many of these novels suggested alternatives to the status quo, such as communities of women.[34] The March household in Louisa May Alcott's *Little Women* or the woman-centered Quaker household in *Uncle Tom's Cabin* are noteworthy examples of such communities. As an example of another alternative to the status quo, before the orphaned heroine of *Alone* by Mary Virginia Terhune marries, she runs a plantation on her own and performs this task with great competence. If patriarchal discourse did its greatest damage by foreclosing the possibility of imagining alternative social arrangements, these novels constituted a powerful counter to that discourse. Clearly, women could not be public actors until they developed a fluency at imagining new possibilities for themselves.[35]

Unquestionably the greatest of the literary domestics was Harriet Beecher Stowe, whose anti-slavery novel, *Uncle Tom's Cabin*, was a veritable primer for public woman. The writing of *Uncle Tom's Cabin* had been inspired by public policy, the Fugitive Slave Act, and sought to influence public response to it. Stowe's most admired characters defy this law, in effect committing civil disobedience. Urged on to the writing by one female relative and supported in the effort by another, Stowe held up the image of the highly competent and deeply political housewife, like the Quaker Rachel Halliday, to the women of the North and urged them to emulate this model. After the outbreak of the Civil War, as we shall be learning, many of them took this advice.

Furthermore, the enormous popularity of these novels meant that the female reform activities in the North during the antebellum period took place in a woman's culture predicated on domesticity but peopled by readers, readers who were accustomed to seeing their domestic activities dignified by much-loved authors. In a larger culture which still denied women public access on a variety of fronts, these writers taught their readers that housewives were capable of great things.

Finally, although the taint of scandal still clung to public women who tried to speak in front of audiences during the early part of the antebellum period, as we shall be learning in the next chapter, the literary domestics published with impunity and were seen as impeccably respectable women. That had not always been the case for writing women. In England in the early eighteenth century, for example, Alexander Pope had launched a virulent attack on Eliza Haywood in his "Dunciad," drawing on "an existing stereotype of the woman writer, according to which she was unclean, untidy, disgustingly sexual, and a whore." [36] In other words, the stereotype had been the prototypical negative view of public woman. The Great Awakening and the ensuing identification of female selfhood with religiosity had done much to counter this stereotype—to the extent that it existed on this side of the Atlantic—as had the ideology of republicanism. Then, too, the subject matter of most of the domestic novels was pious and moralistic. In consequence, by the antebellum period, women writers—as opposed to would-be public speakers—were able to blaze a trail of public exposure and influence, even if with trepidation and sometimes pseudonymously, along which other women could follow.

Turning our attention briefly to the South, we should note that a few of the outstanding women writers of the period hailed from this section. Mary Virginia Terhune, born in Virginia in 1830, lived well into the twentieth century as one of the most loved domestic advice-givers in the country. Caroline Howard Gilman published a journal of fiction, poetry, and miscellaneous prose in Charleston, South Carolina, in the 1830s. [37] Caroline Lee Hentz undertook to write the southern woman's response to *Uncle Tom's Cabin*, *The Planter's Northern Bride*, thus clearly demonstrating her willingness to engage in public controversy. And, as Elizabeth Fox-Genovese argues, Louisa McCord became a forceful and brilliant pro-slavery advocate. Although we stray from the subject of the novel in discussing McCord, what Fox-Genovese has to say about her is so insightful about southern womanhood more generally that we do well to pay heed to it. Fox-Genovese contends that although southern women kept journals, they were more reticent about publishing than their northern counterparts. She then suggests that McCord found her voice in a neoclassical mode and thereby avoided the self-representation being explored by the literary domestics. In other words, McCord's strategy was to present her pro-slavery arguments as emanating from a neuter mind rather than as bearing any relation to a woman's special concerns.[38] In sum, there were southerners who took the literary route to public womanhood, but they were less numerous and generally less outspoken than in the Northeast.

Just before the outbreak of the Civil War two books appeared by black women, one fiction, although clearly autobiographical, and one openly autobiographical, which can be taken as marking a new epoch in the self-representation of black womanhood. Indeed, both authors did what Louisa McCord shrank from—they revealed difficult aspects of their own experiences in making their political points. In both, one set in the North and one largely in the South, the authors launched powerful indictments of racism, attacking with special force its impact on the life of a sensitive woman. Both record such cruel suffering that they can be painful to read.

Virtually unknown from its publication in 1859 till its recent rediscovery, Harriet Wilson's Our Nig was the first novel by a black woman in the United States and one of the first to be published anywhere in the world.[39] Although very little is known of Wilson's life, her rediscoverer, Henry Louis Gates, Jr., has been able to establish that such few facts as are known closely parallel the circumstances of Frado, the heroine of Our Nig. An abandoned child from a biracial marriage, Frado becomes the servant and de facto slave of the cruel Mrs. Bellmont. Kicked, beaten, overworked, and barely educated, Frado nonetheless manages to hang on to her humanity and to her spiritual yearnings. A few of the white people in the New England farm community are kind to her, but the members of the Bellmont family by and large call her "Nig" or "Our Nig" and treat her accordingly. Most of the narrative is devoted to her life with the Bellmonts, with a very brief final chapter describing Frado's marriage and her abandonment by a similarly impoverished husband—but not before the birth of a son. We then learn from an appendix that the author Harriet Wilson was in a similar predicament and had written her story so as to raise money for the maintenance of her own son.

That a woman who had been so abused and whose life was so difficult would have had the sense of self to write at all, let alone to write the first novel by a black woman, is truly miraculous. We can surmise that her books and her religious faith must have sustained Harriet Wilson as they sustain her heroine—and as they have sustained many other women whose suffering may have been less extreme but was no less real to them. Moreover, in trying to fathom Wilson's achievement, it is important to realize, as we shall be learning in the next chapter, that black women were becoming public women in a variety of ways during this period, but especially via their preaching. Summing up Wilson's feat, Gates says that "her legacy is an attestation of the will to power as the will to write" and that she transformed the black-as-object into the black-as-subject.[40]

Harriet Jacobs's pseudonymous *Incidents in the Life of a Slave Girl* appeared in 1861, with a preface by the noted abolitionist Lydia Maria Child in which Child vouched for Jacobs's veracity and respectability, a step which presumably assured it a wider readership than that of *Our Nig*. Certainly, the book is a compelling narrative. Interestingly, although *Incidents* is about the heroine's harsh treatment at the hands of slave owners, it is also about a slave community, and therefore the heroine's life is less unremittingly devoid of kindness and love than is that of Frado. Indeed, "Linda Brent" 's free grandmother plays a role that is very reminiscent of that of the notable housewife figure in many of the domestic novels. The narrator enumerates her feats of cookery, by which she was able to purchase her freedom, describes her beautiful preserves, and establishes her high repute among

whites and blacks both. Clearly, she was a towering figure of strength
to her granddaughter.

Indeed, it is possible to outline many points of similarity between
these two books and the novels by white women.[41] For example, that
mixture of fierce anger directed against unjust social arrangements and
pecuniary motivation for picking up the pen that characterized Harriet
Wilson also characterized Parton, Southworth, and many others. The
latter may or may not have had the imagination to see black women
as their sisters, but they were, in fact, united by their mutual economic marginality in a society with so few opportunities for women,
white or black. In other words, for women of both races becoming a
public woman as a writer was often based on financial necessity.

One can also point to similarities in the rhetoric employed by
Wilson and Jacobs and their white counterparts. Wilson's tone echoes
that of the sentimental novels of the day, although her subject is much
harsher. Jacobs's tone more closely resembles that of Susanna Rowson
in *Charlotte Temple*; that is, Jacobs is out to teach her readers a lesson
about the evils of the slave system, and she is by no means shy about
underlining her major points with long asides to the reader.

> Reader, I draw no imaginary pictures of southern homes. I am telling
> you the plain truth. Yet when victims make their escape from this wild
> beast of Slavery, northerners consent to act the part of bloodhounds,
> and hunt the poor fugitive back into his den.[42]

But if Wilson's and Jacobs's books had much in common with
those by their white counterparts, there was one major area in which,
perforce, this was not true, the area of sexuality and romantic love.
Some of the white women novelists adopted the "waiting for Prince
Charming" mode; others did not. But for the black women, the toll
taken by racism, impoverishment, and the lack of legal binding force
for the marriage contract under slavery all combined to make romantic
love of the till-death-do-us-part variety extraordinarily difficult to achieve.
Frado's husband, from all we know based on Mr. Wilson, may have

been a decent and honorable man, driven to the desperate act of abandonment by his inability to provide adequate support for his wife and
child. Jacobs speaks of a young black man with whom she fell in love
as a young woman; her master, however, refused to give her permission to marry him.[43]

After telling of this episode, the slave narrative then recounts the
central formative experience of Linda Brent/Harriet Jacobs's life: in her
determination to preserve herself from her despised master Dr. Flint,
she gave herself to another white man, Mr. Sands, the lesser evil, and
gave birth to two children. In a book clearly designed to rally anti-
slavery opinion, the author revealed an episode that was sure to make
her white women readers appropriately angry at the sexual exploitation
inherent in the system of slavery, but might well also have caused
them to look askance at the author herself as a "fallen woman." Jacobs
managed to find a tone for writing about this experience that was both
chagrined and dignified.[44] It is important to understand how courageous her self-revelation was. The community of women—white or
black—who shared her experience of sexual exploitation was *not* a
community of readers, let alone of writers. Therefore, in her desire to
go public with the worst facts of slavery, she was exposing herself to
possible censure from the very group of women least likely to have
shared a similar experience. Moreover, she was asserting that when a
slave woman was subject to victimization by a slave owner, she had
the right to give herself to another man as an alternative, so as to
preserve her right to choose.[45]

This bold assertion of sexual selfhood stood the invidious stereotype of public woman on its head: a woman wrote and published a
book in which she freely admitted to the very behavior the merest hint
of which was used to drive women out of the public arena. By such
acts of courage, the bugaboo might lose its power to determine wom-
en's conduct—although it must be conceded that the readership of
Incidents was probably not extensive enough to have great impact.

In 1861 came the first fiction written by an American woman,
Rebecca Harding Davis, to deal sympathetically with the plight of a
white working-class woman, when *Life in the Iron Mills* appeared in

the *Atlantic Monthly*. Starkly realistic about the brutal circumstances of mill workers' lives, the novella drew upon the first-hand observations of Harding Davis, a child of the middle class, who was raised in such a town and who identified with the thwarted lives she saw around her. Like many other works of woman's fiction from these years, it had been largely unknown until its modern rediscovery, in this case by Tillie Olsen.[46]

Harriet Beecher Stowe, who had been born in the early nineteenth century and had begun to publish during the heyday of the literary domestics, wrote the novel with the biggest political impact of all. Indeed, no American, man or woman, has ever written a novel with similar impact. *Uncle Tom's Cabin* appeared in the early 1850s and instantly propelled its author into international celebrity. She then began to correspond with Republican congressmen such as Charles Sumner who were opposing the extension of slavery. During the Civil War she met with Abraham Lincoln, who reputedly said, "So this is the little woman who started this big war." In short, she became a public woman with a prominence no other had yet enjoyed at a time when women still had no formal role in the polity.[47]

With this achievement behind her and having published several other works of fiction, in the late 1860s Stowe took up an enterprise that was bold indeed: in her novel *Oldtown Folks* she mounted an assault, albeit an admiring one, on a powerful bastion of patriarchy, her father's Calvinism—thus revealing herself to be the rightful heir of Anne Hutchinson. Moreover, like Jacobs, she also dealt unconventionally with the theme of a seduced woman.

It has often been remarked that all of Lyman Beecher's children needed to stage a religious rebellion; one of the prime reasons apparently was the death by drowning of the oldest sibling Catharine's fiancé and Lyman's resolute refusal to give her the comfort of assurance that he had died a Christian. Catharine herself then went on to forge her own independent set of religious beliefs. And many years later this tragedy helped motivate Harriet to write about Calvinism, a conclusion that can be safely reached because a thinly disguised version of the drowning provides a central episode in another of the New England novels, *The Minister's Wooing*.

In brief, *Oldtown Folks* is set in a small New England village shortly after the American Revolution had ended. Narrated by Horace Holyoke, it is the story of three orphans, of their upbringing, and of the way their fate intersects with that of the mysterious Emily Rossiter, the seduced woman in question, and the fascinating Ellery Davenport, modeled on Aaron Burr. In setting her stage and peopling it, Stowe gives a precise account of the religious beliefs of all her characters and then demonstrates what their beliefs have to do with their behavior.

The first thing a reader is likely to notice about *Oldtown Folks* is its brilliance, the sheer intellectual achievement it represents. Henry May calls it "the most penetrating and imaginative account ever written of New England Calvinism and the society it formed and reflected."[48] The young girl who at the age of twelve wrote an essay entitled, "Can the Immortality of the Soul Be Proved by the Light of Nature?"—an essay that won approval from her father—grew up to have a sophisticated grasp of theology.

The second thing one notices may well be Stowe's ambivalence about many of her themes and her characters. Aware of the toll taken on the sensitive by a too-strenuous adherence to Calvinism, she also admired the intellectual and emotional rigor it called forth in New Englanders. Indeed, Grandmother Badger, the character who represents Stowe's central values—as did Rachel Halliday in *Uncle Tom's Cabin*—is perhaps the most devout Calvinist in the book. Stowe is also ambivalent about many of her male characters. For example, she gives a memorable portrait of the lovable but shiftless Sam Lawson. Married to the long-suffering Hepsy, Sam would rather play games with Oldtown children than assume the responsibilities of the family man he is. Yet Sam charms the reader as he undoubtedly charmed the author.

Attacking patriarchy both in the guise of the religion of the fathers and in the guise of irresponsible or cruel husbands, Stowe goes further in this novel than she had in *Uncle Tom's Cabin* in setting forth a woman-centered alternative to patriarchy. The earlier novel depicted competent housewives who took strong action against slavery, and it showed Rachel Halliday's kitchen as a haven of harmony and social justice. Grandmother Badger's kitchen is a haven in this sense— Stowe goes to great lengths to demonstrate to the reader that class and racial barriers do not matter in this sacred precinct—but she and her kitchen are both filled with intellectual vitality, too. We are told what Grandmother reads—Rollin's *Ancient History* and Hume's *History of England*, for example—and Horace, the narrator, frequently extols the "wisdom of grandmothers." In other words, in *Uncle Tom's Cabin* Stowe strongly criticizes the social and economic system that would condemn human beings to bondage because of other human beings' greed and posed the loving, Christian home as an alternative. In *Oldtown Folks* she criticizes the intellectual system that condemned many people to lifelong despair and poses the wisdom of grandmothers and the egalitarian social order of Grandmother Badger's kitchen as an alternative. Moreover, she also presents an impassioned plea for co-education and creates a woman character, Miss Nervy Randall, who combines the roles of housekeeper to the schoolmaster and instructor of a class in Virgil.

Yet another achievement was Stowe's vivid rendering of the daily life, the diet, the holiday customs, of her beloved New Englanders. As *Moby-Dick* is "about" whaling as well as about profound moral and existential questions, so *Oldtown Folks* is about New England Thanksgiving rituals as well as about the benefits and liabilities of Calvinism.

> When the apples were all gathered and the cider was all made, and the yellow pumpkins were rolled in from many a hill in billows of gold, and the corn was husked, and the labors of the season were done, and the warm, late days of Indian Summer came in, dreamy and calm and still, with just frost enough to crisp the ground of a morning, but with warm trances of benignant, sunny hours at noon, there came over the community a sort of genial repose of spirit,—a sense of something accomplished, and of a new golden mark made in advance on the cal-

endar of life,—and the deacon began to say to the minister, of a Sunday, "I suppose it's about time for the Thanksgiving proclamation."[49]

In paying tribute to New England housewives, Stowe focused public attention on the "hidden" daily activities of ordinary women.

To suggest that Stowe presents a picture of a completely symmetrical gender system—something her greatniece Charlotte Perkins Gilman wrestled with in a number of *her* books—would be an overstatement. But the boldness of Stowe's imagination and her extraordinary respect for female experience and female wisdom represent a highwater mark in the enterprise of valorizing both female subjectivity and also the woman's culture based on domesticity.

Finally, the sympathetic depiction of Emily Rossiter, whose "fall" into being Ellery Davenport's mistress is depicted at least in part as an act of rebellion against the harshness of Calvinism, also represented an act of authorial generosity to women.[50] Unlike Eliza Wharton and Charlotte Temple, a chastened Emily Rossiter lives at the end of the novel. This stance toward a seduced woman character serves to undermine the notion that women are either pure as the driven snow or whores. This dichotomy has, of course, been at the heart of the invidious stereotype of public woman.

Thus, within less than one hundred years of the publication of the first novel by an American woman, the genre had enabled a broad range of women to find a public voice about a broad range of female experiences. For many of them from marginal economic or social positions, the mere act of picking up a pen was in and of itself a politically significant act. In addition, several of them produced explicitly political novels dealing with social injustice or with the ravages of untrammeled male privilege. From their books, generations of women readers could draw courage to act in the world.

That such a process did, in fact, take place is borne out by Barbara Sicherman's study of the reading habits of the Hamiltons of Fort Wayne, Indiana, a family which produced two remarkable women, the classicist Edith and the pioneer in industrial medicine Alice. While the Hamiltons can hardly be considered typical—Sicherman calls them

"intensively and self-consciously literary"—the influence of their reading on the young women was so pronounced as to suggest a pattern
that did not merely pertain to one family. Sicherman found that the
young women were especially drawn to "socially conscious" heroines;
in fact, Alice Hamilton claimed to have been inspired to her medical
career by such a heroine. Sicherman concludes that "a reading culture
such as the one maintained by the Hamiltons provided a means for
accustoming and encouraging women to imagine new possibilities for
themselves."[51] She further concludes that this process led them into
the "innovative behavior associated with the Progressive generation."
In other words, their reading of novels encouraged Alice and Edith
Hamilton to become public women. Surely, they were not alone.

"Woman's Place" and Public Space, 1800–1860

I have blushed for my sex when I have heard of their entreating ministers to attend their associations, and open them with prayer. The idea is inconceivable to me, that Christian women can be engaged in doing God's work, and yet cannot ask his blessing on their efforts, except through the lips of a man.

SARAH GRIMKÉ

In the antebellum United States women created the first woman's movement, and state legislatures began to grant married women the right to own property in their own names. As is well understood, both of these developments represented radical departures from the status quo. What is less well understood is the fact that they were part of a larger process by which, during these years, American women were gaining public access in a variety of areas, not only the political and the legal but also the cultural—as with the novel—and the social geographical.

It is important to acknowledge at the outset of this discussion the extent to which Quakers had pioneered such changes, especially in the latter two arenas. From their earliest arrival in the New World, Quaker women had been traveling to preach the Word, sometimes at the cost of their lives. They had organized women's meetings within the church, and they had organized for benevolent social purposes on their own. But at the beginning of the nineteenth century, they were a group which was dwindling in numerical significance, as the growth of evangelical denominations swamped that of older groups. Quakers would still supply many of the greatest women of the century such as Lucretia Mott, but they were no longer numerous enough to provide grass-roots energy for reform, except in a limited way.

The South, which had seen a certain number of outstanding public women in the colonial period, as we have noted, would become the country's main bastion of a conservative social order, including with respect to the position of women, in the antebellum period. This was because opinions about slavery were becoming much more sharply polarized than they had been earlier. Opposition to slavery in the North was becoming more fervent and more moralistic. Moreover, abolitionist sentiments often belonged to the same persons who held other reform-oriented ideas such as those pertaining to women's rights. In consequence, defenders of the southern way of life and the "peculiar institution" began to take a dim view of any reform at all as potentially dangerous.

Thus the antebellum advance of women into public roles was less equally distributed around the country than had earlier been the case. Paradoxically, however, it ultimately involved far more women, because in this instance, the sources of change came from explosive and broad-scale economic developments in the North that redefined public space and gender roles alike. At the same time, the Second Great Awakening released a democratizing burst of religious enthusiasm that also brought reform in its wake. In short, the social change of the antebellum period was both narrower in terms of regional distribution and deeper in terms of the number of women involved in unprecedented public activity than anything that had gone before.

As the first factories producing thread and textiles began to be built in small New England towns in the 1820s, entrepreneurs turned to young farm women to be their employees, thus necessitating a new set of ground rules for female behavior outside of home. As steamboats and railroads supplemented or replaced stage coaches, another new set of rules had to be forged to govern conduct on board the changed modes of transportation. As cities grew and became much more heterogeneous, they changed character and became more chaotic and potentially threatening to women than the small-scale cities of the colonial period. Other changes were more positive for women: urban growth also facilitated the development of women's voluntary associations. The conventional wisdom that men's work moved outside the home under the impact of industrialization and that the two spheres in consequence became more highly differentiated does not begin to convey the actual complexity of early nineteenth-century social geography.

Let us begin with the area of gainful employment for women. The overwhelming majority of women who were employed in the antebellum United States worked as domestic servants, thus carrying forward time-honored modes of approved female behavior. Indeed, domestic service remained the single largest category of female employment until well into the twentieth century. But significant numbers of women were employed in other capacities, too, even if only for a few years. So many women were employed in unprecedented ways, in fact, that it became necessary for defenders of propriety to think of an appropriate rationale for this situation. For example, in 1853 Sarah Josepha Hale, editor of *Godey's*, mused: "Home is woman's world; the training of the young her profession; the happiness of the household her riches; the improvement of morals her glory. Such would be her position were the world rightly ordered." But Hale recognized that many women found themselves needing to support a family. She thought that any indoor employment was sufficiently akin to home so as to render it proper and mentioned type-setting and waiting on tables as two instances in point. In fact, "Louis A. Godey employs now eighty-eight female operatives in the different departments of the *Lady's Book!*" [1] She had earlier given a ringing endorsement on similar grounds to both teaching and medicine as female professions. [2]

So rapid and bewildering was the change in these years that we read over and over again about attempts to cloak woman's public activity with the aura of woman's sphere, attempts such as Hale's contention that all indoor employment is akin to home. Mary Kelley quotes what one woman had to say about the public performances of another, a singer, in Savannah in 1819:

Her public concerts are marked by this peculiarity, that she enters the room with a private party, for she is greatly noticed, and seats herself with the other ladies. When the company has assembled, she is led to the piano by private gentlemen of the first respectability, and after every song, again takes her place among the ladies, one of whom keeps a shawl ready to throw over her.[3]

The most important woman's occupation other than domestic service in these years was schoolteaching. One estimate suggests that between 1825 and 1860 about one-quarter of all New England women spent at least a small portion of their lives in the classroom.[4] Horace Mann and others pioneered the transformation of teaching into a true profession. Catharine Beecher and Emma Willard were the best-known woman educators, building schools and tirelessly promoting female education.[5] Of course, these developments fostered the cause of public womanhood in a variety of ways, directly, because more women were standing up in a classroom—as opposed to teaching in dame schools in their homes—and indirectly because educated women were likelier to seek public influence than their less-educated sisters.

Of the antebellum schoolteachers who were stepping into more visible public roles, none displayed more courage than those who went west. Polly Welts Kaufman has written about them in her *Women Teachers on the Frontier*. In the 1830s Zilpah Grant sent fifty-seven teachers west from Ipswich. Then in the late 1840s Catharine Beecher organized a much more ambitious undertaking whereby several hundred went to frontier areas lacking basic institutions. The teachers traveled by railroad to Buffalo and then by boat on lakes, rivers, or canals. The last stage was by coach or farm wagon. Staying together for as much of the journey as possible, the women nonetheless were apt to be on their own for at least part of the trip.[6] In so doing they faced the twin dangers of encountering boisterous and drunken men or of conducting themselves in such a way as to garner criticism. A woman could not be too careful. Traveling in a boat on the Mississippi, Arozina Perkins sat talking to a man about "religious duties and responsibilities. Time passed very swiftly, and it was nearly eleven before I tho't of the im-

propriety of sitting there so long with him."[7] Reporting back to headquarters, Augusta Hubbell wrote from bitter experience. She had been
recovering from an illness and had received occasional calls from a
gentleman, who never stayed past 9 p.m., according to her account.
Malicious gossips claimed that the hour of his departure was closer to
midnight and tried to have her dismissed.[8]

In the eighteenth century women had traveled, but rarely distances of this magnitude and rarely so much on their own. Moreover,
they had usually journeyed from the protection of one family group
to that of another. The hundreds of schoolteachers who went west
might well have found themselves living alone. Sometimes, they also
found themselves engaged in closely fought negotiations about sal-
ary—this, while hundreds of miles away from friends and family. Theirs
was not an undertaking for the cowardly. Says Kaufman: "As the pioneering women teachers grappled with their professional problems of
where and what to teach and how much to be paid, many of them
took actions that demonstrated a sense of personal autonomy. Because
they acted while serving as teachers, a woman's role acceptable to the
broader society, the model so many of them presented of a woman as
an independent individual capable of acting on her own was more
easily accepted."[9]

By 1860 more than 60,000 women were employed in cotton textile manufacturing in New England. At first they were native-born,
but by the 1850s they were much more likely to be of immigrant
background. Like the teachers, the first cotton textile operatives were
pioneers of changing gender roles. Recruited from farm families to live
in mill towns, they were the first substantial group of women to live
away from home—not just their own homes but away from any type
of family governance, to which domestics, for example, were subject.
Cognizant that this was an unprecedented situation, mill owners built
company boardinghouses for their women workers and instituted strict
rules for their personal conduct. The women were required to observe
a curfew and to attend public worship. Such virtues as cleanliness and
punctuality were enjoined upon them, and boardinghouse keepers were
expected to enforce the rules and in general to supervise the young

women. Nonetheless, their living situation away from male authority qua father of the family fostered a collective identity that soon led to developments that the employers had probably not anticipated.

Their pride in that collective identity almost immediately led some of the Lowell women to begin to write for their own newspaper, the *Lowell Offering*. Though sponsored by the factory owners, the *Offering* nonetheless published work that reflected the authentic voices of the workers as they sought to counter negative stereotypes of the woman who must work for a living. In the mid-1840s the Lowell Female Labor Reform Association began to support a labor newspaper, the *Voice of Industry*, which then became a vehicle for furthering their cause. Thus, for a while these women workers had two outlets for writing about their lives, one of which also served more overtly political purposes.

Writing an autobiography many years later, mill worker Harriet Robinson recalled her fellow workers as "wide-awake" and interested in the public issues of the day: "Some of us took part in a political campaign for the first time in 1840, when William H. Harrison, the first Whig president, was elected; we went to the political meetings, sat in the gallery, heard speeches against Van Buren and the Democratic Party, and helped sing the great campaign song. . . ."[10]

More important, within not much more than ten years after the mills were built, women workers went on strike and publicly protested what they deemed to be unjust treatment by their bosses. In February 1834, after employers reduced their wages for piece work, 800 women "turned out" or struck and then paraded to other mills to try to enlist further support for their cause. The Boston *Evening Transcript* described the situation:

> The number soon increased to nearly *eight hundred*. A procession was formed and they marched about town. . . . We are told that one of the leaders mounted a pump and made a flaming Mary Woolstonecraft [sic] speech on the rights of women and the iniquities of the *"monied* aristocracy," which produced a powerful effect on her auditors, and they determined "to have their own way if they died for it."[11]

What is more, this extraordinary example of all-female collective protest, among the first in American history, although women had earlier participated in mixed crowds, was carried on in the name of the republicanism of the revolutionary war period.[12] As we have seen, this political ideology had afforded an opportunity for women to define themselves as political beings. A few women had begun to refer to themselves as "politicians" in the early Republic, and now hundreds were marching forthrightly onto the public stage to defend their interests in the name of the same tradition.

Thus republicanism furnished an ideological framework; the increasing access to writing by and about women enhanced the dignity of female selfhood; and antebellum economic change further eroded patriarchal control over women, because it created new living arrangements and gave a few women some money of their own.

That the operatives' protest was collective was pathbreaking. In a recent article Linda Kerber compares women in revolutionary France with women in the revolutionary United States. The former situation saw many collective protests by women; the latter saw women organizing but in a much more decorous and limited way, except for a very few instances. "It is this absence of a collective dimension to most of their activities that marks the greatest difference between the female experience of the French and American Revolutions, and between the experiences of American women and their brothers," says Kerber.[13] She points to the fact that there was no American tradition of women's guilds such as existed in France as an important part of the explanation for the differences. By the 1830s, on the other hand, there were if not guilds at least groups of women working in close proximity and sharing common economic interests.

The early nineteenth century saw not only the beginnings of industrialization in textiles and also in shoes—in both of which industries there were women operatives—but also a rapid geographic expansion, fueled by the Louisiana Purchase in 1803 and other territorial acquisitions. This, too, brought changing gender roles, although not to the extent that one might suppose. The scholarly consensus is that westering women were eager to re-establish their familiar domestic patterns, both because the familiar brings comfort in a new environment and because domesticity empowered women in this period.[14] Nonetheless, as with the women teachers, the process of moving west over long distances sometimes in a wagon with a family group but other times by herself created a new social geography for a woman.[15] It is impossible to gauge accurately the number of women who journeyed alone but we are fortunate enough to have accounts by several women travelers themselves. Were they seen as "public women" with all the negative connotations, or were they accorded the same respect as men on a similar journey?

First of all, in this area as in so many others, the South was the most conservative part of the country. In her impressive study of black and white women in plantation households, Elizabeth Fox-Genovese states that "a woman alone on the public thoroughfares was a woman at risk."[16] Reading the journals and letters of southerners convinced her that white southern women ventured out without a male escort on only the rarest of occasions. Although married women had more freedom than the unmarried, they seem not to have exercised it. Even as late as the 1860s women still feared traveling alone. For example, after the unmarried Rebecca Harding published *Life in the Iron Mills* in 1861 to great acclaim, she wanted to travel north from Virginia to receive the plaudits in person but felt she could not do so without a male escort. She wrote to Annie Fields, the wife of her publisher, "Oh, Annie, how good it must be to be a man when you travel."[17]

Because steamboats and then railroads created so unusual a type of public space with an unknown etiquette, there were various attempts to segregate the sexes, both on board and in waiting rooms, so as to regularize a potentially "promiscuous" assemblage.[18] Travelers' accounts vary as to how thoroughgoing this segregation may have been. No doubt there were regional variations as well as those having to do with the scale of operations of the vehicle in question. Traveling with her children on a southern steamboat in the late 1820s, the English writer Frances Trollope encountered a milieu calculated to make a woman feel as if she had strayed into male public space, a milieu to which a woman was likely to react with at best discomfort and at worst disgust and fear. Trollope's fellow passengers included Kentucky flat-boatmen, who were seldom sober, and "gentlemen of the cabin," who were not much better. To her eyes, the latter seemed to claim spurious military titles and to spend most of their time talking about politics—punctuated with oaths—spitting, and cleaning their teeth with pocketknives. No doubt she would have been delighted that the sexes were on the whole segregated, except for the fact that the gentlemen's cabin was relatively well appointed and "their exclusive right to it is somewhat uncourteously insisted upon." [19] On another occasion she remarked that the segregation of the sexes on board a steamboat was so complete that husbands and wives could not be together except at mealtimes. [20]

Traveling extensively throughout the country twenty years after Mrs. Trollope and her entourage—and all alone—the Swedish writer Frederika Bremer also provided detailed accounts of her journey. Because she was a well-known writer, she had introductions to the leading people in most of the cities on her route. She was, therefore, frequently able to provide herself with an escort. For example, arriving in New York, she went to visit Andrew Jackson Downing, the noted landscape architect, and his wife, and they then took her sightseeing. She describes an episode that took place in a boat on the Hudson as follows: "Just beside us sat two young men, one of whom smoked and spat incessantly just before Mrs. D. and myself. 'That gentleman needs a Dickens!' said I softly to Mr. D. 'But then,' replied Mr. D. in the same undertone, 'Dickens would have committed the mistake of supposing him to be a gentleman.' " [21]

On other occasions, and particularly in the West, she was on her own. In Wisconsin, for example, she was planning to take a "diligence" or public stagecoach: "The diligence came. It was full of gentlemen; but they made room; I squeezed myself among the strangers. . . ." [22] On another leg of her trip, to Galena, Illinois, she had an even more unnerving experience: "There were three or four gentlemen in the diligence; I was the only lady. It was so dark that I could not see their countenances; but their voices and their inquiries told me they were young and of an uneducated class." She says that they overwhelmed her with cheerful but somewhat rude questions such as, "Are you scared, Miss Bremer?"[23] That the roads were rough and diligences often overturned added to a woman passenger's uneasiness.

By the time of the Civil War an unmarried young woman in the North could travel alone on the railroad with impunity. This can be gleaned from Louisa May Alcott's vivid description of her travel experiences in *Hospital Sketches*, an account of her brief career as a Civil War nurse. She set out to get a pass so as to ride for free on the railroad from Boston to Washington, D.C., where she would take up her work as a nurse. The president of the railroad sent her to the governor of Massachusetts for the pass. "Though the apartment [in the state house] was full of soldiers, surgeons, starers, and spittoons," she forced herself to persevere and was successful. Nonetheless, the ordeal was trying: "I'm a woman's rights woman, and if any man had offered help in the morning, I should have condescendingly refused it, sure that I could do everything as well, if not better, myself. My strong-mindedness had rather abated since then, and I was now quite ready to be 'a timid trembler' if necessary."[24]

Having procured the pass, Alcott set out on her journey, once again filled with the spirit of adventure: "Having heard complaints of the absurd way in which American women become images of petrified propriety, if addressed by strangers when traveling alone, the inborn perversity of my nature causes me to assume an entirely opposite style of deportment." She proceeded along this line, determined to be forthright in her self-presentation. Particularly taken with the way an Englishman treated his cross wife, she engaged him in conversation: "He answered very civilly, but evidently hadn't been used to being addressed by strange women in public conveyances; and Mrs. B. fixed her green eyes upon me, as if she thought me a forward huzzy, or whatever is good English for a presuming young woman."[25]

There are several things worth noting about these passages, such as Alcott's utter fearlessness about traveling alone and her humor about the etiquette of speaking to strangers under such circumstances. But most noteworthy of all is the fact that she sees her dauntless conduct as a "public woman" as part of her commitment to women's rights.

The first women travelers ventured out on their own because economic necessity or perhaps even a spirit of adventure dictated that choice. Without necessarily doing so consciously, they were pioneering an important new freedom for women—before the creation of what we would call a feminist ideology. By the 1860s that ideology had begun to be articulated and a woman traveler could see her journey as part of a larger enterprise.[26]

New types of employment and a new capacity to move about the country were not the only sources of change for women in these years, however. Among the most important catalysts for public womanhood was the religious upheaval known as the Second Great Awakening, whereby the number of believers grew, the number of denominations proliferated, and enthusiastic religion profited at the expense of established denominations. A recent student of the phenomenon, Nathan Hatch, points out that between 1775 and 1845 the population of the United States went from 2.5 million to 20 million while the number of Christian clergy went from 1,800 to 40,000. Perforce this development meant a change in the character of the clergy, a diversification in its social and educational base. Hatch calls the result "religious populism," because it reflected "the passions of ordinary people" to an unprecedented extent.[27] The leaders of this mass religious movement rose from the ranks and "proclaimed compelling visions of individual self-respect and collective self-confidence," an appeal which reached countless thousands.[28] Clearly, this was also a message well suited to encourage women to take a more active religious role.

In addition, the issue of social geography comes into play here, too. In terms of the use of public space, the most innovative development associated with the Second Great Awakening was the camp meeting, especially suited for frontier areas, but by no means confined to them. Many hundreds of people would flock to a clearing and set up tents so as to attend several days' worth of revivals. Itinerant ministers were often the featured attractions on such occasions. If the architecture of a church could frequently reinforce a sense of hierarchical authority, then the informal setting of the camp meeting served the opposite purpose.[29] In consequence, many people, women included, saw it as appropriate to engage in more spirited public behavior than under any other circumstances. An unfriendly witness, Frances Trollope, described a revival in Cincinnati, a revival which she thought to be coarse and melodramatic:

> It is thus that the ladies of Cincinnati amuse themselves; to attend the theatre is forbidden; to play cards is unlawful; but they work hard in their families, and must have some relaxation. For myself, I confess that I think the coarsest comedy ever written would be a less detestable exhibition for the eyes of youth and innocence than such a scene.[30]

Her denunciation makes it clear how liberating such occasions must have been for women. Not yet able to claim much in the way of public space of their own, women who attended a camp meeting had the opportunity to behave in public with a spontaneity forbidden them under other circumstances.

In addition, women's more active public role during the Second Great Awakening manifested itself in two other principal ways. In the first place, a small number of women, both black and white, began to preach in some of the newly forming denominations; not surprisingly, camp meetings were a favorite venue. Hatch tells, for example, of Nancy Towle, a young New Hampshire schoolteacher who was converted in 1818 owing to the efforts of another woman, Clarissa Danforth. In her memoir of 1833, Towle estimated that she had traveled 15,000 miles in the space of a decade as she spread the word, and that she had encountered approximately twenty other women preachers of various denominations along the way. Her path was difficult, because both family and community opposed what she was doing. Nonetheless, she persevered. Hatch summarizes her career as follows: "This ordinary woman of meager prospects found explosive potential in the settled conviction that she was called to thwart social convention and to accomplish great and mighty things."[31]

So far as is known, the first black woman to make a career of her preaching was Jarena Lee, who also published the first autobiography by a black woman in 1836. Born in New Jersey in 1783, Lee was a servant until her marriage. Four or five years after being converted, she heard a voice that said, "Go preach the Gospel!" She went to see Richard Allen, the leader of the African Methodist Church in Philadelphia, about her experience, and he gave her permission to exhort but not to preach. Some years later, after her husband had died, she was in church, and it seemed to her that the preacher had "lost the spirit: . . . in the same instant I sprang, as by an altogether supernatural impulse, to my feet, when I was aided from above to give an exhortation on the very text which my brother Williams had taken."[32] She was fearful about Allen's reaction to the episode, but rather than disapproving, he was sufficiently impressed by her fiery exhortation that he endorsed her occasional preaching at Bethel in Philadelphia and her full-time career as an itinerant. Jarena Lee was thus the first in a tradition of powerful black women speakers that included Sojourner Truth and Frances Harper later in the century.

In the second place, the Second Great Awakening played a major role in stimulating women to form voluntary associations. More clergy were telling more people, especially women inasmuch as congregations were becoming increasingly feminized during this period, that they were competent and efficacious, and their female parishioners were taking them at their word and forming societies for charitable, educational, and missionary purposes. In just the short period of 1817–18, for example, the Boston Female Society for Missionary Purposes corresponded with 109 other societies of a like nature.[33] In *Cradle of the Middle Class*, Mary Ryan describes the connection she traced between female conversions in Oneida County, New York, and the women's subsequent involvement with associational activity. She found that more than half the female converts of 1814 joined the earliest evangelical organization, the Oneida Female Missionary Society, an organization that would play a major role in promoting the ministry to the frontier by raising money and funding auxiliaries. "These women orchestrated the revival and devised a sphere for women that had not been anticipated. . . ."[34]

Another scholar, Joanna Gillespie, has immersed herself in women's religious memoirs from the period and has found confirmation of the extent to which their religion empowered many women. As she puts it, "Religion was the first public arena for the traditional woman's discovery of individuality and self-management."[35] She found that the memoirs reflect a powerful sense of autonomy which helps to explain how it was that women were propelled into public action—albeit usually of a limited nature, stopping short of occupying a pulpit, for example. Interestingly, six of her memoirists went so far as to lament their lack of access to public preaching, while one of the six developed the strategy of marrying an itinerant preacher who would allow her to "exhort the congregation before and after his sermons."[36]

To sum up the impact of the Second Great Awakening on public womanhood, its main benefit for women was to ratify and consolidate the valorization of female subjectivity which had begun in the seventeenth century. In conjunction with other developments in the culture such as the high respect for domesticity[37] and the growing power of female expressiveness in the novel, the net result was to increase female self-confidence for acting in the world. Many women converts in the early nineteenth century then took the step of forming voluntary associations, at first confined to religious and charitable purposes, but with potential for a broader range of interests. A handful of women went further and began to preach in public, mainly in frontier areas. And everywhere, revivals and camp meetings constituted a much less formal public setting for religious activity than did churches—and one with a different set of ground rules for public behavior.

Social change of the magnitude we have been discussing does not often go unopposed. As women claimed new terrain, both literally and metaphorically, they frequently faced what we would now call turf wars. By looking at the issue of social geography, we are able to see how such wars played themselves out. The larger point is that attempts to keep women in their place, in every sense of the word, often manifested themselves as attempts to deny women access to public space.

Indeed, we do not need to leave the home to see the presence of gender turf wars over the use of space, in this case private space. As women began to make new claims to power and influence in the name of their domestic role, both within the family and in the larger society, they also began to assert their power to dictate acceptable male conduct in the sacred precinct of the parlor. We have much literary evidence of male aversion to the use of the parlor, because small boys and grown men knew that this was the locale where they had to be on their very best behavior as defined by a wife or mother. At the same time that domesticity was empowering women and encouraging them to control the rules of conduct in the parlor, women were also gaining the use of a new space, neither wholly public nor wholly private—the front porch.[38] Here they could carry on various domestic tasks—doing needlework, shelling peas—while maintaining a public presence and monitoring the activities of others in the community.

If home itself might be subject to gender turf wars, then how much more so the new types of urban space in the rapidly growing cities.[39] We now have a literature that speaks to this issue in many different locales. Christine Stansell, for example, discusses the interplay between unmarried working-class women or "Bowery Gals" in New York in the antebellum period and the young "bloods" who saw them as "rightful prey on the streets."[40] Despite being subject to this harassment, the women were filled with high spirit and a sense of fun as they claimed their own right to be on the streets. "Her very walk has a swing of mischief and defiance in it," one observer wrote of the Bowery Gal.[41] Those women who were brave enough to pioneer as public speakers might well face both an unruly crowd and the authorities, as one female evangelist found to her sorrow in New York in 1810, after she had taken to the streets with her message.[42] Several decades later, in 1857 a woman tried to speak at a public meeting of unemployed, but a band of boys drove her away.[43] Matilda Joslyn Gage was the only "strong-minded" woman in her village of Manlius, New York. "When walking down the street she would often hear some boy, shielded by a dry-goods box or a fence, cry out 'woman's rights.' "[44]

It should be noted that, under the influence of revivals, middle-class women founded the New York Female Moral Reform Society in 1834 to reform prostitutes, in so doing claiming the right to visit brothels—with a male escort—and to chastise male patrons.[45] In other words, women might be the victims of male harassment, but they could also go on the attack themselves.

A major locus of change in woman's public access had to do with her capacity to stand up before an audience and retain her reputation as a respectable woman. Let us begin with the situation of actresses. As is well known, women had not appeared as actresses on the English-speaking stage at all until 1660 and the Stuart restoration, a time when moral standards became generally more relaxed. Even then, the first English actresses invariably were stigmatized as "public women" in the invidious sense of the term. Colonial America, on the other hand, saw few actresses, because there were few theaters until the late eighteenth century. By that time cities, north and south, began to house theaters, and both sexes acted in plays. But actresses were not seen as respectable women—one scholar says that as late as 1857 a woman named Mary Ann Duff was buried in an unmarked grave because of her "dark secret of having been an actress".[46]—and prostitutes occupied the third tier, thus making the theater a dangerous place for a respectable woman to visit. By the 1860s prostitutes had been banished, respectable women were becoming theater-goers, and actresses could be received in polite society.[47] It seems very likely that such changes were related to the fact that women were beginning to legitimate the role of public speaker and to claim access to the lecture stage or podium at about the same time.

The career of the famous—not to say notorious—Frances Wright affords a lens through which we can observe many of these changes taking place—and being resisted—because Wright was a highly determined public woman. While a few women may have spoken publicly on ceremonial occasions before Wright—presenting a flag to a regiment, giving a graduation address—she was the first to give lectures on controversial subjects.

Born in Scotland in 1795 to an upper-middle-class family and orphaned at an early age, Fanny, as she was known, came to maturity possessing financial independence. In addition, she was tall, strikingly attractive, and blessed with a powerful personality. In 1818 she and her younger sister came to New York, where they took up residence. Wright then wrote a play, *Altorf*, which was produced in February 1819. Attending the opening performance, she made the concession to propriety of keeping her identity as author secret. She was, therefore, unable to respond to the audience's calls of "author, author," by which they greeted the play's success. This episode marked the beginning of her fame—the secret did get out—and also demonstrated her propensity for flirting with dangerous situations, dangerous in terms of the approved standards of female behavior in public.[48]

Returning to England, she published her *Views of Society and Manners in America* in 1820—without a name on the title page. Once again, however, the secret got out, and the book's enthusiasm for democracy brought her friendship with such well-known men as Jeremy Bentham and the Marquis de Lafayette. Indeed, her friendship with the latter was so close as to render her the protégé of the famed Frenchman. When she next came to the United States, again with her sister, she had access to men such as Jefferson, Madison, and Jackson because of her friendship with Lafayette, in whose entourage the two young women were traveling. Nonetheless, the hint of scandal was beginning to cling to her name. Another European visitor the following year had this to say: "I was told that this *lady* with her sister, unattended by a male protector, had roved through the country, in steam-boats and stages, that she constantly tagged about after General L. . . . "[49]

It is impossible to do more than give the sketchiest outline of Wright's career as a reformer, an activist, and a public woman. Founder of Nashoba in Tennessee, an idealistic if short-lived experiment in setting up a model community where slaves could earn their freedom. Author of a treatise into which "she put an affirmation of sexual experience that no one else in nineteenth-century America would approach."[50] Freethinking advocate of rights for workers. So indefatigable a traveler that on one trip she spent two months traveling on horseback, an unheard-of journey for a woman. This list of her remarkable activities is by no means exhaustive.

After the failure of Nashoba, she moved to New Harmony, Indiana, where the reformer Robert Owen had established another model community. On July 4, 1828, Wright made a speech at New Harmony in which she gave a rousing call for reform and attacked mindless patriotism and militarism. On this occasion she became perhaps the first woman in the United States to speak before so large a mixed audience.[51] Her initial success was sufficiently great that she was soon speaking regularly. Frances Trollope described one of her speeches— on the nature of true knowledge—that took place in Cincinnati. Somewhat fearful of attending so daring an event, Trollope bucked up her courage and went anyhow. She was rewarded with being able to witness a notable performance. Majestically clothed in white muslin, Wright had attracted a considerable crowd of gentlemen and ladies who heard her display her "extraordinary gift of eloquence."[52]

Having spoken to large audiences in several cities, Wright moved to New York in 1829 where she frequently drew audiences of more than one thousand to her lectures. A witness described the scene as follows:

> As the appointed hour sounded from St. Paul there was a general turning of heads. She came up the aisle, and attained the platform, accompanied by a bevy of female apostles and a single thick-set and well-constituted Scotchman. He helped her in little matters, received her cloak, and also her cap a la Cowper, which she took off as men do, by grasping it with a single hand.[53]

By all accounts, her presence was electrifying, and her speeches revivified the freethinking tradition among New York's workingmen.[54] But as time went on and her espousal of free love became known, the attendance at the lectures fell off, and she became a pariah, unwelcome on social occasions. Her last years were spent in relative obscurity. In their comprehensive survey of American sexual attitudes, John D'Emilio and Estelle Freedman have this to say about Fanny Wright: "No matter which reform Wright supported, whether universal public education or a decentralized banking system, the charge of free love was invoked to discredit her, and for years when women spoke in public, critics hurled the accusation of 'Fanny Wrightism,' intimating sexual immorality."[55] In other words, those who opposed changing gender roles employed Fanny Wright as a symbol of "public woman," in the invidious sense of the term, and then attempted to discredit other would-be public women with a similar stigma.

But too many women were experiencing too much public access, whether in the classroom, via religious activism, by sisterhood in organized groups, or by various new types of gainful employment for this particular genie to be put back in the bottle. Other women soon followed Fanny Wright on the lecture platform. Her successors would not, however, follow in her footsteps on the free-love issue for many years to come. Rather, they would take scrupulous pains to maintain their reputations as "respectable" women so as to make their public voices on other issues more credible.

If Wright was a flamboyant, freewheeling individualist, we can locate other pioneering public speakers in a social matrix that helps to explain their motives and also how they could persevere, given the extraordinarily trying situations they often faced. For example, while the first black woman to speak in public on political issues, Maria Stewart, followed Wright by a mere four years, she was the beneficiary of the substantial growth of free black communities and organizations in northern cities. By 1832 there were dozens of mutual aid societies for black women; there was also an anti-slavery society founded by black women in Salem.[56] Although Boston's Stewart gave the first overtly political speech, in Philadelphia, as we have learned, the African Methodist Church had already experimented with allowing occasional preaching by Jarena Lee. It is not unreasonable to suppose that Stewart knew about this.

Nonetheless, what she did took rare courage. Born in 1803, Maria Stewart had been a bound servant in a clergyman's family until her marriage. Widowed young and deprived of her inheritance by the machinations of a small group of unscrupulous white men, she underwent a transformative religious experience that intensified her opposition to slavery. In the fall of 1831, she took a manuscript on the subject to William Lloyd Garrison at *The Liberator*. She then went on to give three eloquent abolitionist addresses, attacking colonization and espousing a more militant anti-slavery posture. But this public career evidently took its toll in stress, and she soon retired from such exertions.[57] Noteworthy is the fact that she, like so many other women, felt compelled to reply to St. Paul: "Did St. Paul but know of our wrongs and deprivations, I presume he would make no objection to our pleading in public for our rights."[58]

The next breakthrough for public womanhood, by Sarah and Angelina Grimké, also owed directly to the growing strength of abolitionist sentiment. In Boston, for example, women like Maria Weston Chapman and Lydia Maria Child were beginning to oppose slavery publicly, founding the Female Anti-Slavery Society. The two Grimké sisters, who had been raised in South Carolina in a slave-holding family but had moved north as they became disaffected with the mores of their native region, became the first female abolitionist agents in 1837 and embarked on a lecture tour of New England. Although they, like Stewart, were the beneficiaries of being part of a network of social activists, all of these pioneering women speakers faced such vilification that they had to pay a high personal cost for their public stance.

As it happened, Sarah and Angelina Grimké were at first going to speak to all-female audiences, but within two weeks men were coming in substantial numbers, too. Soon, the Grimkés, like Wright before them, were speaking to audiences of one thousand. And almost as quickly, they were embroiled in controversy owing to a pastoral letter denouncing them, circulated by the Massachusetts Congregational clergy. Authored by the Reverend Dr. Nehemiah Adams of Boston, the letter made the following point: "We cannot therefore, but regret the mistaken conduct of those who encourage females to bear an obtrusive and ostentatious part in measures of reform, and countenance any of that sex who so far forget themselves as to itinerate in the character of public lecturers and teachers."[59]

In addition to the pastoral letter, the two women faced a storm of ridicule from the press. Unlike Fanny Wright, the Grimkés had done nothing unusual to call attention to their sexuality. Moreover, again unlike Wright, they were profoundly religious and their speeches

reflected this. Nonetheless—as had happened to so many of their predecessor public women—the opposition engaged in sexual innuendo:
"The Misses Grimké have made speeches, wrote pamphlets, exhibited
themselves in public, etc. for a long time, but have not found husbands yet. We suspect that they would prefer white children to black
under certain circumstances, after all."[60]

The reason that the Grimkés were so significant, so inspirational
to many other women who prepared to follow them on the lecture
stage, is that they showed such staying power and such calm courage
under extraordinary circumstances. Most noteworthy was the occasion
when Angelina spoke in Philadelphia while a mob rioted outside. (The
mob burned down the building later that night.) Then again, there
was the fact that Sarah published a reply to the pastoral letter in which
she defended their rights as public activists and replied to the Pauline
injunction. She argued that Paul was referring to very specific circumstances in Corinth, rather than issuing a blanket condemnation of all
speaking in church by women. Making the common-sense observation
that if Paul were to be taken literally, this would preclude the use of
female Sunday school teachers and female choir members, she went
on to say: ". . . young and delicate women are engaged in all these
offices; they are expressly trained to exhibit themselves, and raise their
voices to a high pitch in the choirs of our places of worship. I do not
intend to sit in judgment on my sisters for doing these things; I only
want them to see that they are as really infringing a *supposed* divine
command, by instructing their pupils in the Sabbath or day schools,
and by singing in the congregation, as if they were engaged in preaching the unsearchable riches of Christ to a lost and perishing world."[61]
For her part, Angelina testified before a committee of the Massachusetts state legislature in 1838, becoming the first American woman to
address a legislative body and thus increasing the sisters' notoriety.

Although Sarah and Angelina Grimké retired from the front lines
after the latter's marriage to fellow reformer Theodore Dwight Weld,
subsequent historians have pointed to them as the two who did more
than anyone else to legitimate a woman's right to be a public speaker—
even on controversial subjects. There were still, of course, attempts at

counter-revolution. For example, in 1843 the Hopkinson Association of Congregational Divines of New Hampshire attempted to apply the Pauline doctrine so literally that women were prohibited from sighing in church or from uttering the words "Glory, Glory."[62] But after the trail blazed by the two sisters from South Carolina, there was a steady stream of women committed to being public speakers.

Two other women who fought for this right were Lucy Stone and Antoinette Brown Blackwell, college friends, sisters-in-law—they both married members of the Blackwell family—and lifelong allies in the fight for women's rights. Students at Oberlin (the first coeducational college) in the late 1840s, they were appalled to learn that the all-male faculty opposed training women as public speakers. Stone challenged this prohibition by speaking at a celebration of the tenth anniversary of West Indian emancipation. Shortly thereafter, Blackwell and others organized a Ladies Literary Society as a forum for training themselves in public speaking. In the winter of 1846–47, during Oberlin's vacation, Brown taught at a private academy in Rochester, Michigan, where the headmaster encouraged her to give her first public speech in the village church. So encouraging was the response that she returned to Oberlin and convinced her theology professor, the noted evangelist Charles Grandison Finney, to allow her to give oral presentations in his classes.[63]

Blackwell's ambition was to become an ordained member of the clergy. Not surprisingly, given this ambition, she, too, felt compelled to grapple with St. Paul. For one of her classes she wrote an exegesis of the famed passage in his letter to the Corinthians, taking the position that Paul's words had been misunderstood by later generations. She thought that he had meant only to warn against excesses and irregularities. She then attended the first national woman's rights convention in Worcester, Massachusetts, in 1850—here we are slightly ahead of our story—and delivered a speech based on this paper to an enthusiastic audience.[64] Following the convention, she decided to join Stone on the lyceum circuit and to support herself as a lecturer. Even before she was ordained at a small Congregational church in South

Butler, New York, in 1853, she received invitations to preach from liberal ministers and was able to occupy a pulpit from time to time.

By the 1850s, then, less than twenty years after the pastoral letter denouncing the Grimké sisters, women were regularly giving public speeches to mixed audiences throughout the Northeast. They could anticipate large enough audiences that they could even expect to support themselves in this fashion. They chiefly spoke against slavery, for temperance, and for women's rights. It should be noted that many of the ideas *about* women's rights were being developed to justify a woman's right to speak in public about important issues.

Two African-American women were active on the lecture circuit in the years just before the Civil War, Sojourner Truth and Frances Harper. Sojourner Truth was, by any standard, one of the truly remarkable women of the nineteenth century. Born in slavery in upstate New York in the late eighteenth century, she never had the opportunity to attend school and was, in consequence, illiterate. Nonetheless, she became one of the most powerful public speakers of her day. Deeply religious, she had received the call to travel and preach in 1842, in the tradition of Jarena Lee and others. But unlike the others, she went on to deliver explicitly political messages. Tall and with a sonorous voice, she made a strong impression on all who heard her.[65]

Frances Harper, on the other hand, was born to free black parents in Baltimore in 1825. Over the course of a long life, she published poetry, short stories, and, in 1892, a novel about Reconstruction, *Iola Leroy*, of which more later. During the 1850s she lectured extensively for anti-slavery societies in Massachusetts, Maine, New Jersey, New York, Pennsylvania, and Ohio. Thanks to the activities of all these women, white and black, the public discourse about abolition was not an all-male discourse, the first time that this had been true about a major policy issue in American history.

These women were famous without being notorious—unlike Fanny Wright. At the same time, there were also breakthroughs into public womanhood being engineered by "ordinary" women, women who were not famous, although one was destined to become so. For example, in 1853 four New York women gave Fourth of July speeches in small towns, accompanied by all the traditional paraphernalia of a celebration of the grand and glorious Fourth.[66] In 1852 Clara Barton, completely unknown at the time, appeared before the school board in Bordentown, New Jersey, and convinced that body to set up free public schools.[67] At more or less the same time, two young women who had gone west to teach were asked to perform church duties in the absence of a clergyman. Without consulting one another, they each came up with the same solution to the perplexing dilemma of how to minister to a real need without transgressing the boundaries of propriety: they read aloud from prayers and lectures published by men.[68]

This tiny sample shows the context for the breakthroughs made by well-known women. In towns and cities throughout the North and West, women were taking small—and in some cases big—steps into the public arena. No doubt many of them were inspired by reading about Sarah and Angelina Grimké or other pioneers. It also seems likely that they were inspired by reading novels featuring formidable female protagonists. Most of the women, white and black, drew on the reverence for domesticity that reached its apogee during this period as well as on their rootedness in evangelical Christianity. Together these helped neutralize the older connotation of public woman. The most significant exception to this pattern—other than Fanny—was the behavior of the women strikers at Lowell and a few other similar cases.[69]

By the 1840s, in addition to the acts of particular individuals, women were organized into thousands of societies for charitable purposes and a certain number for more controversial reforms like abolition. Anne Firor Scott provides the figure of seventy-seven all-female anti-slavery societies as of 1837, for example.[70] The research of Nancy Hewitt into the women's associations of Rochester affords us the opportunity to examine how the members of such groups viewed the issue of public womanhood. Dividing her women activists into three groups, benevolent, perfectionist, and ultraist, she points out that the women in all three categories were perforce required to do public fundraising, a profound challenge to prevailing sex-role stereotypes. All her subjects belonged to the bourgeoisie, roughly defined, but the women in the category she styles benevolent had the most claim to upper-middle-class status and were the most respectful of societal taboos against "public woman." Indeed, they "prided themselves on never ascending public platforms."[71] Yet in the end, their drive to help others and the need to raise money to support this activity required them to step out of woman's place, too.

Thus the bold step undertaken by Elizabeth Cady Stanton and Lucretia Mott when they summoned other activists to the conference at Seneca Falls in 1848 represents merely the best-known—and deservedly so—of a myriad of activities whereby women were staking out the claim to public space, public roles, and public influence. One day in the summer of 1848 the two women were enjoying a visit and soon began to discuss the problems of their sex. So angry did they become as they talked that they decided to hold a meeting on the subject and to issue a public call for participation in the local newspaper. Less than one week later, 300 people answered the call. After wide-ranging discussion, one hundred of them signed the declaration drafted by Stanton, a declaration calling for suffrage, for an improvement in the legal position of married women, and for more equitable laws governing divorce.[72]

Two facets of the Seneca Falls conference intersect directly with the issue of the social geography of gender. In the first place, although the Quaker minister Lucretia Mott was an experienced public speaker, she did not feel equal to the task of chairing the meeting, and neither did any of the other women. Therefore, James Mott was the chair. Stanton, who would become one of the most eloquent public speakers of her day, made her debut at Seneca Falls: "I should feel exceedingly diffident to appear before you at this time, having never before spoken in public, were I not nerved by a sense of right and duty, did I not feel that the time had come for the question of woman's wrongs to be laid before the public. . . ."[73]

In the second place, along with the call for the franchise, the first time women made this demand in a public way, Stanton wrote into the Declaration of Sentiments that emerged from the convention the following resolution: "*Resolved*, that the objection of indelicacy and impropriety, which is so often brought against woman when she addresses a public audience, comes with a very ill-grace from those who encourage, by their attendance, her appearance on the stage, in the concert, or in feats of the circus."[74] In short, in drawing up her list of key demands, Stanton recognized the importance of legitimating access to the lecture stage and the significance of the social geography of gender.

Two years later, as we have seen, there took place the first of a series of national woman's rights conventions, to which came outstanding reformers, men and women both. Members of this generation, who had so bravely pioneered woman's public presence, could now take stock of what had been achieved and what, besides the franchise, was still to come. But despite the fact that women were regularly speaking on the lecture platform, it was not yet possible for those attending a public meeting to discuss woman's rights with impunity. The national convention of 1852 saw women subjected to shouting and hissing from the floor. The following year, there was an attempt to hold a convention in New York, but organizers adjourned it because of "mob disturbances."[75]

Despite such lingering episodes of harassment, by the time of the Civil War there would be no turning back from woman's right to speak publicly on most of the important issues of the day, including such controversial matters as abolition and women's rights. There was, of course, one notable exception to this and that was the whole area of sexuality. None of the outstanding public women except Fanny Wright was prepared to deal with sex, and she became a pariah owing to the fact that she was.[76] But sex aside, and despite their lack of the franchise, during the Civil War, northern women took it upon themselves to lecture politicians, generals, and their fellow citizens about what was on their minds. And as we shall be learning, what was on their minds was a very inclusive category. Moreover, there is reason to believe that by the time of the war, women were routinely attending political events. For example, in his research on the small town of Sugar Creek in Illinois, John Mack Faragher found that in the early period, "[p]ublic life was dominated by men and their rituals," and the public culture was "ultra-male." But by the late 1850s, newspapers were inviting women to attend political events, and women were taking them up on the invitation.[77]

Before leaving the antebellum period, we should take note of certain developments that foreshadowed the changes of the late nineteenth century. In 1846 in New York City A. T. Stewart opened the country's first department store.[78] The department store represented an entirely new type of urban public space—grand, ceremonial, and consecrated to the largely female activity of shopping. There had never been so impressive a built environment so much intended for women, and, in consequence, women's experience of living in a city would be permanently altered. They would also have access to new types of employment: in the late 1850s, Clara Barton obtained employment as a clerk in the U.S. Patent Office in Washington, D.C., one of only four women employees. After approximately one year her sponsor left and his successor dismissed the women because of the "obvious impropriety in the mixing of the two sexes within the walls of a public office."[79] After a short period, Barton won reinstatement. Now the only woman employee, she was subject to harassment from her fellow workers and began to acquire a "reputation for lax sexual conduct" that followed her throughout her life.[80]

The department store and the office would both revolutionize the social geography of gender in the Gilded Age. But as the episode involving Barton so clearly reveals, any advance into new public roles still ran the risk of a counterattack involving charges of sexual impropriety. Anne Hutchinson's enemies had called her "Jezebel," and two centuries later Connecticut clergymen hurled the same epithet at feminist-abolitionist lecturer Abby Kelley.[81] In other words, those women who led the advance into public womanhood in the antebellum years had to possess courage of a high order, because they were marching into contested terrain and risking charges that might give them much pain. But they carried with them new sources of dignity and strength.

6

Northern Women and the Crisis of the Union

> Need I tell you that the women were always ready to press into these places of horror, going to them in torrents of rain, groping their way by dim lantern-light, at all hours of night, carrying spirits and ice-water; calling back to life those in despair from utter exhaustion, or again and again catching for mother or wife the last faint whispers of the dying?
>
> FREDERICK LAW OLMSTED

That women were deeply involved with the conduct of the American Civil War was not new. Women have always accompanied armies, perhaps as officers' wives but more likely as laundresses and/or camp followers. In the latter capacity they have, of course, been "public women." What was new about the Civil War was the fact that a few women were presuming to suggest to various generals how best to conduct the war. In addition, in both North and South, women nursed with devotion—without sacrificing their respectability—and saved lives. In the North they organized for relief on a completely unprecedented scale. A smaller group organized the Women's National Loyal League to pressure Congress to pass the Thirteenth Amendment. Inspired by Stowe's great novel *Uncle Tom's Cabin*, northern soldiers marched off to battle singing Julia Ward Howe's "The Battle Hymn of the Republic." In other words, women's writing was central to the culture during this period. And when the war ended, a plethora of books appeared, celebrating the heroic efforts of all these remarkable women. In short, despite the dearth of overtly feminist activity while the war raged, women were highly successful in legitimating a variety of public roles as a consequence of the war—and then they achieved postwar fame for so doing.

Clearly, the older connotation of public woman still lurked in people's minds, ready to be invoked as a weapon should the occasion present itself to do so. The best-known example of this phenomenon was the treatment meted out by Union General Benjamin "Beast" Butler to the women of New Orleans after Union victories led to the occupation of the city in 1862. Loyal to the Confederacy, many women went out of their way to show disdain for the northern soldiers by a variety of gestures, including spitting at them. Incensed, Butler ordered that any woman who insulted an officer of the United States "by word, gesture, or movement" would be subject to treatment "as a woman of the town plying her vocation."[1] In other words, women who violated decorous norms of public behavior would be treated like public women.

Another cultural stereotype of these years that could be invoked to discourage public activity by women, particularly the type of activity needed to deal with the carnage of battle, was that of "strong-mindedness." When modern men and women use the word "feminist,"[2] either to praise or to blame, they are getting at something quite similar to what was meant by "strong-minded" in the nineteenth century, that is, a woman who was/is independent, eager to obtain her rights, and highly motivated. As we have seen, for example, Louisa May Alcott referred to her "strong-mindedness" when describing her valiant attempts to secure a railroad pass. The word shows up repeatedly in unflattering discussions of the woman's movement. As a consequence, a young woman who went off to nurse for the first time, usually without training, and found herself at Gettysburg, say, and who needed all the strength of mind she could muster, might well feel ambivalent about this trait inasmuch as the term was used pejoratively to discredit woman's rights activists. As an instance in point, we find a young woman writing in 1864 of the ill treatment visited on nurses by their male medical colleagues: "No one knows who did not watch the thing from the beginning how much opposition, how much ill-will, how much unfeeling want of thought, these women nurses endured." The writer found this to be all the more inexplicable and unfortunate in that "none of them [the nurses] were 'strong-minded.' "[3]

Thus despite the changes during the antebellum period and the personnel needs generated by the first modern war, a war which mobilized hundreds of thousands of soldiers, the path to public womanhood was not without its obstacles. On the other hand, the cultural potency of domesticity in the 1850s—the dignity granted to female subjectivity—and the organized strength of northern women in their church groups and other voluntary associations gave thousands the self-confidence to engage in activities that took them out of woman's accustomed sphere.

Although the focus is on the North, it is important to acknowledge that changes were taking place in the South, too, albeit of an attenuated nature relative to what was occurring in the Union. Happily, we are beginning to have a literature about women in the nineteenth-century South. To summarize, the first substantial modern treatment of southern women, Anne Firor Scott's overview, The Southern Lady, emphasized the extent to which the war constituted a force for change by undermining the basis for patriarchy.[4] Writing a community study of the free women of Petersburg, Virginia, some years later, Suzanne Lebsock found a much more complex pattern and called for more research to test the accuracy of Scott's generalization about the erosion of patriarchy.[5] Now scholars are producing specialized studies that permit a more fine-grained analysis. Jacqueline Jones demonstrates that during the Civil War, "[b]lack women's priorities and obligations coalesced into a single purpose: to escape from the oppression of slavery while keeping their families intact."[6] In other words, they were, if not public women, at least agents of their own history to the extent possible. The first modern analysis of the experiences of white women to be confined to the Civil War itself, George Rable's Civil Wars, suggests that the war did little to disrupt the South's gender hierarchy. Thus he adheres to Lebsock's view, rather than Scott's. Like Fox-Genovese, he emphasizes the constraints on southern public womanhood, relative to contemporary developments in the North. He says of the pro-slavery writer Louisa McCord, for example: "Thus despite her great interest in public questions, Louisa McCord drew the line at delivering public speeches."[7]

Finally, the darkest view of the position of southern women during the war comes from Drew Faust. She argues that Confederate women became disaffected during the war, because "[t]he way in which their interests in the war were publicly defined—in a very real sense denied—gave women little reason to sustain the commitment modern war required."[8] The burden of current research confirms, then, that the dynamic for change with respect to public womanhood was not emanating from this part of the country.

In confining the discussion to the North, we are by no means limiting it to the activities of a northeastern elite, however, for during the war the seeds planted by women during the Second Great Awakening and nourished by broad-scale economic and technological change came to fruition throughout the Union. Annie Wittenmyer of Iowa and Mary Ann Bickerdyke of Illinois played roles equivalent to those of Cornelia Hancock of Pennsylvania or Georgianna Woolsey of New York—to say nothing of the unsung heroines of the thousands of soldiers' aid societies scattered throughout the nation.

As soon as the war began—indeed, even before the official outbreak of hostilities at Sumter on April 12, 1861—northern women became concerned about how they could help. In December 1860, for example, after Lincoln's election stirred the call for a secession convention in South Carolina but before any of the other major developments had taken place, the prescient Almira Fales had started to collect hospital supplies.[9] After Sumter, she was joined by many others. The initial focus of women's activity was to produce an abundance of "havelock" hats, whose long flaps were intended to protect men from the southern heat. As it happened, the havelocks proved valueless, but the women soon found better outlets for their energy.

The need for citizen involvement with the health and welfare of the men in arms could not have been more urgent. At the commencement of hostilities, the U.S. Army employed a mere twenty-six doctors and a surgeon general to minister to the needs of its 15,000 soldiers.

The surgeon general Clement Finley was superannuated and bitterly opposed to citizen involvement in his operation, no matter how inadequate that operation may have been. Moreover, there were no general hospitals, and, as a consequence, a wide range of buildings would be employed for this purpose before the fighting had ended. In short, there was a critical lack of trained personnel, supplies, and facilities, a situation crying out for remedy. And the women of the North had the edifying example of Florence Nightingale to suggest to them that *they* could do something to provide the remedy.

Less than two weeks after Sumter, upwards of fifty women and a few men met at the New York Infirmary for Women to discuss what they could do. Present were a number of outstanding members of the community, including Dr. Elizabeth Blackwell, the first American woman physician.[10] In his report of the event, Henry Bellows, the man who would become the president of the relief organization that emerged out of this meeting, wrote of an "uprising of the women of the land." He, a Unitarian minister, and the other well-connected men involved in the formation of what became the U.S. Sanitary Commission then sold it to a skeptical Abraham Lincoln and the Army establishment as a way of taming and controlling the enthusiastic but potentially bothersome women.[11]

It was a tough sell. According to another of the men, the Sanitary Commission's historian Charles Stillé, in the first interview between organized benevolence and the Medical Bureau, ". . . it was manifest that the officers of the Medical staff thought the zeal of the women and the activity of the men assisting them, superfluous, obtrusive, and likely to grow troublesome and that the sphere of the public in the work of aiding and relieving the army was predestined to be a very small one." Stillé further stated that Dr. Bellows had taken those objections seriously, but that the women were undeterred.[12] And in the end, the need was simply too great for the medical establishment to continue to oppose any but a token citizen effort. On June 9, 1861, Secretary of War Simon Cameron issued an order setting up the Commission and appointing Bellows and his male colleagues to be its officers. They were to serve without pay, although the government would

furnish them with a room. Several doctors and several clergymen were
on the board as well as Samuel Gridley Howe, husband of Julia Ward
Howe and the only commissioner to be a member of the reform community. As George Fredrickson pointed out in *The Inner Civil War*,
this was an elite group of men, expected by the government to keep
the women in check, an expectation the men themselves fully shared. [13]
But as we shall be learning, events and the women themselves con-
spired to give the women a much more active role than had been
anticipated. Soon the Sanitary Commission deployed paid agents to
visit battlefield and hospital alike, distributing supplies and checking
up on sanitary conditions.

As for woman's desire to nurse—and let it be remembered that at
the time nursing was not yet a profession, hence there existed no formal training programs from which to recruit—Secretary Cameron sought
to deal with the issue by appointing the well-known reformer Dorothea Dix to be the Superintendent of Female Nurses in April 1861.
Cognizant of the danger that women who went off to tend the wounded
might be seen as camp followers, Dix required her nurses to be over
thirty, plain in dress, and "by no means liberally endowed with personal attractions." [14] Like the Sanitary Commissioners a volunteer, Dix
served devotedly and eventually installed hundreds of nurses. But she
proved difficult to get along with—testimony to this comes from women
as well as from the male doctors who were her adversaries—hence her
effectiveness suffered.

There were, thus, two major organized efforts to mobilize northern women for the war effort, the Sanitary Commission and the
government-sponsored program to recruit women nurses, administered
by Dorothea Dix. In addition, countless women served as freelances,
so to speak, the best-known being Clara Barton. Barton, at the time a
federal employee, began to throw herself into relief work fairly soon
after Sumter. Before long a woman's network had taken shape whereby
others sent her supplies to be distributed to the troops encamped around
the capital. But she held back from personally visiting the battlefield
despite a strong desire to do so, because she feared for her reputation.
In February 1862 she attended the bedside of her dying father, and he

advised her to go to the front, telling her that a respectable woman would be treated with respect.[15] This was all the encouragement she needed. Within a few months she had obtained permission to take hospital supplies and food to the front. Before long, she had dropped the practice of taking another woman along for propriety's sake. Making a point of being fearless, she made herself so useful that she began to receive privileged information about anticipated battles. As a consequence, she was able to be at Antietam "just behind the cannon."[16]

It would be impossible to calculate the exact dimension of the female contribution to the war effort. Women were urged to form soldiers' aid societies under the ultimate direction of the Sanitary Commission so as to provide a variety of supplies. They responded so enthusiastically that "[t]he estimated value of the stores distributed to the army during the war was about fifteen millions of dollars," about four-fifths of which was the value of contributions in kind from American homes.[17] Women conceived of the idea of staging sanitary fairs as fund-raisers—and made the needlework to sell at the fairs—by which the sum of three million dollars was raised for the Commission. Women were employed as agents, and women ran regional offices. They procured vegetables so as to protect the soldiers from scurvy, becoming "capital foragers," and one Sanitary agent, Mary Ann "Mother" Bickerdyke, supervised a cattle drive down the banks of the Mississippi so that the recovering soldiers hospitalized in Memphis would have fresh milk.[18]

Mary Livermore, who with Jane Hoge and two men ran the Chicago office of the Sanitary Commission, wrote a memoir of her war work in which she described their activities and catalogued what had been sent to the army from just the one office. She and Hoge received packages from the entire region. Homemade garments arrived for recuperating men, in the folds of which women had tucked loving notes of encouragement. Working women pledged a portion of their salaries, and children brought in their contributions. As a consequence of all this, Hoge and Livermore shipped 77,660 packages to hospitals and battlefields with a cash value estimated at $1,056,192.[19]

James McPherson, the most distinguished modern historian of

the Civil War, contends that "[t]he U.S. surgeon general was right when he wrote proudly that the union army's mortality rate from disease and wounds was lower than had been observed in the experience of any army since the world began."[20] For this the thousands of women nurses north and south and the female "foot soldiers" of the Sanitary Commission deserved much of the credit. The army establishment resented all the volunteer help, especially from women, but proved unable to prevent it. This was because "so popular was the Sanitary Commission with the soldiers, so obvious its effectiveness, and so great its influence with Congress," that it was able to defend itself.[21]

The phrase "influence with Congress" is indicative of the way in which women's service for the Sanitary Commission enhanced the stature of public womanhood. Despite the fact that much of the work for the Commission seems an extension of traditional female activity—nursing, cooking, sewing—in defending their right to carry on these activities, and as they saw fit, many of the women became adept politicians. Invariably, those who survived the challenge of running a regional office also became able administrators. Neither of these skills—at least on the scale described by Livermore—was part of the usual repertoire of the housewife.

In her memoirs, Livermore tells of a trip to Washington in November 1862. She and women from throughout the country attended a Woman's Council, called by the staff of the Sanitary Commission. En route to the capital, Livermore and her colleague Jane Hoge encountered a young soldier in convulsions. They brought him around, and then Hoge sought out his commanding officer and denounced the officer's negligence: "The mother of this youth would have held you to account, had he died."[22] Once in Washington, the two women had the opportunity to meet Abraham Lincoln as well as other high officials and to speak their minds with some candor.[23] The women were genuinely important to the war effort, they knew it, and male public officials knew it. As a result, the women could find the courage both to confront a military officer and to consult with the President of the United States.

In working for the Sanitary Commission and in going to the front, women enjoyed an unprecedented public visibility. But there was another way in which women's public visibility was at an all-time high during the Civil War and that was in terms of their cultural influence. We have already discussed *Uncle Tom's Cabin*, the most influential American novel of the nineteenth century, in considering women's use of the power of the word. Julia Ward Howe's "Battle Hymn of the Republic" became the unofficial anthem of the union forces, and she, a reformer and suffragist, became one of the best-known and most beloved women of her time.[24]

Even before the outbreak of the war, women had begun to inscribe themselves on certain public rituals and to claim a few holidays as their own,[25] most notably Thanksgiving as the chief festival of sacralized domesticity. In 1863 Abraham Lincoln officially proclaimed Thanksgiving to be a national holiday, the culmination of many years of lobbying to achieve this goal by Sarah Josepha Hale of *Godey's*. The most influential American woman editor of the nineteenth century, Hale had concluded that it would have a salutary effect on the entire country should all Americans break bread together and give ritual thanks on the same day. (Before 1863, there had been local variations in the date for celebrating the occasion.) She then mounted a letter-writing campaign directed to Presidents, secretaries of state, and governors. For example, we find her writing to thirty-one state governors in October 1852, asking each to use his influence to promote a National Thanksgiving Day on the last Thursday of November: "Would not the effect of such a National Festival be promotive of sectional harmony and a closer Brotherhood among our assemblage of States?"[26] That her crusade achieved success during the war itself was surely not a coincidence.

Yet another manifestation of the new potency of the female cultural presence lay in the career of one of the most famous orators of the day, Anna Dickinson. Where before the war women had spoken about reform to audiences made up largely of those sympathetic to their point of view, Dickinson spoke on behalf of the Republican party at political rallies. As we have learned, women had only recently begun to appear in the audiences of such rallies before, in the early 1860s, Dickinson starred on such occasions.

A Quaker from Philadelphia, Dickinson gave her first public address in 1860 at the age of seventeen. Late in 1861, she lost her job at the U.S. Mint. According to her own account, this owed to her public expression of abolitionist sentiments. In any event, she soon wrote to William Lloyd Garrison to request his help in setting up lectures in Boston.[27] Complying with her request, he wrote to her about the size of the hall: "Most of the female lectures fail for lack of voice and this has led those who are opposed to female speaking to say that if God had intended it, he would have given the necessary vocal powers. I am pretty confident that you will be able to make yourself heard."[28] Her stint in Boston launched the lecturing career which made her, if only briefly, one of the most famous women in the country. Radical Republicans sought her as a speaker, because they knew her as a forceful advocate of the causes they believed in such as the centrality of the slavery issue to the war. On one occasion she addressed an audience of five thousand at Cooper's Union, having been introduced by Henry Ward Beecher, brother of Harriet Beecher Stowe and a clergyman without peer in public esteem. No doubt the climax of her career came on January 16, 1864, when at the age of twenty-one she spoke on the subject of the Freedmen's Bureau to the House of Representatives—with Lincoln in attendance.[29]

Dickinson's voluminous papers at the Library of Congress bear witness to her celebrity, because the correspondents constitute a remarkable range of mid-century Americans. Susan B. Anthony wrote frequently, telling Dickinson at one point that for the success of the suffrage campaign, "[a]ll that is wanting is a voice that has the public ear to take the lead. Would that voice might be the *one* and *only woman* the nation now deigns to hear." A physician in Ottawa, Illinois, having heard that she was dangerously ill, offered to come with his wife to treat her, for expenses only. It is clear from such letters that she loomed large in the public imagination.[30]

Yet she could not entirely escape the chief hazard that beset ear-

lier public women—that is, a certain vulnerability where issues of sexual propriety were concerned. For example, one of her correspondents, Henry Homes of Albany, wrote to her about what he deemed
the "blemishes" in her performance. An ardent admirer, he had been
commending the speech he had just heard to a clergyman, who responded that he had been told "there were coarsenesses in it." Homes
explained what the coarsenesses had been: "The kind of blemish to
which I refer is the occasional indulgence of the speaker in the use of
a word or phrase, which however frequently employed by politicians
addressing mass meetings, do not need to be used in halls where a
lady addresses persons of both sexes, but do rather create a temporary
revulsion of feeling." The two phrases he had in mind were "making
to eat dirt" and "this filthy sheet. . . . They might be uttered by a
lady speaking in a dramatic part, but should they be chosen by a lady
speaking in her name and character?" He clearly thought not.[31]

All in all, it was quite a record of contribution for American
women. But women's wartime activism was by no means limited to
noble service and inspirational writing and speaking. Instead, one of
the most noteworthy achievements of these years was the way in which
a small group of women led by Elizabeth Cady Stanton and Susan B.
Anthony constituted themselves as a political force weighing in on the
side of ending slavery. Calling this undertaking the Woman's National
Loyal League, Stanton and Anthony determined to try to collect one
million signatures on a massive anti-slavery petition. So pressing did
this issue seem that Stanton insisted they must put aside woman's rights
conventions for the time being. Nonetheless, Stanton was evidently
not without feminist motivation for organizing the League. Indeed,
she and Anthony hoped that they could legitimate female activity in
the political arena, thus furthering the goal of gender equality in the
postwar period. By May 1864 the League had 5,000 members nationwide and had collected 265,314 signatures. By the time the Thirteenth
Amendment, ending slavery, had passed both houses of Congress in
early 1865, the League had gathered nearly 400,000 signatures.[32]

Finally, another significant development of the wartime years was
the increasing presence of women as office employees, including those

working for the government itself. Because this topic will receive substantial attention in the next chapter, we will merely note it here, by way of suggesting how much the Civil War did to enhance public womanhood.

Women themselves took note of the war-wrought change they saw in themselves and others. For example, Elizabeth Cady Stanton and her co-authors of *The History of Woman Suffrage* came to this conclusion:

> The social and political condition of women was largely changed by our civil war. Through the withdrawal of so many men from their accustomed work, new channels of industry were opened to them, the value and control of money learned, thought upon political questions compelled, and a desire for their own personal, individual liberty intensified. It created a revolution in woman herself. . . .[33]

Acting in the world in so many unprecedented ways, women were learning a variety of new skills and becoming comfortable with a new level of public exposure. In the first place, as Stanton realized, the type of familiarity with political questions that had been displayed by an Abigail Adams or a Mercy Otis Warren, elite women whose family connections placed them at the center of discussions about the fate of the new nation, now became much more widely diffused. If one reads women's diaries and letters from these years, one soon encounters sophisticated discussions of politics. Following secession, for example, Abby Woolsey of New York wrote to her cousin in Alabama to deplore what had happened. Referring to the attempted Crittenden Compromise, she queried why southern demands had so increased since the preceding year. There ensued a very knowledgeable discussion of individual politicians and their stances. Woolsey was particularly incensed by the demand for a slavery code in the Constitution. "We can never eat our principles in that way. . . ."[34]

Perhaps the most significant evidence on this point comes from Henry Bellows, who began his work for the Sanitary Commission assuming that one of his main jobs would be to curb the misguided zeal of his female constituency. In the end, Bellows acknowledged how well women understood the underlying issues of the struggle. Writing the introduction to a book about women and the Civil War that came out in 1867, Bellows argued that women had been as well equipped as men to discuss "the public questions involved in the war," ascribing this to the widespread availability of public education in the antebellum years.[35]

Thoroughly familiar with the politics of the war—and in a few instances with the military strategy[36]—many women were prepared to assume public responsibility and even to challenge male authority in order to comfort and save the lives of the men in their charge. There are numerous examples, but a handful will suffice to make the point. Early in the war, two young sisters from New York, Georgianna Woolsey and Eliza Woolsey Howland, went to Washington to nurse. Horrified to learn that such hospitals as existed had no regular chaplains, the young women took it upon themselves to rectify the situation. They wrote to General Van Rensselaer and to Lincoln, urging the appointment of at least one chaplain, and Georgianna then personally delivered the letter to the White House. For her part, Eliza wrote to a professor at Union Theological Seminary to inquire who might be available for this duty. As a result, Henry Hopkins, son of President Mark Hopkins of Williams College, arrived in Washington to take up the post.[37]

Half a continent away and many battles later, Annie Wittenmyer, elected by the state legislature to be Iowa's sanitary agent, arrived in Helena, Arkansas, in August 1863. The hospital there seemed to her to be in a dreadful condition, and the men complained that they had been left to die. Hearing this and with the evidence of her own eyes to confirm what the men told her, she took the next steamboat to Memphis to confront the commanding general. When he seemed to her to be temporizing about what he could do to relieve them, she told him, "I want the order issued before I leave this office. I want to go back and tell the men the boats [to evacuate them] are coming—it may save lives." The general having capitulated and left, she then explained to his adjutant that if the boats did not arrive on schedule, her only recourse would be to the newspapers of the North. Recounting this episode in her memoirs, she proudly states that she hurried back to Helena to inform the men that help was on the way, and that the general fulfilled his part of the bargain.[38]

Hannah Ropes of Massachusetts was already a seasoned reformer when she arrived in Washington to nurse in 1862. Abandoned by her husband, she and one of her two children had spent a year in Kansas as part of a free-soil contingent in the mid-1850s, but had returned to Massachusetts because of the violence in that strife-torn region. Her assignment in Washington was to a hospital that had been converted from being a hotel. Here she shared duty with Louisa May Alcott, who called their place of employment "Hurly-Burly House." Soon after her arrival, Ropes began to do battle with the stewards who were in charge of supplies. In her opinion, a few were dishonest and were more interested in lining their own pockets than in providing for the wounded men. To document their misdeeds, she started a diary. Eventually she took her complaints all the way to Secretary of War Edwin Stanton and used every bit of political capital she could muster to straighten out the situation.[39] But her triumph was short-lived, because she died of typhoid fever in 1863.

It is difficult to reconstruct more than one hundred years later how many of the women who wrote of such incidents were being genuinely helpful to the recovery of their charges and how many were merely busybodies. From the women's own standpoint, they fought the good fight. Male doctors, for their part, tended to prefer working with Catholic sisters, trained to submit to male authority.[40] Yet we also have documents from men in which considerable admiration for women, even interfering women, shines forth. Frank Bacon (who would marry Georgianna Woolsey) was a surgeon in New Orleans and wrote to describe one such woman:

> I reluctantly confess that I am subjugated and crushed by a woman who sings The Star-Spangled Banner copiously through all the wards of my hospital. . . . She weighs three hundred pounds. She comes every morning, early. She wears the Flag of our Country pinned across her

heart. She comes into *my* room, my own office, unabashed by the fact that I am the Surgeon in Charge, and that an orderly in white gloves stands at the door. She looks me in the eye with perfect calmness and intrepidity. . . . She nurses tenderly, and feeds and cries over the bad cases. . . . Of course I do not encourage the visits of this creature with the Flag of our Country and the National Anthem. On the contrary, they encourage me.[41]

Of all the women who saw themselves as tribunes of the enlisted man, on whose behalf they would challenge any and all authority, none was more famed than Mary Anne Bickerdyke of Galesburg, Illinois, affectionately known to the men as "Mother." Indeed, she achieved the postwar status of legend as this passage from Mary Livermore's memoir will attest:

Among the hundreds of women who devoted a part or the whole of the years of the war to the care of the sick and wounded of the army, "Mother Bickerdyke" stands pre-eminent. Others were as heroic and consecrated as she, as unwearied in labors, and as unselfish and self-sacrificing. But she was unique in method, extraordinary in executive ability, enthusiastic in devotion, and indomitable in will. After her plans were formed, and her purposes matured, she carried them through triumphantly, in the teeth of the most formidable opposition. She gave herself to the rank and file of the army—the private soldiers,—for whom she had unbounded tenderness and developed almost limitless resources of help and compassion.[42]

Another postwar writer claimed: ". . . the name of Mother Bickerdyke will be spoken with reverential love, until her boys are mustered out and their tongues are all silent in death."[43]

A widow with two young sons when the war began, Bickerdyke heard a sermon by the Reverend Edward Beecher in which he adverted to the great needs of the wounded men in the western theater. Securing care for her sons, she went off to serve, first as a freelance nurse and then on behalf of the Sanitary Commission, with which she had a somewhat troubled relationship.[44] Her passionate determination to save lives no doubt made her an uncomfortable, if powerful, ally.

The stories of Bickerdyke and her exploits appear in many memoirs. There is, for example, the account of the officer who bragged because Mother Bickerdyke was good to him—even though he was not an enlisted man. Her willingness to confront inept or drunken doctors furnished a popular theme. Livermore, for example, talks of the surgeon given to debauches who was dismissed at Bickerdyke's instigation. He then went to General Sherman to complain. " 'Who was your accuser?' asked General Sherman; 'who made the charges?' 'Why—why—I suppose,' said the surgeon reluctantly, 'it was that spiteful old woman, Mrs. Bickerdyke.' 'Oh, well, then,' said Sherman, 'if it was she, I can't help you. She has more power than I—she ranks me.' "[45] Livermore also provides myriad details about Bickerdyke's indomitability—the aforementioned cattle drive, for example, and another time when she visited a battlefield the night after the battle, haunted by the thought that one or more of the bodies might still have life in it.

Contemporary letters reinforce the tenor of the memoirs. We find Bickerdyke reporting to a correspondent, for example, that she needed to get vegetables delivered to invalids, but that the road had been barred to all but military uses. "But I have obtained orders from the authorities which will enable me to bring them *all* very soon." Two months later one of her co-workers wrote, ". . . I joined Mrs. Bickerdyke, at Ringgold just in time to go through to aid the wounded on the first day of the conflict and the goods taken through by Mrs. Bickerdyke's energy and the few [illegible] taken in our ambulance was all we have for our poor suffering men."[46] Despite her willingness to buck authority, Bickerdyke usually got the ear—and also the respect—of commanding generals. Livermore reports that she had an especially close relationship with Sherman, perhaps because her character was "akin to his own. Both were restless, impetuous, fiery, hard-working, and indomitable."[47]

Beyond the increased conversance with public issues and the increased willingness to challenge male authority, public women grew in self-confidence because of the scale on which some of them were

carrying forward their activities. Once again, Henry Bellows had admiring things to say about the women whose work he observed in the
Sanitary Commission: "Hundreds of women evinced talents there,
which, in other spheres and in the other sex, would have made them
merchant princes, or great administrators of public affairs." He thought
that "[t]he distinctive features in woman's work in this war were magnitude, system, thorough co-operativeness with the other sex, distinc-
tiveness of purpose, business-like thoroughness in details. . . ."[48]

For the women themselves, all this constituted a revelation about
what their hitherto hidden resources might be. It seems likely that no
more than a handful of American women had ever before run enter-
prises on the scale of one of the regional offices of the Sanitary Commission. For example, Bickerdyke organized a work detail of 50 to 70
freed people so as to operate laundry services for as many as 10,000
recuperating soldiers in Memphis.[49]

In her memoirs, Livermore describes the genesis of the first great
sanitary fair in Chicago in 1863. The expenses of the northwestern
office had been heavy, and money was badly needed. She and Hoge
recalled earlier fund-raising fairs on a smaller scale and decided upon
"a grand fair in which the whole Northwest would unite." Their male
colleagues "languidly approved our plan but laughed at the promise to
raise $25,000." Hoge and Livermore then went into a whirlwind of
activity in preparation for the fair only to find that neither of them
could enter into a contract without a husband's signature. "Here was
a revelation. We two women were able to enlist the whole Northwest
in a great philanthropic money-making enterprise in the teeth of great
opposition, and had the executive ability to carry it forward to a successful termination," yet could not function autonomously. Vowing
to take up women's rights after the war ended, Livermore proceeded
with the planning, securing from Lincoln the original copy of the
Emancipation Proclamation to be auctioned off. This first fair raised
nearly $100,000—the men became believers, too—and as we have
seen, fairs in various cities eventually raised approximately $3,000,000
for the Sanitary Commission.[50]

Still another way in which the status of public womanhood changed during these years was in certain women's acceptance of publicity, their willingness to see their activities reported in the press. This represented a significant departure from traditional norms of decorous feminine conduct. In his book about southern women, for example, George Rable reports that a group of South Carolina women went to a ceremony for the Palmetto Guards and were horrified to find their names printed in a newspaper account of the occasion.[51] Inevitably, the women who were wartime heroines had to learn to accept publicity. Mrs. Woolsey wrote to Georgianna and Eliza: "I fear we are beginning to feel proud of you, as we hear your praises sounded in various quarters, and read paragraphs in the papers of your doings."[52] Bellows states it this way in the introduction to a book celebrating the heroines' exploits:

> A record of the personal services of our American women in the late Civil War, however painful to the modesty of those whom it brings conspicuously before the world, is due to the honor of the country, to the proper understanding of our social life, and to the general interests of the sex whose rights, duties and capacities are now under serious discussion. Most of the women commemorated in this work inevitably lost the benefit of privacy, by the largeness and length of their public service. . . .[53]

This process, by which women lost "the benefit of privacy," can be observed particularly well in the case of Cornelia Hancock, a young Pennsylvania Quaker who became a nurse. Only twenty-three at the time of Gettysburg, and thus too young to meet Dorothea Dix's strict standards for lack of personal attractions, Hancock went to the railroad station at Baltimore where potential nurses were assembling—and where she was explicitly rejected by Dix. Undeterred, she got on the railroad car and rode to Gettysburg. Once there, she encountered so powerful a need that there was no further squabbling about her youth. After performing valiantly at Gettysburg—she received a medal—she spent several months nursing at a hospital for contrabands in Washington. Shocked by the terrible conditions there, she sought out Senator Charles

Sumner of Massachusetts to tell him about the problems.[54] She then proceeded further south.

But her most outstanding service came at the Battle of the Wilderness during the last terrible days of the war. Grant had taken charge of the Army of the Potomac, and she and other civilians had been sent home from their posts in northern Virginia. Hearing of savage fighting, she resolved to go back to the front. Her brother-in-law was a physician, and each medical man was allowed one assistant. This then became her authority to return, although she still had doubts about whether a woman would be granted a pass. "I sat upon my trunk perfectly easy. There has always been a way provided and I always expect there will be, so never concern," she wrote to her sister.[55] As a result of her insistence on being near the men, she found herself in a situation that called forth every resource of energy and initiative she possessed. She accompanied two surgeons to a hospital in Fredericksburg:

> On arriving here the scenes beggared all description and these two men, eminent as they are in their profession, were paralyzed by what they saw. Rain had poured in through the bullet-riddled roof of the churches until our wounded lay in pools of water made bloody by their seriously wounded condition. On these scenes Dr. Detmold and Dr. Vanderpool gazed in horror and seemed not to know where to take hold. My Gettysburg experience enabled me to take hold.[56]

In the letter to her sister describing this episode, Hancock explained that the two men quickly "got their nerve" and performed admirably.

But Dr. Vanderpool was unwilling to let the matter rest there. He wrote an article for the *New York Tribune* in which he glowingly described Hancock's "indefatigable labors," and she became a celebrity. Her sister wrote to say, "[t]hee is a real heroine." Her mother wrote that the *Tribune* article had been reprinted in their hometown newspaper and was "creating a sensation in the neighborhood." There had earlier been a series of letters from her mother intimating that certain neighbors were gossiping about the propriety of Cornelia's conduct. Now those same people were "foremost in extolling you." But the surest badge of her credentials as a heroine was the fact that her young nephew was imitating her when he played with other children. "It is all right Eddie's nose should bleed if he undertakes to be like me," Hancock wrote to her sister.[57]

More than a few of these women were permanently transformed by their experiences, because they so magnificently rose to the occasion during the crisis of the Union. Indeed, it would be difficult to overstate the significance of the theme of rising to the occasion, which emerges repeatedly in the contemporary accounts.

Perhaps the most remarkable example of this phenomenon other than the foregoing account of Cornelia Hancock can be found in the letters by Georgianna Woolsey—as well as those about her. We have already met Woolsey, who took it upon herself to arrange for a military chaplain while quite a young woman. In 1862 she joined Frederick Law Olmsted, who, on behalf of the Sanitary Commission, had fitted out hospital ships. The ships were to transport wounded men who needed a lengthy period of recuperation to northern hospitals. Olmsted's project would eventually serve thousands of men, but at the time Woolsey and her sister Eliza Woolsey Howland joined him, the ships were not yet completely outfitted but were nonetheless receiving the wounded, because the need was so great. The two women had arrived on board the *Ocean Queen* a short while earlier when 150 men were brought on board. Olmsted wrote that he was appalled to return to the ship himself and find ". . . that the miserable first officer had given way, and every man who could walk of the patients had been taken on board. The glorious women had hunted out a barrel containing some Indian meal from some dark place where it had been lost sight of . . . and were already ladling out hot gruel, which they had made of it; and the poor, pale, emaciated, shivering wretches were lying anywhere on the cabin floors, crying with sobbing, trembling voices, 'God bless you, Miss! God bless you.' "[58]

By 1864, Woolsey was nursing in northern Virginia. She wrote to her sister Jane about one day's labors: "I cooked and served today 926 rations of farina, tea, coffee, and good rich soup, chicken, turkey, and beef, out of those blessed cans [from the Sanitary Commission]." [59] A few days later, she saw men marching off to what she knew would be a fierce battle and impulsively picked roses to hand to them as they marched by. After the war had ended, a friend wrote to her: "Levi Thatcher . . . sat with me a long while the other day, and we talked of you dear Miss Georgy. He says the most beautiful moment he has ever seen in his life was at Fredericksburg, last summer, when you were giving roses to the regiment who were marching to almost certain death, and a soldier stepped from the ranks and seized your hands. . . ." [60]

Young women who had never seen a male body were suddenly called upon to bathe and dress strange men. Unmarried women who had never needed to cook for a family were suddenly cooking for hundreds of people. Alcott described how she felt the first time she had to wash the wounded: "If she had requested me to shave them all, or dance a hornpipe on the stove funnel, I should have been less staggered; but to scrub some dozen lords of creation at a moment's notice, was really—really—. However, there was no time for nonsense." [61]

Another type of rising to the occasion came from Charlotte Forten, a young woman from one of the most prominent free black families in the country, the Fortens of Philadelphia. [62] Sent to an academy in Boston and thus given as good an education as the country offered a woman in the antebellum United States—with the rare exception of those who made their way to a college like Oberlin—Forten was nonetheless far from exempt from the effects of racism. She wrote: "I wonder that every colored person is not a misanthrope. Surely we have something to make us hate mankind. I have met girls in the schoolroom—they have been thoroughly kind and cordial to me,—perhaps the next day met them on the street—they feared to recognize me." [63]

Acutely sensitive to such omnipresent slights and in delicate health, Forten nonetheless responded to what she saw as the call of duty and went south in 1862 to teach freed people in the sea islands of South Carolina, while the war raged not far away. Union forces had taken Port Royal, and the decision had been made to educate the 10,000 or so freed people who remained after their masters had fled. Forten accompanied other northerners on this challenging mission, a social experiment without precedent in American history. But unlike her largely white colleagues, she also had to endure such personal indignities as listening to white soldiers "plentifully" using the word "nigger" in her presence. She stuck it out for nearly two years, going home in May 1864 after having participated in proving that freed slaves, who had been forbidden to read and write, were fully capable of being educated.[64]

With so much growth by public women and in so many areas—conversance with public issues, entrepreneurial activity on a mammoth scale, acceptance of public exposure, a new willingness to challenge male authority—it is not surprising that one of these women became an internationally known figure. In many ways, Clara Barton's life furnishes a model—albeit an exaggerated one because her life was so extraordinary—of how the Civil War could impact a woman. She had already shown signs of a willingness to break out of woman's sphere in the antebellum years. Then her humanitarian work during the war made her into a household name. After the war had ended, she used her fame to gain a hearing from various Presidents and secretaries of state—as we shall be learning in the next chapter—on behalf of the International Red Cross and became the first American woman to serve as an official representative of the federal government.[65]

The other figure besides Barton who became a leading public woman in the late nineteenth century directly owing to her war work (according to her own testimony) was Mary Livermore. Like Barton, Livermore had shown signs of becoming a public woman even before the war broke out, covering the Republican convention in Chicago that nominated Lincoln, for example. But once she went to work for the Sanitary Commission, the range of her activities grew exponentially. We have already noted many of them, such as the trip to see Lincoln, the supervisory work in Chicago, and the initiative taken where the sanitary fairs were concerned. In her memoirs she provides details of other personal victories or turning points, too. For example, she visited her first hospital after the battle of Fort Donelson. Overcome by the sights and sounds, she needed to be led out three times. "But was I to shrink from the sight of misery which these brave men were so nobly enduring. The thought was a tonic. . . ." Never again would she be overcome by a hospital visit, and her courage grew in other ways, too. Before too much longer, she was able to march in to see General Grant himself so as to get him to grant permission to discharge two dying men.[66]

Experiences such as these helped give her the courage to make her first public address to a mixed audience in Dubuque, Iowa, in 1863. Despite the increasing public acceptance of women on the lecture platform, Livermore was horrified when she learned that what she had supposed to be a speech to a small, female audience was, in reality, going to be something else. Billed as "A Voice from the Front," her speech had attracted a huge crowd:

> I was appalled and dumbfounded. At that time, I had never attempted a public address to a promiscuous audience. I had only addressed audiences of women, sitting in a chair decorously before them, and trying with all my might to keep my hands folded on my lap. I had no idea whether I had voice to reach an audience such as the ladies had invoked—or courage to bear me through the ordeal.[67]

At first, she refused to go on, but she eventually relented, and the event netted $8,000 for the Sanitary Commission—as well as bushels of supplies.

Like Barton, Livermore will reappear when we discuss the Gilded Age. For now, we should note that this Unitarian minister's wife who was terrified by the ordeal of her first speech to a large audience would subsequently criss-cross the country many times speaking on behalf of the causes she believed in. Organizer of a suffrage convention, editor of a woman's rights newspaper, Livermore became so well known that her memoir of the war sold 60,000 copies. Late in life, she and her devoted husband Daniel returned to their native Massachusetts where a school in the community of Melrose was named after her. Moreover, the Massachusetts Women's Christian Temperance Union commissioned a bust of her.[68] Truly, she was a public woman.

Triumphant though this record of female achievement was, it should not stand without an acknowledgment that it was also shot through with instances of class and racial prejudice and with nods to Mrs. Grundy, that figure denounced by Charlotte Forten when fulminating in her diary against the rigid propriety that prevented her from going further south to teach black soldiers.[69] Moreover, Cornelia Hancock and Georgianna Woolsey may have been able to tolerate publicity, but this was by no means a universal attitude. For example, we find the upper-class Katharine Wormeley writing a small book about the Sanitary Commission, designed to raise money for that body, but not allowing her name to be used. We also find her writing to her mother expressing strong disapproval of the fact that a congressman who had visited the hospital ship where she was working wanted to move that Congress give official thanks for the undertaking. "Mr. Olmsted, mindful of our feelings, promptly declined."[70]

If Wormeley resisted becoming a public woman, despite her record of achievement for the Sanitary Commission, no doubt this owed much to the traditional linkage between public womanhood and the aura of sexual misconduct. The women who went to the war knew that they risked being seen as partaking of that aura. For some of them, this was as terrifying as the hazards of battle. For example, Adelaide Smith of New York and her colleague Miss Bain were in a camp other than the one to which they were attached when suddenly they found themselves under fire. What to do? Physical safety lay in staying put, but that course of action was clearly risky for their reputations. Smith said to Bain: " 'Should we brave the comment of staying all night in a strange camp, or must we risk our lives in attempting to escape the shells falling on our route?' Without a moment's hesitation the courageous girl said firmly and briefly: 'I'd rather risk the shells and drowning.' "[71] Happily they both survived.

Courageous about some aspects of their lives, in other words, upper-middle-class white women who went to the war were not necessarily uniformly courageous; they knew full well the penalty they might pay for attracting gossip. Nor were these women, so humane in their sympathies for the soldiers, necessarily enlightened about other women of a different class or race. Wormeley, for example, frequently enunciated the opinion that women should be "guided by the wisdom of men" and that those women who were in a supervisory position should be of the right class.[72] Mary Phinney, a nurse, went to one African-American religious service and wrote home: ". . . we went to the negro meeting, where we laughed our fill. How I wish you could go to a real nig meeting and hear them exhort."[73]

For their part, the African-American women themselves compiled an impressive record of wartime and postwar service, despite being forced to deal with people like Phinney. Elizabeth Keckley, Mary Todd Lincoln's seamstress, participated in organizing a Contraband Relief Association.[74] Josephine St. Pierre Ruffin worked with the Sanitary Commission and also devoted her energy to recruiting black soldiers.[75] Maria Stewart, the first black woman in the country to give a public address, became the Matron of the Freedmen's Hospital in Washington, D.C., in the 1870s.[76]

No black woman did more for the war effort and for humanitarian causes than Sojourner Truth. Celebrated for her powerful and impassioned oratory before the war broke out, Truth devoted herself to the freed people during the conflict. She instructed newly freed slave women in the domestic arts, and she also nursed. On October 29, 1864, she met Abraham Lincoln, who told her that he knew about her work and commended her for it. Despite her service and the recognition she received for it, however, she had to endure constant abuse when she tried to   self of public transportation. On such occasions, she always made a point of insisting that she was a lady and thus entitled to ride on the horse-drawn streetcar, and she usually prevailed—but not without much unpleasantness.[77]

For working-class white women, the stresses of war—which fell disproportionately on poor people—occasionally resulted in their participating in public displays of anger, both south and north. As the Confederate economy faltered and food became ever more scarce, women in Richmond engaged in bread riots, for example. Moreover, even in rural areas of the Confederacy there were episodes of law-breaking that had "strong overtones of class conflict."[78] During the last winter of the war there were also two strikes by women ordnance workers.[79] But these episodes pale in comparison with the violent uprising of the largely Irish working-class of New York in July 1863, in which women took part.

It is not possible to give more than the sketchiest background for the July Days. Scholars have shown that Irish and free black workers competed for the lowliest jobs in northern cities, and that Irish people were, as a result, massively unsympathetic to the plight of enslaved African-Americans and massively disaffected from the war. Copperhead Democrats played to these sentiments. When the federal government instituted a draft from which a rich man could buy his way out, there were several antidraft riots, the bloodiest of which took place in New York City. Indeed, with an estimated death toll of 120 people this was the worst domestic disorder in American history. A largely Irish mob attacked defenseless blacks, burned an orphanage for black children, and lynched at least twelve people. Mary Ryan's research has established that although women made up less than 10 percent of those arrested, their presence was strongly noted at the time. "Women were reputedly well represented in the crowds that assaulted and abused Negroes, besieged the Colored Orphan Asylum, and attacked the homes of abolitionists."[80] In short, by no means were all of the public women of the Civil War era, on either side, engaged in actions on behalf of the war effort.

Nonetheless, when one surveys the whole picture, the most striking impression is the epochal nature of woman's involvement with the war. Women, as half of humanity, have always had a history, but before the mid-nineteenth century they have rarely had a political history, that is, a record of their public activity. Northern women created such a history between 1861 and 1865. And after the war had ended, there was also a historiography devoted to their heroism. The ever-quotable Henry Bellows said in a letter to Hoge and Livermore in 1863: "The time will surely come when the great uprising of the women of America—nay, their systematic organization and co-operation in a common work, will be regarded as the most marked social feature of the war, the most splendid achievement on record of spontaneous humanity, the brightest augury of perpetual peace and unity in our Nation."[81]

Moreover, for the first time in American history, there was public art, statuary, for example, representing heroic individual women and not merely an abstraction—Liberty—or a mythical figure. We have already noted the bust of Livermore. In addition, the women of Galesburg commissioned a statue of Mary Ann Bickerdyke. Carved on its base is the quotation from General Sherman. "She outranks me."

This, then, was the record women carried into the postwar era, when the nature of citizenship and of suffrage constituted the most pressing public issues of the day, given the emancipation of millions of former slaves. That women were unable to parlay their war work into enfranchisement should not blind us to the magnitude of their achievement.

Wrote Bellows to Hoge and Livermore:

> The women have constituted themselves as a great national quilting party; the States so many patches, each of its own color or stuff, the boundaries of the nation the frame of the work; and *at it* they have gone, with needles and busy fingers, and their very heart-strings for thread, and sewed and sewed away, adding square to square, and row to row; allowing no piece or part to escape their plan of Union; until the territorial area of the loyal states is all of a piece, first tacked and basted, then sewed and stitched by women's hands wet often with women's tears, and woven in with women's prayers; and now at length you might truly say the National Quilt—all striped and starred—will tear anywhere sooner than in the seams, which they have joined in a blessed and inseparable unity![82]

Phillis Wheatley—from the frontispiece of her book of poems. *(Courtesy of the Rare Book Collection, Wilson Library, University of North Carolina at Chapel Hill)*

Mercy Otis Warren in about 1763—a portrait by John Singleton Copley. *(Bequest of Winslow Warren, courtesy of Museum of Fine Arts, Boston)*

Elizabeth Freeman. This portrait was done by a member of the Sedgwick family. *(Courtesy of the Massachusetts Historical Society)*

Frances Wright. *(Courtesy of the Library of Congress)*

Elizabeth Cady Stanton with her sons, Henry and Daniel. *(Courtesy of the Vassar College Library)*

Susan B. Anthony. *(Courtesy of the Nebraska State Historical Society)*

Harriet Beecher Stowe at home in the mid-1860s. *(Courtesy of the Stowe-Day Foundation, Hartford, Connecticut)*

Statue of Mary Ann Bickerdyke, Galesburg, Illinois. *(Photograph by Peter Bailley, courtesy of Knox College)*

Frances Willard. *(Courtesy of the Frances E. Willard Memorial Library, Evanston, Illinois)*

Victoria Woodhull. *(Courtesy of the Schlesinger Library, Radcliffe College)*

Emma Goldman speaking on birth control in New York in 1916. *(Courtesy of the Bettmann Archive)*

Emma Goldman in uncharacteristically bourgeois garb. *(Courtesy of Brown Brothers)*

Ida B. Wells. *(Courtesy of Troy Duster)*

Ann Burlak, sometimes called the Red Flame, speaking to striking silk workers in Pawtucket, Rhode Island, in 1931. *(Courtesy of Wide World Photos)*

Cannery workers and growers joining in a protest against food processors, Sunnyvale, California, 1939. *(Courtesy of the Sourisseau Academy, San Jose State University)*

Labor organizer Dorothy Healey. *(Courtesy of the Labor Archives and Research Center, San Francisco State University)*

Helen Gahagan Douglas in costume for *She,* about ten years before she ran for Congress. *(Courtesy of the Western History Collections, University of Oklahoma Library)*

Helen Gahagan Douglas speaking at the United Nations in 1946. *(Courtesy of the Western History Collections, University of Oklahoma Library)*

Dolores Huerta in 1973. *(Photograph by Hans Ehrmann)*

Wilma Mankiller addressing the Cherokee Nation. *(Photograph by Sammy Still, courtesy of the Cherokee Nation)*

Mary Oyama in 1943. *(Courtesy of Vicki Littman)*

7

Public Womanhood and the Incorporation of America

If the beginning of industrialization in the early nineteenth century had had a profound impact on public womanhood—and it surely had—then it is not surprising to discover that the development of a corporatized industrial economy in the late nineteenth century had at least as strong an impact. The changed scale of doing business in the United States created a vast number of new jobs, many of which were filled by women. As a consequence, increasing numbers of women began to be able to live apart from traditional families. Further, women pioneered institutions to help those suffering from the dislocations of urbanization and industrialization—and in so doing transformed their own lives. On the cultural front, thousands of temperance activists became public women in these years so as to combat the evils of alcohol.

Yet not all the changes were positive for women. To the considerable disappointment of many, women failed to win the vote at the time black men secured it. And that was not all. The hyper-competitive, even brutal, new rules of the economic game fostered ideologies like Social Darwinism, antithetical to the values that had traditionally been championed by women, as they had advanced into the public arena. In short, there were defeats as well as victories for women in the Gilded Age. But on balance, the fact that a few public women of the period, most notably Emma Goldman and Ida B. Wells, began to speak publicly about sex, without losing the ability to command an audience, represented an extraordinarily significant breakthrough for all women, the first indication that women might someday speak on the same range of public issues as men. Moreover, public womanhood, which had been largely middle-class Protestant white with a small admixture of Protestant black, became much more diverse in its social composition in these years.

In the decades following the Civil War, the American economy went from being owned by single individuals or partnerships to being dominated by corporations, which developed elaborate bureaucracies to oversee their massive holdings. Office work, which had been a male preserve, then metamorphosed into women's work as personnel needs soared. The typewriter was invented in 1867 and seemed to employers eager to save money to be especially well suited to the nimble fingers of women—who could be paid less than men. The upshot of all this was that women began to be increasingly employed as stenographers, or typewriter girls, as they were called. Their numbers soared to over 200,000 by 1900 (see Table 7.1).

As several scholars have demonstrated, when office clerks had been male, they had been seen as apprentice managers. After the work was feminized, secretarial work became a dead-end job. The significant point for our purposes is not how much the jobs did or did not do to advance women, however, but rather how revolutionary a development the Gilded Age office was in terms of social geography. The business office hitherto had been almost as much a quintessentially male space as had been the polling place on election day. Now that thousands of women were marching into the terrain, this could no longer be the case. What would be the rules of conduct for interaction between male and female employees? Should they treat one

TABLE 7.1. Number of Women
Employed as Secretaries

1870	9,982
1880	28,698
1890	168,808
1900	238,982

Source: Barbara Wertheimer, *We Were There:*
The Story of Working Women in America (New
York: Pantheon, 1977), 159.

another as neuters? Could they? If not, what would happen to the
reputations of the women employees?

Cindy Aron has studied the offices of the federal government during the late nineteenth century and is able to provide a case study of
the process by which the office became sexually integrated. As was
invariably the case, the federal offices had been male turf, containing,
for example, a plethora of spittoons. What is more, "[m]en also smoked
in the office, used rough language, and occasionally appeared for work
in an intoxicated condition."[1] As she points out, women who went to
work for the government, working side by side with men, needed to
learn to behave in a more competitive fashion than was permitted by
the usual norms of approved female behavior. For their part, the men
needed to modify their language and tone down *their* behavior so as
not to offend their female coworkers.

Moreover, during the initial stages of women's entry into this
male sphere, gossip about sexual misconduct swirled if there was the
slightest reason for suspicion. Many people apparently thought that no
"good" woman would seek such employment, and therefore the stigma
of "treasury courtesan" was attached to those who did. Aron found
that "[o]ften just the rumor of wrongdoing on the part of a female
clerk was sufficient to cause—at the minimum—her dismissal from
office."[2]

That the sexual valence, as it were, of the typewriter girls was a
subject of no small interest, both to her coworkers and to the general

public, is borne out by an examination of selected periodicals from the late nineteenth and early twentieth century.[3] One reader wrote to the *Illustrated Phonographic World* in 1895, for example, that she, considered by her friends to be a pretty girl, had to listen to constant compliments from employers, to her great annoyance. "This familiarity is brought about, I presume, by dictation. Any stenographer will admit that dictation leads very easily to conversation, which very naturally brings a girl on a nearer level with her employer than if she were a bookkeeper or clerk."[4] A newspaper editorialized: "The pretty typewriter girl is becoming very numerous in the land. It has come to pass that faithful wives no longer pray that their husbands may not be led into temptation, but that they may not be led to elope with their typewriters."[5]

Not surprisingly the onus was placed on women to behave with such dignity that they would be beyond reproach. One letter writer, a woman, stated: "The woman stenographer has it in her power by steering well between the Scylla of prudery and the Charybdis of familiarity, to raise the standard (and in this generation, even establish the standard) by which men will judge her sex in this profession."[6] The typewriter girl was supposed to be all business, but also to retain "that quality without which all other feminine attractions sink into insignificance, and to which they are always secondary—Womanliness."

As thousands of offices were becoming sexually integrated and tens of thousands of women were finding employment in them, the city sidewalks themselves were changing in character. *The National Stenographer* of May 1897 reprinted an article from the *New York Recorder* on this subject:

> Ten years ago a woman visible in the flesh "down town" was a natural curiosity; she was a gracious vision without reference to age, color or costume. Now it is the writer's opinion that there are 53,721 girls in the noonday procession and as 20,310 are pretty, young and fairly dressed the spoiled sons of fortune who stand in doorways to see them go by are as critical and hard to please as if they were baldheads at a ballet . . .
>
>   She [the typewriter girl] is a gregarious animal. By preference she

walks four abreast and drives men to the gutter if not to drink, with every step of her triumphal progress.

While offices and city sidewalks were emerging as sexually integrated spaces, the department store was coming into its own as *the* grand public space for women. By the late nineteenth century, owners were authorizing architects to employ lavish materials like stained glass and marble, to use rotundas and galleries as part of the design, and to build on a huge scale. Women then formed both the bulk of the sales force and the preponderance of the customers in this palatial environment. Moreover, as Susan Porter Benson points out in *Counter Cultures*, the department store also represented a kind of democracy in action in its openness to women of all classes: "A certain heady democracy obtained: the humblest daughter of the working classes could rub shoulders with the city's wealthiest grande dame—both would of course not be equally courted by managers, but there were few other places where it was possible or even likely for the two to meet."[7]

Although the department store was not sexually integrated in the same way that the business office was, nonetheless department-store clerks were "public women" and as such were open to suspicion about their sexual conduct. Benson writes of repeated scrutinizing of the work force between the 1880s and the 1920s by various investigators: "Perhaps the most damaging and certainly the most sensational charge was that department store saleswomen were in special peril of prostitution, whether professional or occasional. The public nature of the store, its sumptuous atmosphere, and its low wages combined, so the argument went, to make the transition from the counter to the bordello all too easy."[8]

The economic changes of the Gilded Age thus had a profound impact on public womanhood because they transformed urban public space—though the women taking their places in the new spaces were still at risk to be labeled as "public women" in the invidious sense. The surge in female employment—factory work, teaching, and nursing besides what we have just discussed—then created a much more substantial number of women who not only earned money but used their income to exercise the option of living apart from a family group. As a consequence, it began to be possible, at least in theory, to predicate a women's politics on a basis other than domesticity. Speculations aside, what can be stated with certainty is that more working women began to be more independent than ever before and that this social fact would have inescapable political ramifications.

Joanne Meyerowitz has written about independent women wage earners living in Chicago between 1880 and 1930 in her *Women Adrift*. She provides the following figures to demonstrate the growth in the phenomenon: in 1880 there were 3,800 women living alone in Chicago; in 1910 there were 31,500; and in 1930 there were 49,100.[9] These figures reflect not only an overall growth in the number of wage-earning women but also a decline in the percentage of women working as domestics (particularly live-in domestics) and consequently subject to family governance for that reason.

The pattern uncovered by her research suggests that in the early stages of this development women lived apart from their families because of unhappy or abusive relationships with parents or stepparents. As time went on, women more frequently spoke of their choice in positive terms: "Women adrift, however, were not simply the victims of poverty, stigma, and abuse. Increasingly in the early twentieth century, women actively chose to leave home to escape the restrictions routinely imposed upon daughters in the family economy."[10] In short, young women were opting for freedom, even if this meant that they lived very near the poverty line. Meyerowitz estimates that by 1900 about 20 percent of wage-earning women nationally were "adrift."

No doubt changing cultural norms—such as increasing secularization or the dawning of the culture of consumption—and the new economic possibilities reinforced one another to affect women's choices. In any event, it was now possible for a young woman to live a life with much more sexual freedom than if she were under the paternal roof. This meant in turn that the ancient dichotomy between "good" or "respectable" women and "bad" or "public" women was beginning to break down.

Recent scholarship underlines the magnitude of the change taking place. For example, Mary Blewett studied shoemakers in the Northeast in the mid-nineteenth century and found that male workers projected upon their female coworkers a view of women's power "as moral, unselfish, and spiritual not as material, self-interested, or political."[11] Moreover, the women themselves seem to have shared this view of the matter. Blewett quotes a diarist by the name of Sarah Trash, whose self-image as a moral woman was her dominant characteristic.[12]

By contrast, the young working women in turn-of-the-century New York who are the subjects of Kathy Peiss in her *Cheap Amusements* were eager to devote themselves to pleasure. Not only did they work outside the home—no doubt occupying sidewalks for part of the day!—but also they sought public entertainment, providing clientele for Coney Island amusement parks, for example, as well as for dance halls. Dressing flamboyantly, they pioneered a new kind of female self-presentation whereby it became much more difficult to look at a woman and assess accurately whether she was prepared to sell her body. This, too, served to break down the distinction between good and bad girls upon which the invidious connotation of public womanhood had rested.

So bold was the departure from traditional norms launched by working women that reformers fought back by attempting to regulate behavior at dance halls. Indeed, one of the best-known political women of the early twentieth century, Belle Moskowitz, first came to prominence working for dance-hall reform[13]—although it should be said that the reform had very little impact. Working women continued to go out on the town in search of a good time and to allow men to "treat" even though this practice resulted in a level of sexual byplay that would have horrified their parents. That so many more of them were "adrift" made all this the more possible.

What this meant was that a new type of female subjectivity was emerging, a more sexually assertive subjectivity. The "new women" of the working class were less likely than their predecessors of any class to be driven from public space or public roles by aspersions on their chastity. Says Peiss, "[t]hese young women pioneered new forms of public female behavior which the dominant culture ultimately incorporated and popularized."[14]

If female subjectivity was changing its character in these years, this also owed to the fact that the Gilded Age was a cultural as well as an economic watershed. Millions of immigrants from southern and eastern Europe had poured into the country. Cities were larger, denser, more dangerous, and more anonymous than ever before. The concentration of wealth was increasing and seemed to be out of control. For all these reasons the values appropriate to an overwhelmingly Protestant, rural nation were giving way.

Educated Americans of the late nineteenth century were reading, if not Charles Darwin himself, then one of his popularizers.[15] They were learning to accept scientific rather than providential explanations for the universe. The social sciences emerged as distinct disciplines, aiming to provide rigorous explanations of human behavior. Literary tastes, too, began to change as first naturalism and then modernism taught the cultivated to despise the kind of emotion-laden novels most often written by women. In other words, "sentimental" became a pejorative word.

Mid-nineteenth-century woman's culture, which underlay the powerful politics we have been discussing in preceding chapters, had been Protestant, pious, domestic, predicated on the passionlessness of women—at least in public discussions—and largely middle-class in its orientation. These characteristics account for its strength in a country like the antebellum United States and also for its limitations. The economic and cultural changes of the late nineteenth century undermined the basis of that woman's culture. While the changes were positive for public womanhood insofar as they made it more possible for women to control their own sexual destiny and to develop a politics that was not wedded to traditional norms of family life, the changes would also take away some of the classic means for building gender solidarity among women such as a common Protestant affiliation.[16] Moreover, after the emergence of modernism, it was much more difficult as a general proposition to employ the novel straightforwardly to valorize female subjectivity than heretofore. Indeed, the domestic novel and the zenith of woman's culture substantially overlapped in time, not least because the former provided the best means for propagandizing on behalf of the latter.

How, then, were women going about their advocacy for women's issues in these years? Many women had come out of the Civil War experience anticipating that their war work—to say nothing of the years of dedicated service to the cause of abolition—would be rewarded with the franchise. By 1867 Elizabeth Cady Stanton and Susan B. Anthony were campaigning for suffrage in Kansas, where the voters were considering a proposition which would have extended the franchise to both blacks and women. In her memoirs, Stanton writes humorously of the down side of being a public woman—of having to sleep in rooms crowded with strangers, fighting off vermin, and easing the pangs of hunger by chewing the bark of slippery elm. More important, she also furnishes a memorable description of a stay with Mother Bickerdyke, who had resettled in Salina, Kansas, and who provided an antidote to the rigors of being on the road. "There we had clean, comfortable beds, delicious viands, and everything was exquisitely neat. She entertained us with her reminiscences of the War."[17] The point is that as soon as the war had ended, the campaign for woman suffrage began in earnest, and the best-known activists on behalf of suffrage formed an alliance with some of the best-known of the women who went to the war. If black men had proven their valor on the battlefield, where nearly 200,000 served the Union cause, then so, too, had the loyal women of the North, absolutely vital to the war effort, demonstrated their capacity to be citizens in every sense of the word, including at the ballot box.[18]

It is important to understand this intellectual connection, echoes of which can be found in the volumes on the history of woman suffrage written by Stanton and others in 1881,[19] because then the bitterness felt by many of the women when suffrage failed to materialize is easier to fathom. This is not the place to go into a detailed narrative of the events in the latter 1860s, because they have been superbly recorded and analyzed by others.[20] Briefly stated, virtually to a man, the male members of the reform community told women that it was the "Negro's hour," because the Civil War had been fought to free slaves, who then needed to be able to defend themselves with ballots in the postbellum South. Thus, women were to wait their turn for enfranchisement. One wing of the women's movement accepted this advice and the ensuing Reconstruction amendments, and one, championed principally by Stanton and Anthony, did not. The latter were especially incensed, because the Fourteenth Amendment placed the word "male" in the Constitution for the first time. Eventually, a rapprochement between the two sides took place in 1890, and Elizabeth Cady Stanton, by then the grande dame of the suffrage campaign, was elected to head the newly merged organization. Not until 1920, again in the aftermath of a war, did the campaign for an amendment to the Constitution enfranchising women finally succeed.

The Civil War record of heroism and service represented the most substantial contribution by American women to their country to that time—and still stands as remarkable. The failure to achieve suffrage in the late 1860s given the high tide of women's activism preceding it demonstrates that the strategy for achieving public womanhood based on nineteenth-century woman's culture, with its strong service component, could go only so far. Women needed to be able to conceive of themselves as having interests as well as duties. Hence while the cause of public womanhood seemingly lost ground in some respects in the Gilded Age owing to the erosion of the strength of woman's culture, in the last analysis the growth of a class of independent wage earners pointed the way to the achievements of the twentieth century—the franchise and public policy that actively promotes women's access to higher education and to a full range of employment opportunities, for example.

Although the classic nineteenth-century woman's culture would eventually be undermined by the new values, in the Gilded Age it was still capable of inspiring women to remarkable public activism. Indeed, the temperance movement that developed in the 1870s represented the most impressive grass-roots mobilization of women for reform—as opposed to the mobilization during the war years which had

had no specific policy goal—to date in American history. Further, by the 1880s, the Woman's Christian Temperance Union (WCTU) had become the largest organization of American women. A temperance movement had first taken shape in the 1830s with participation by both men and women but with male leadership. By the 1860s women were becoming more assertive about male drinking, and elements of women's war work anticipated the mood of the postwar temperance movement. Disgust with drunken surgeons or inebriated officers is a leitmotif running through various memoirs, which also describe an occasional strong initiative by a woman. Mother Bickerdyke's willingness to go after a drunken doctor became the stuff of legend. Then in 1873 midwestern women spontaneously began a campaign to close down saloons that partook of the same confrontational spirit.

In her *Women and Temperance*, Ruth Bordin describes the personal transformation whereby one midwesterner became a public woman and helped launch the crusade in Hillsboro, Ohio, that ignited the "Western Prairie Fire." "Eliza Thompson . . . came from an influential Ohio family. She attended Catharine Beecher's school in Cincinnati as a child and there met Harriet Beecher Stowe. Her father had been governor of Ohio and her uncle a United States senator. She saw herself as a lady and was accustomed to behaving like one. Taking public positions was not a part of her self-image. And while she was an ardent supporter of the temperance cause, she was not in the habit of expressing her convictions in a public way."[21] While her husband, a judge, disapproved of her stepping out of the traditional role, her children encouraged her to do just that. She decided to accept a leadership position in the band of singing, praying women that marched to hotels and saloons to ask that proprietors pledge to stop selling alcoholic beverages. Within a few weeks, the number of businesses selling liquor in Hillsboro had gone from thirteen to four.[22] Soon the crusade had spread to many other communities, and hundreds of women like Eliza Thompson began to taste public power for the first time in their lives. As for Thompson herself, "[s]he always retained some of her original reticence, but she also could and did address hundreds formally from public platforms for the rest of her life."[23]

The midwestern crusade led directly to the founding of the WCTU in 1874, the first president of which was Annie Wittenmyer of Civil War fame. Over the course of the next twenty-five years this organization not only drew countless women like Eliza Thompson into public roles but also produced a truly visionary leader in Frances Willard, who became president in 1879 and remained in that capacity until her death in 1898. With the motto "Do Everything," Willard led her organization into many other types of reform besides agitation for temperance, including the pursuit of woman suffrage so as to protect the sanctity of the home. Beloved by thousands throughout the country, in communication with labor leaders, Populists and Fabian socialists, Willard enjoyed a new kind of public visibility for a woman.[24] No doubt Stowe had partaken of this level of fame after the publication of *Uncle Tom's Cabin*, but the fame had been more for the book than for its author or her leadership.

Another significant mobilization of women on the basis of woman's culture in those years was the settlement house movement. Less of a grass-roots phenomenon than the temperance movement because it was necessarily confined to cities, it was nonetheless extraordinarily important for public womanhood, because the settlement house workers had so strong an impact on public policy, pioneering much social legislation. Like Willard and others in the WCTU, those who founded settlement houses had a transcendent vision of the middle-class home and its virtues, which they wanted to share with others less fortunate than themselves. Yet the homes they created in slum neighborhoods, models of harmony and peace, differed from the usual middle-class home in being headed by women. This, too, made them significant for public womanhood, because patriarchs were noticeably absent from these environs.

Kathryn Kish Sklar begins an article on Hull House, no doubt the best-known of the settlement houses, with these queries: "What were the sources of women's political power in the United States in the decades before they could vote? How did women use the political power they were able to muster?"[25] She then gives an account of the successful campaign waged by Hull House to achieve the passage of anti-sweatshop legislation in Illinois in 1893 and the subsequent effort to see that the legislation was enforced. Sklar argues that the Hull House community of women was so emotionally gratifying for its residents that this enhanced their capacity to be public women and to undertake campaigns like the one in 1893. Writing of Florence Kelley, who came to Hull House in 1891, she says: "Somewhat paradoxically, perhaps, her autonomy was the product of her affiliation with a community."[26] In short, the settlement houses permitted women to have active public lives and well-nurtured private lives at one and the same time.

Finally, in assessing the organizational strength of public womanhood based on woman's culture during this period, it is important to take note of the development of the women's club movement. Originating as religiously based charitable organizations in the early nineteenth century, some women's clubs had become more overtly political and secular by the end of the century. Women saw them as vehicles for training themselves about public issues and for making an impact on the world. Between the WCTU, the still significant denominational groups, the two suffrage associations, and the burgeoning number of literary and educational societies, it was the rare American woman who had no access to a club in the late nineteenth century. For example, Anne Firor Scott cites research on the black community of postwar Memphis where laundresses and domestics belonged to clubs along with the wives of skilled workers and professional men.[27] In another article she states that in 1890 Portland, Maine, contained at least fifty women's clubs.[28] In short, women's clubs, already significant in the antebellum period, became more diverse, more numerous, and even more significant by the end of the century.

Moreover, many of the women who came out of the woman's culture tradition blazed new trails in these years. Clara Barton, whose Civil War heroism had given her an international reputation, worked on relief during the Franco-Prussian War. Convinced that the United States should be a signatory to the Geneva Convention and join the Red Cross, she came home and began to lobby forcefully toward this end. Eventually successful in the early 1880s, she then conceived the idea of broadening the work of the Red Cross to include relief for domestic disasters as well as for military suffering. In 1884 Secretary of State Frederick Frelinghuysen persuaded her to attend the Third International Conference of the Red Cross as the official representative of the American government, the first woman to have a diplomatic appointment. The only one of her sex among the ninety-five delegates, she enjoyed such high repute that she was able to persuade her colleagues to adopt the principle of domestic relief for the new organization.[29]

Mary Livermore was one of many Gilded Age women who adopted political positions outside the framework of the two-party system—which was failing lamentably to deal with the problems created by the incorporation of America. Women were leaders of Bellamy Nationalism, spokespeople for Populism, and actively engaged with socialism.[30] Livermore became the outstanding woman in the wing of socialism which came out of the Protestant tradition and was nourished by woman's culture—as opposed to that based in cities and tied to immigrants. Traveling throughout the country to lecture on women's rights and on temperance, Livermore linked her analysis of these issues to social and economic ills created by an exploitative capitalism.

Like Livermore, Frances Harper spoke publicly on behalf of temperance and women's rights in the postbellum years, having made her debut before the war, as we have seen. But as an African-American woman, she had another set of concerns to address, too. In these years, black women were organizing clubs in the South as well as in the North and, with very limited resources, working to combat the pernicious effects of racism.[31] Harper was a leader in the nascent club movement and a well-known author as well as a public speaker; she was in the forefront of those who attempted to provide an African-American presence at the Chicago World's Fair of 1893, from which blacks had been excluded. Constantly confronted by the hypocrisy of white reformers in the temperance and suffrage movements, who backed away from a full-fledged endorsement of the inclusion of blacks in their organizations—and more often than not accepted their formal exclusion—Harper put the fruits of her experience and her wisdom into her novel *Iola Leroy*, published in 1892 when she was sixty-seven years old and a seasoned political veteran.

Didactic and employing many of the conventions of the woman's novel of the nineteenth century—not surprisingly—*Iola Leroy* suffered a long neglect. Featuring a refined mulatto heroine, the novel was seen by generations of black critics to represent a failure of vision on the part of the author. But recently the black feminist critic Hazel Carby has published her re-evaluation of *Iola Leroy* in *Reconstructing Womanhood* and has also written an introduction to a new edition of the novel.[32] Carby argues, convincingly, that Harper anticipated W. E. B. Du Bois in envisioning a vital role for black intellectuals in the community of the future. Moreover, the heroine, who has been raised in ignorance of her racial identity, rejects a well-placed white suitor after learning of her true background, because of her feelings of solidarity with black people. In other words, she chooses to use her talents and energies toward the uplift of her people rather than a life of ease.

> "And yet," said Iola, earnestly, "I believe the time will come when the civilization of the negro will assume a better phase than you Anglo-Saxons possess. You will prove unworthy of your high vantage ground if you only use your superior ability to victimize feebler races and minister to a selfish greed of gold and a love of domination."[33]

Iola Leroy is the first novel by a black woman to have so marked a political stance.[34] Its author represented a combination of many facets of public womanhood, including public speaking, organizing, and writing a pathbreaking novel. Harper also combined the quintessential program of a Gilded Age white woman reformer—temperance and suffrage—with a visionary program for African-Americans.

Both Susan B. Anthony and Elizabeth Cady Stanton, stalwarts of the antebellum suffrage movement, leaders of the Woman's National Loyal League during the Civil War, and then leaders of the National Woman's Suffrage Association in the Gilded Age, pioneered bold new public activism during these years. Their activism was not based on woman's culture, hence anticipated developments that would come to fruition in the twentieth century. Anthony cast a ballot in the presidential election of 1872 and two weeks later found herself the subject of arrest on the grounds that she had violated a civil rights law aimed at unreconstructed southern men. Touring the county in which the trial would take place and speaking on the issues, Anthony was so convincing that the U.S. District Attorney sought a new venue for the trial on the grounds that it would be impossible to find an unprejudiced jury.[35] In her defense, Anthony argued that inasmuch as women are citizens, they necessarily possess the right to vote in a democracy. Thus no specific enabling legislation would be required for their exercise of the franchise. She also gave vivid examples of the burden that coverture still placed on married women, telling about a woman in Illinois whose false teeth turned out to be unsatisfactory. The dentist sued for payment of the bill; the judge refused to allow her to testify at the ensuing trial. Proclaimed Anthony: "Think of it, ye good wives, the false teeth in your mouths are a joint interest with your husbands, about which you are legally incompetent to speak!"[36]

For her part, Stanton spoke out on a broad range of issues in these years, including divorce.[37] But her boldest public act was her work on the *Woman's Bible*. Convinced that orthodox readings of the Bible had served to reinforce woman's relegation to a separate sphere and an inferior status, Stanton recruited a team of women to provide critiques of particularly misogynist portions of the Old Testament. Only the bravest were willing to cooperate because the project was sure to attract both notoriety and censure. In her memoirs, Stanton explains:

> The more I read, the more keenly I felt the importance of convincing women that the Hebrew mythology had no special claim to a higher origin than that of the Greeks, being far less attractive in style and less refined in sentiment. Its objectionable features would long ago have been apparent had they not been glossed over with a faith in their divine inspiration.[38]

Part I of the *Woman's Bible* appeared in November 1895 and met a firestorm of criticism. The following year a convention of Stanton's own National American Woman's Suffrage Association disavowed the project by a vote of 53 to 41.[39]

The transition from reform based on woman's culture to other sources of authority for public womanhood is well exemplified in the realm of charitable institutions. In the antebellum period Dorothea Dix had promoted the founding of a number of asylums for the mentally ill, becoming the leading reformer in the country in this arena. After the war, Josephine Shaw Lowell took up the mantle. The sister of one fallen Civil War hero and the widow of another—at the age of twenty—Lowell was determined to make a contribution to her society as they had. She moved from work with freed slaves to work with paupers in New York. In 1875 she prepared a report on the subject of able-bodied paupers that Governor Samuel Tilden found to be so impressive that he appointed her to the State Board of Charities as the first woman member of this body. Unlike the earlier Dix, a freelance, Lowell worked well within an institutional framework. Owing to this and her voluminous writing, she became "one of the most influential persons in the charity movement of her generation"[40] and a pioneering advocate of professionalizing social work. While women had been engaged in charitable activities throughout the nineteenth century, what was new about Lowell was the fact that she was employed by the state and that she was a partisan of the tough-minded approach to helping others, rather than merely a mother figure to those in need.[41] In short, she was truly a transitional figure between those public women through the Civil War and slightly beyond who justified their activism on the basis of woman's culture and the neutral "experts" who were the dominant figures in the Progressive Era.

On the one hand, women had failed to get the vote and were beginning to see domestic values under at least oblique assault.[42] On the other hand, hundreds of thousands of women were gaining a measure of economic independence. Moreover, a galaxy of remarkable women had managed to achieve public influence. In no area was the outcome for public womanhood more noteworthy, the change more dramatic, than in woman's capacity to speak openly about sexuality. We can best gauge the magnitude of this transition by looking at Victoria Woodhull, who rose to prominence in the 1870s and plummetted after she made public a sexual scandal, and comparing her with others of a slightly later period.

Victoria Woodhull was a woman with unconventional stances on both politics and personal life, including a belief in free love and a membership in the International Workingmen's Association, a Marxist group. In 1871 she was a newspaper publisher in New York, and in that capacity she testified before Congress, arguing that women had already been enfranchised by the Fourteenth and Fifteenth amendments. This bold maneuver caught the attention of Stanton and Anthony, and they took an immediate interest in the charismatic Woodhull. (Indeed, some scholars suggest that Woodhull's argument was the source for Anthony's defense in 1872.) But Woodhull's views on free love rendered her notorious, and other New York newspapers began to print scandalous stories about her. Before long, she was subject to such severe harassment—eviction from her home, the withdrawal of financial support from her paper—that she resolved to fight back in a particularly outrageous manner, in so doing precipitating the most publicized scandal of the Gilded Age.

Henry Ward Beecher was the best-known clergyman of the day, so beloved that his visage was used to sell patent medicine.[43] What is more, he had been a leader of the more conservative wing of the woman suffrage movement. For some time, gossip had linked him to an attractive parishioner, Elizabeth Tilton, who was, like Beecher himself, married. In November 1872 Woodhull published a special issue of the weekly which was devoted to the scandal, evidently because she wanted to expose the hypocrisy of the sexual double standard.

Even before this, Woodhull had inspired feelings of outrage and revulsion in many women's rights advocates. For example, the Reverend Phebe Hanaford denied her pulpit to Isabella Beecher Hooker (sister of Catharine, Harriet, and Henry) because of her adherence to Woodhull.[44] Stowe satirized Woodhull as "Audacia Dangereyes" in *My Wife and I* and regarded her with what can only be described as loathing—even before Woodhull published the rumors about her brother.[45] And these women were favorable to suffrage and reform.

No doubt those on the other side were even more strongly negative about Woodhull.

In truth, Woodhull had lived her life as a high-wire act, becoming a protégée of Commodore Vanderbilt in a stock-brokerage house shortly after her arrival in New York, for example, by which means her ascent to notoriety was insured. A public woman in being the first to announce for the presidency (in 1872) and in her stock brokerage business, Woodhull almost seemed to go out of her way to reinforce the connection between public activity and sexual impropriety by flouting decorous standards and doing little to disguise her behavior. As an instance in point, she briefly shared an abode with both her first husband Dr. Canning Woodhull and her apparent second husband Colonel James Blood.[46] Thus she willingly gave scandal-mongers ammunition to be used against her.

Following her public exposure of the gossip about Beecher and Tilton, Woodhull and her sister (and colleague) Tennessee Claflin were arrested on the charge of passing obscene material through the mails. Acquitted after seven months of litigation, the two were clearly chastened by the harassment they had undergone. In the late 1870s they departed for London and for quieter lives. For those who had defended them—Isabella Beecher Hooker and Elizabeth Cady Stanton, among others—it would be years before the whiff of scandal surrounding them, too, had entirely disappeared. Like her predecessor Fanny Wright, Victoria Woodhull was briefly a phenomenon as a public woman but soon lost her credibility and her access to a public.

The first American woman to command large audiences as a speaker over a long period of time while openly living an unconventional personal life was Emma Goldman, born in 1869, about the time Woodhull and Claflin arrived in New York. By the time Goldman launched her speaking career in the 1890s, the United States had become a very different place than it was for the Claflin sisters. Millions of immigrants had arrived from southern and eastern Europe—like the Goldman family themselves—and tens of thousands more women were gainfully employed outside the home. Thus Goldman did not need to derive her public legitimacy from her acceptance by middle-class Protestant arbiters, as both Wright and Woodhull had been forced to do to pursue a public career.

Born in what is now Lithuania to a Jewish family, Emma Goldman came to the United States with a sister in December 1885. Shortly thereafter, their parents followed. Goldman arrived in the New World just in time for the unfolding of the Haymarket drama, at which time several anarchists were convicted of a heinous crime on the basis of highly dubious evidence. Drawn to the anarchist cause, Goldman was soon enmeshed in the life of political activism on behalf of radical causes which she pursued till her death in 1940. Says her biographer Alice Wexler, "Almost from the moment she entered the anarchist movement in 1889 at the age of twenty, Emma Goldman enjoyed a notoriety unequalled by any other woman in American public life."[47]

Johann Most, the anarchist editor of *Freiheit*, identified Goldman as having the potential to be a gifted orator and coached her extensively in her early twenties, so as to prepare her for this undertaking. She first came to widespread public attention as a speaker at hunger demonstrations in New York City in 1898. Arrested and convicted for inciting to riot, she spent ten months in prison. The famous journalist Nelly Bly of the *New York World*—another noteworthy public woman of these years—interviewed Goldman while she was awaiting trial and wrote a very favorable article about her which helped turn an anarchist firebrand into a celebrity. Nearly three thousand people packed an auditorium to greet Goldman following her release from prison, and she was immediately swamped by invitations to lecture.[48] She was soon traveling extensively throughout the country on the lecture circuit.

What is most significant about Goldman for our purposes is the fact that she believed in making sexuality a central concern of her politics. Not only did she publicly advocate the use of birth control and the freedom of sexual expression, but she saw sexuality itself as a source of "creative energy."[49] Moreover, her public persona united passionate and combative political stances with a vibrant physical presence—as had several of her illustrious predecessors such as Wright and Woodhull as well as the Civil War orator Anna Dickinson. Yet despite her controversial stands on a multitude of public issues, despite more than one imprisonment, despite a series of love affairs, and despite her deportation during the Red Scare, Emma Goldman never suffered the kind of marginalization to which earlier female sexual radicals had been subject. Whether A. Mitchell Palmer and J. Edgar Hoover liked it or not, Goldman was a player on the international stage for most of her adult life.

The relationship between her public and private lives is exceptionally interesting and has recently been the subject of scholarly attention. Far too peripatetic to lead a conventional domestic life, she nonetheless liked to cook and frequently played a motherly role with her lovers. Bold and seemingly fearless as she was in her public addresses, she used a much different voice when writing to the great passion of her life, Ben Reitman. To him she wrote letters filled with abject craving for his presence and for his love.[50] So devoted to her cause that the novelist Theodore Dreiser wrote to her that she was "more of a public than a private person even in your own room," she nonetheless inspired devoted friendships.[51]

Thus the life of this extraordinarily courageous—and fortunate insofar as her timing was concerned—public woman reveals how many contradictions remained for such an individual. "Public woman" was no longer an oxymoron and was losing its character as an epithet. Yet the status of being a public woman still was more problematic for those to whom it applied than was "public man" for men. Public men had wives to create a private life for them and to bear most of the responsibility for maintaining it. Public women did not.[52]

Although Ida B. Wells did not publicly flout conventional sexual morality as did Goldman, she was no less courageous, because she, an African-American woman, publicly discussed one of the nation's most strongly tabooed subjects, interracial sex, in order to denounce the crime of lynching. Born in the waning days of slavery, Wells was orphaned in 1878 at the age of sixteen and forced to support herself and her younger siblings. Within the next decade, she had become first a schoolteacher and then a newspaper editor. In March 1892 a mob in her home town of Memphis lynched three young black men whom she knew and admired. Horrified and outraged by this event, Wells launched her crusade against mob violence, although she had to leave the South—and briefly leave the country—in order to pursue this activity. Three months after the Memphis lynching she wrote this editorial:

> Eight Negroes lynched since last issue of the *Free Speech*. Three were charged with killing white men and five with raping white women. Nobody in this section believes the old thread-bare lie that Negro men assault white women. If Southern white men are not careful they will over-reach themselves and a conclusion will be reached which will be very damaging to the moral reputation of their women.[53]

After the editorial's publication, a mob destroyed her press (she happened to be in the North at the time) and she began a new phase of her life, going to lecture in Britain because there it was possible to talk freely to white audiences about lynching and its context. She explained to her audiences abroad that during slavery white men had had access to sexual favors from black women, but that they were unwilling to admit now that slavery had ended that their women might be similarly attracted to black men. In the event of sexual intercourse between a white woman and a black man, the only explanation according to the vast majority of southern whites was that a rape had taken place. Hence the savagery of white mobs: they felt justified in executing summary justice against the putative black rapist. Wells toured extensively in Britain with this message, trying to stir up British public opinion to put pressure on Americans to do something about so monstrous an evil. The southern press attempted to vilify her reputation, but without success. In her autobiography she enumerates all the well-placed British people who accorded her both a hearing and respect.

Returning to the United States in 1894, after two trips abroad, she was able to obtain better access to American audiences because she carried letters from British clergymen urging their American counterparts to open their pulpits to her. Once again, she was proclaiming that "white women have been known to fall in love with black men, and only after that relationship is discovered has an assault charge been made."[54] She then launched a career of extraordinary public activism, interrupted for a few years while she raised the four children to whom she had given birth after her marriage to an attorney in Chicago. She wrote a pioneering expose of lynching entitled A *Red Record*. She founded several women's groups, including, after the turn of the century, a suffrage club for black women. In 1930 she ran unsuccessfully for the Illinois state senate. Moreover, her autobiography demonstrates that she had a feel for the importance of public presence, whether that presence was as a member of an all-white crowd at a football game or as a defender of due process for black people in a town where a race riot had taken place.

About the same time that Wells and Goldman were touring to give lectures on subjects that would have been unheard-of just a short while earlier, Kate Chopin published her novel *The Awakening*, the awakening in question being that of the Creole heroine to both her autonomy and her sexuality. Using prose that conveys an atmosphere of sensuality, Chopin describes Edna Pontellier's growing awareness of the limitations of her husband and her willingness to explore erotic experiences with other men. That an American woman would write about such a topic in the late 1890s was an indication of the dawning freedom of expression about sexuality that would be so consequential for public women. Yet the book's immediate fate was harsh. Condemned by reviewers as vulgar, the novel and its author were marginalized as early women lecturers who tried to deal with "free love" had been marginalized. Only in the late 1960s would *The Awakening* be recognized as an American classic.

To sum up the status of public womanhood as the Gilded Age ended, let us once again refer to the four analytical categories with which we began. In terms of the social geography of gender there had probably been more change in the nineteenth century than in any preceding century in human history. New means of transportation, new modes of employment, and new types of living arrangements had given American women an unprecedented freedom to travel on their own and to be agents of their own history. What is more, in the late nineteenth century another liberating vehicle, the bicycle, had appeared on the scene to increase a woman's freedom of movement. Women might still be denied entrance into restaurants and clubs if unescorted by a man, a woman alone on the street at night might still be treated like a "public woman" à la Lizzie Schauer, but consider the places to which women *had* gained access. They could go to the factory, the office, the department store, the amusement park, the dance hall, and the theater. They could attend political rallies. They could stand up in front of audiences and in front of church congregations; indeed, the Pauline injunction seemed to be a dead letter. They could travel alone on ships, railroads, and other vehicles. They could work side by side with men to whom they were not related, and they could walk in a group down a city sidewalk.

In no other area was the progress quite so substantial. In the realm of politics, women reformers were beginning to have a strong impact on public policy even without the vote, an impact that would reach a crescendo at local and state levels during the Progressive Era, and at the national level during the New Deal. Moreover, a few women like Josephine Shaw Lowell in New York were beginning to hold important appointive positions at the state level. Yet as of 1890, decades of agitation for suffrage had produced meager results. That year Wyoming entered the union as the first state fully to enfranchise women. By 1900 only Colorado, Utah, and Idaho had followed suit.

With respect to the legal foundations of public womanhood, here, too, the situation was one of undoubted but halting progress. It is impossible to give more than the sketchiest outline of changes in the legal sphere inasmuch as this is not a treatise in legal history. Nonetheless, it is important that we have a sense of the pace of legal change, as we assess developments in other dimensions of public womanhood. If we enumerate various aspects of the legal situation for women— married women's property laws, access to divorce and to custody of children, laws governing domicile, right to serve on juries—we can begin to grasp the glacial slowness of change in this area. While married women had begun to achieve property rights in the antebellum period, they were still less than the legal equals of their husbands in the United States of the late nineteenth century. Says Amy Dru Stanley, in an article about the laws of marriage in the postbellum period: "In an age that designated contract the embodiment of freedom, the very axis of legal rights and social relations, wives' liberty to contract remained strictly hedged by the bonds of marriage. Registering the effects of the wage system in working-class homes, the earnings statutes established married women's title to their wages. But the entitlement was encased in the paternal rules of marriage; it strained but did not sunder, the abiding conjugal relation of dominion and dependency."[55] It would not be until the civil rights and feminist movements of the 1960s and 1970s that women's right to serve on juries would be fully established and that the Fourteenth Amendment would begin to be applied in cases involving gender inequities so that the law governing domicile, for example, would be more symmetrically applied. In other words, the legal doctrine of coverture was far from a dead letter in the Gilded Age—or for many decades to come.

Finally, we come to the question of culture. In this area public women had enjoyed the earliest breakthroughs, both as authors and as religious leaders. Much was gained in the Gilded Age. In addition to the greater freedom to talk about sexuality, in addition to the enhanced opportunities for cultural influence owing to the new access to the lecture platform, the realm of higher education opened up to women because of the founding of a number of women's colleges and the increasing availability of co-educational public universities.

Yet the erosion of woman's culture, in part owing to changing demographics perhaps but much more because of the respect for the expert, for value-free social science, for tough-mindedness as a virtue, would by 1920 or so make it impossible for women to claim cultural authority as moral arbiters. Indeed, the very idea of a moral arbiter was beginning to seem old-fashioned if not preposterous. Moreover, the religious route to cultural authority was increasingly less important in an increasingly secular society. Hence the story of public women in the first part of the twentieth century is about the loss of one form of public power, however disliked by modern feminists, and the slow gathering of power on a different basis.

8

A Kind of Power: Women and Politics, 1900–1960

In the first decades of the twentieth century women achieved many victories in the public sphere, most important, the suffrage. Moreover, they began to win electoral office, they saw the enactment of major public policy for which they had struggled, and they enjoyed an increasing public presence. It all added up to a new kind of public power. But at the same time, it must be emphasized, women's power and women's access to public influence still fell far short of that exercised by men. What is more, women voted at a lower rate than men and showed no evidence of bloc voting on the basis of perceived gender interest. Those few women elected to high office were frequently widows succeeding their husbands—and they kept a low profile in any event. Before the 1930s, in the rare case where a woman played an important role in government on her own—Belle Moskowitz is the outstanding example of this phenomenon—it was behind the scenes and with a discretion bordering on the heroic. The New Deal then provided women with an unprecedented opportunity to achieve influential positions in the federal government. Yet this influence declined markedly when Dr. Win-the-War replaced Dr. New Deal during the 1940s. As a result, except for women in the work force and in the labor movement—about whom we will read in the next chapter— the major progress for public womanhood between 1920 and 1960 was behind the scenes, in the African-American community or among other groups of ethnic women.

As the twentieth century began, the grand old women who had led the nineteenth-century suffrage movement were reaching the end of their long and remarkable lives. Stanton died in 1902 and Anthony in 1906. The generation who replaced them produced a few remarkable leaders, too. Carrie Chapman Catt has been justly celebrated as the movement's greatest organizer, architect of the Winning Plan of 1916, whereby various states were assigned specific roles so as to put together enough states to ratify a constitutional amendment. Alice Paul and Harriet Stanton Blatch (daughter of Elizabeth Cady Stanton) traveled to Great Britain, observed the tactics of the British suffragists, and came home to lead a suffrage organization which evolved into the National Woman's Party and employed more militant tactics than did the National American Woman Suffrage Association (NAWSA).

Thus, there were two ways in which the successful suffrage movement of the early twentieth century had an impact on public womanhood, beyond the obvious one of securing the franchise in 1920. In the first place, women took to the streets in an unprecedented fashion in these years: they paraded by the thousands and they demonstrated in smaller groups. In one year alone, 1915, suffragists in New York City staged twenty-eight parades, one of which drew more than 25,000 participants.[1] Moreover, women put on plays, pageants, and tableaux. They even sponsored four suffrage films between 1912 and 1914.[2] In short, there had never been a time in American history when so many women had participated in ritualized public behavior, especially public behavior designed to advance female self-interest.

In the second place, led by Catt, some women leaders began to engage in a new—for women—kind of intense politicking of the two parties and of male officeholders. From Mercy Otis Warren on and throughout most of the nineteenth century, white, middle-class women's political culture had been most often decorous and high-minded. Following the failure of the Reconstruction amendments to enfranchise women, Stanton and Anthony had begun to push in a somewhat different direction, willing to anger their opponents, for example, as they demanded justice for women.[3] Under Catt's tutelage, women began to operate in a fashion that was forceful without being confrontational. In New York, Catt's Woman Suffrage party launched a precinct-level campaign for suffrage in 1910. Somewhat later, Catt personally lobbied Woodrow Wilson, asking him for advice and trying to associate him with the cause.[4] If this approach surrendered some of the moral high ground women had been wont to stake out, it may also have ensured the victories of these years.

There were many "firsts" for women in the closing years of the nineteenth century and the early twentieth century. In 1896 Martha Hughes Cannon was elected to the Utah state senate and became the first woman state legislator. By 1921 there were thirty-three women in state legislatures—and approximately 10,000 men. In 1916 Montana voters elected Jeannette Rankin, a Republican, to the House of Representatives, the first woman elected to Congress. In 1925 Wyoming voters elected Nellie Tayloe Ross to take the place of her deceased husband as governor of the state, the first woman to serve in that capacity. These were important milestones yet their rarity is an indication of how unlikely women still seemed as candidates and officeholders. Indeed these figures document the dearth of women in Congress: between 1789 and 1982, 10,000 men served in the House of Representatives, while 100 women served in the House between 1916 and 1982.[5]

Beyond suffrage and the first trickle of women into elective office, the political achievements of public womanhood at the local and state level were extraordinary during the Progressive period. We still lack a study that might provide a summary of how many women played a significant role in how many states to achieve the legislation that gave birth to the welfare state. But proliferating case studies make it clear that the number was substantial.[6] Settlement house workers, women affiliated with the National Consumers' League or the Women's Trade

Union League, and those who pioneered what became the home economics profession were among the women who pushed for—and achieved—protective labor legislation for women workers, laws promoting maternal and child welfare, government inspection and regulation of food products, and child labor laws, to cite a few examples.

Underlying this legislative impact was the grass-roots political mobilization of club women in many locales. For example, in San Francisco between 1906 and 1909 a series of sensational graft trials provided club women with an opportunity to play an important role in the Citizens' League of Justice, an organization that agitated to support the prosecution of grafters. Women held home meetings and mass rallies, made speeches before other women's groups, and attended trials. Worth noting is the contemporary observation that the women who went into courtrooms had to contend with the "opinion of some that women who showed themselves in court were brazen."[7] Nonetheless, at its height the Women's Branch of the Citizen's League of Justice had a membership of between two and three thousand.

Finally, as we contemplate the development of public womanhood in the early twentieth century, we should take note of the fact that in the South there was now a much stronger contingent of public women, black and white, than there had been since the heydey of the powerful upper-class women of the colonial period. The first woman to serve in the U.S. Senate, albeit for the brief period of a few hours in 1922, was Rebecca Latimer Felton, "a political power in Georgia for forty years."[8] But even more remarkable was the appearance of the Atlanta-based Commission on Interracial Cooperation (CIC) in 1920, which very gingerly brought together black and white, men and women, for community betterment. Soon there were Methodist settlement houses with biracial boards and staffs.[9] Given the power of racial taboos in the South, these were unheard-of developments, requiring a courageous group of people for their implementation.

In her biography of Jessie Daniel Ames, the outstanding white leader who emerged from this movement, Jacquelyn Dowd Hall traces the links between the CIC and the later Association of Southern Women for the Prevention of Lynching, which emerged in 1930. A Texas suffragist active in both groups, Ames played a prominent role by speaking out against lynching to "audiences who assumed that no Southern woman of fine sensibilities would speak the word 'lynching' in private, to say nothing of talking from a platform about it by name." [10] Thus, like Ida B. Wells before them, Ames and her colleagues staked out a new terrain of public discourse for women. This was especially valuable because one of the rationales for lynching had been the impossibility of public discussion of rape.

Yet despite all the significant victories, there were almost equally significant losses for white middle-class women between 1900 and 1930. Most noteworthy was the further diminution of gender solidarity among them, a trend that had begun in the Gilded Age. One place to study this development is in the women's colleges. As Helen Horowitz demonstrates in her history of these institutions from their founding through the 1930s, for the first several decades of their existence they had nurtured strong friendships and homosocial bonds. In the early twentieth century this began to change:

> College life had consumed the energies of undergraduates at the turn of the century. In their all-female communities, collegians lived by their own rules, playing out dramas that transformed them. But while a fictional undergraduate of 1900 turned away from a male friend to "Vassar's self-sufficiency," her niece twenty-five years later would have found Vassar alone insufficient—indeed boring, perhaps even a bit threatening. [11]

Horowitz ascribes the change to the fact that "[s]ophisticated Americans learned in the early twentieth century that women had active sexual natures not latent ones." Therefore the intense female friendships that flourished in women's colleges began to garner more scrutiny and even hostility from parents and college administrators. Moreover, women students themselves began to feel deprived and sought contact with male collegians. After World War I the energy that had been focused on the events of the college community began to be focused instead on dating.

As is well known, co-educational campus life in the 1920s also revolved around norms that made the ideals and values of the nineteenth-century women's movement, including gender solidarity, seem old-fashioned and outmoded. Eager to maximize their personal freedom, highly approving of the cornucopia of goods at their disposal, college-age young people of both sexes tended to be apathetic or conformist about politics.[12] Thus, as the veterans of the nineteenth-century women's movement were dying off, they were not being replaced by educated young women with a similar commitment to solidarity among women or to social change in general.

Moreover, the very foundation upon which nineteenth-century woman's culture had stood—the reverence for the home and the respect for the housewife—was being rapidly dismantled.[13] The deconstruction had begun in the Gilded Age and proceeded apace in the early twentieth century as a plethora of "experts" arrogated to themselves the wisdom that had once been the province of older women. Combined with the increasing secularization of American society, this development dealt a death blow to the moral authority of woman based on her sacred duty in the home. In short, woman's sphere was much less likely than earlier to be the source of empowerment for women. Yet the vast majority of American women were still largely confined to work in the home; as late as 1930, only 11.7 percent of married women were gainfully employed outside the home.

In the long run, as women advanced into "new" areas, they wound up in another form of woman's sphere, a more circumscribed one. Those women who achieved graduate training in a variety of fields were most likely to get academic jobs as home economists—unless they chose to teach in a woman's college.[14] The political parties set up separate women's divisions that had little real power.[15] Various jurisdictions, including the federal government, set up women's bureaus where, after the progressive impulse was spent, little progress came about in the area of policy initiatives for women. In other words, women who thought they were establishing a beachhead in male-dominated institutions most often found themselves in some form of female ghetto. But unlike those occupying the woman's sphere of the nineteenth century, they lacked independent moral authority. And most telling of all, they were usually subordinate to an all-male body, which controlled the purse-strings. This was why their power was so limited.

The most important cultural achievement for women of the late nineteenth century, the new freedom to talk publicly and openly about sexuality that had been pioneered by Emma Goldman and others, was also substantially neutralized in these years. Like the home, female sexuality became the province of the expert, in this case, usually a male expert. The public discourse on the subject revolved around "adjustment" and other male-generated therapeutic categories, rather than around explorations of female subjectivity.

Nancy Cott argues in *The Grounding of Modern Feminism* that the most vital arena for organized activity by women after the achievement of suffrage lay in volunteer work and in the clubs. Despite the fall-off in numbers as the National American Woman Suffrage Association (NAWSA) evolved into the League of Women Voters and lost 90 percent of its membership, enough other organizations came into being during the 1920s so that Cott concludes that the net level of organization in 1930 was very comparable to that in 1920.[16] Yet many clubs were losing their political edge. For example, in the 1920s the General Federation of Women's Clubs, the largest single woman's organization and at one time "a decisive voice in the Progressive coalition . . . abandoned politics entirely, choosing to emphasize home economics and the distribution of electrical appliances rather than political action."[17] For that matter the home economics profession itself changed direction and became more interested in trumpeting the latest technological wizardry than in spearheading reform.[18]

Lacking the moral authority possessed by her mother and grandmother as well as a matrix of highly politicized organizations like the Woman's Christian Temperance Union (WCTU) or NAWSA, the middle-class white woman of the 1920s confronted unpleasant realities should she contemplate becoming publicly active. There was no cultural expectation that a woman should be able to "have it all." If she chose serious engagement with politics, for example, she was unlikely to combine this with a husband, let alone with raising children. In

TABLE 8.1. **Percentages of Men and Women Registered to Vote in Chicago, 1914–31**

	1914	1916	1920	1924	1928	1931
Men	68	64	62	62	57	58
Women	32	36	38	39	43	42

Source: Virginia Sapiro, *The Political Integration of Women: Roles, Socialization, and Politics* (Urbana: Univ. of Illinois Press, 1983), 22.

the event that she was brave enough to attempt to combine public life with marriage and children, she was expected to bear the entire responsibility for the maintenance of private life herself. Small wonder that so few women ventured into this terrain.

As for the behavior of the newly enfranchised women voters, the fragmentary data that exist indicate that their continuing greater responsibility for domestic life made it less likely that they would vote than was the case with men. Indeed, American women have voted in smaller percentages than men throughout most of the twentieth century until very recently. (See Tables 8.1 and 8.2.)

The best current information is that while white women voters did not equal male turnouts for many decades, they did mobilize in larger numbers for the election of 1928, which pitted Herbert Hoover against Al Smith. Not only did middle-class women become enthusiastic about the dry Hoover, but those of immigrant stock responded favorably to Al Smith. Indeed, Smith was the first candidate to bring

TABLE 8.2. **Percentages of Men and Women Voting in National Elections, 1948–76**

	1948	1952	1956	1960	1964	1968	1972	1976
Men	69	72	80	80	73	69	76	78
Women	59	62	69	69	60	66	70	69

Source: Sapiro, *The Political Integration of Women,* 23.

these women to the polls in any very large numbers. The election of 1928 was a significant one for women voters because afterward women were never again so remote from the electoral process as they had been in the early 1920s.[19]

It can be said that, on balance, in the immediate aftermath of suffrage the work of promoting female participation in the realm of politics necessarily belonged to a small group of women. Perhaps the most vigorous women's organization in the 1920s was Alice Paul's National Woman's Party, which more or less by Paul's design operated as a vanguard group, rather than one which recruited a cross-section of American women. Single-issue in its orientation—first concentrating on suffrage and then after 1923 on the achievement of the Equal Rights Amendment (ERA)—it was also controlled from the top down. Members of the Woman's Party possessed gender solidarity—with a vengeance some might say—but defined that solidarity so narrowly as to repel interest on the part of many who might otherwise have been attracted to feminist politics. As Nancy Cott puts it:

> The NWP's "appeal for conscious sex loyalty" . . . was directed toward members of the sex who could subordinate all other identifications and loyalties—class, ethnic, racial, religious, political—to a "pure" sense of themselves as women differentiated from men. That meant principally those who belonged to and were privileged by the dominant culture in every way except that they were female.[20]

In consequence, the Woman's Party dropped from a membership of 60,000 at its height to a few thousand after suffrage.

One final problem, which should be mentioned before we examine the achievements of the '20s, stemmed from the aforementioned ERA. Championed by the largely upper-class women of the NWP, the ERA was anathema to individuals and groups who had worked for protective labor legislation for women. The latter included the newly born League of Women Voters, the National Consumers' League (NCL), and the Women's Trade Union League (WTUL), as well as organized labor. These groups were unprepared to see the overturning of legislation for which they had struggled for many years. Thus in a time when the strength of public womanhood was already declining, a schism over deeply held principles made a bad situation worse.[21]

Amidst so much gloom, there were of course a few bright spots. Many of the settlement house veterans were still active in the '20s. In no state were they more influential than in New York, where Eleanor Roosevelt, Molly Dewson, and Frances Perkins were part of an organized network that also included the aging Florence Kelley, who had been for decades an inspiration to younger women. Of Kelley, it was said, "Everybody was brave from the moment she came into the room."[22] Nourished by these contacts, Roosevelt, Dewson, and Perkins, each in her own way, then spearheaded the remarkable advance of women into government positions during the New Deal years.

Moreover, during the '20s women had a substantial impact on American foreign policy, because they agitated so determinedly for peace. Carrie Chapman Catt and Jane Addams were the best-known Americans in the international peace movement of women. Scholars generally credit this movement—at least in part—for the adoption of the Kellogg-Briand Pact of 1928, a multinational agreement renouncing the use of force to solve international disputes.

Finally, another New Yorker, Belle Moskowitz, played an unprecedented public role during this period. Moskowitz, the scourge of dance halls in the early twentieth century, became during the 1920s the first American woman to have direct, daily impact on the governance of a large state—albeit as the right-hand-woman of Governor Al Smith and not as one elected to office herself. Elizabeth Israels Perry, her biographer and granddaughter, tells of how Moskowitz came to public life through her involvement with women's organizations as well as her commitment to reform. By the time of Smith's first gubernatorial campaign in 1918, Moskowitz had the connections and the savvy to organize the women's vote for him. (New York granted women the vote in 1917.) This was no mean feat inasmuch as Smith had risen through the ranks of Tammany Hall, a route to office little calculated to endear him to reform-minded women voters.

Eventually, the Irish pol from the sidewalks of New York and the reform-minded Jewish woman developed a true partnership. He respected her brains, her tact, and her diligence. She gave unstintingly of herself to him and to his administration—her official capacity at first was executive secretary of the commission to reform state government—because she saw this, no doubt correctly, as her best chance to make an impact on policy. Robert Caro describes her vividly in his biography of Robert Moses, who also worked for Smith:

> She wasn't "Mrs. M." then [in 1918] or "Moskie" or "Lady Belle." Nicknames would come later when, all but unknown to the public but an almost legendary figure among politicians, she would be possessed of more power and influence than any woman in the United States. She would be called "Mrs. M." by the man who had given her that power and influence, Alfred Emanuel Smith, and by the young social workers and reformers she had recruited to Smith's service. That nickname would be used in an attempt at familiarity by politicians who, on favor-seeking visits to Albany, would notice her sitting unobtrusively in a corner of the Governor's office, a short, plump, and motherly woman who sat placidly knitting and waiting for the Governor to turn to her, as he did before making any important decision, and ask: "What do you think Mrs. M.?"[23]

It should not pass by without comment that the most powerful woman in the United States was "all but unknown to the public." Shrewd enough to realize that no male politician could be publicly seen as reliant on a woman, she settled for "the reality, but never the appearance (except to insiders), of power."[24] Never occupying an official position after the disbanding of the Reconstruction Committee, she involved herself in "editing his [the Governor's] public papers, writing speeches, monitoring legislation, ferreting out information, [and] finding the right person for a vacant post."[25] In other words, she made herself indispensable and could enjoy a concomitant influence.

Belle Moskowitz first garnered Al Smith's attention and interest as a potential liaison to women's organizations that in 1918 were quite powerful. Although these organizations would lose clout and members over the course of the decade, they were still potent enough in the early '20s to convince Congress to pass a controversial piece of healthcare legislation, the Sheppard-Towner Act, over the objections of the American Medical Association. A coalition of groups from the League of Women Voters to the NCL, the WTUL, the General Federation of Women's Clubs (GFWC), and the Business and Professional Women formed a Women's Joint Congressional Committee to lobby Congress on women's issues. In 1921 Congress responded to the pressure with a landmark bill that allocated federal funds to welfare for the first time, providing money to states to fund public health programs such as visiting nurses and education on prenatal care. After this triumph, and absent any evidence of female muscle being exercised at the polls, women's organizations lost ground. According to William Chafe:

> Beginning in mid-decade, however, women's standing in the eyes of politicians dropped precipitously. A Congressional supporter urged the Women's Joint Congressional Committee to reduce its pressure for a home economics measure because Congress was tired of being asked to pass women's legislation. The Child Labor Amendment, which had engaged the energies of so many reform groups, failed ratification in the key states of Massachusetts and New York as Catholic bishops joined the opposition with claims that the amendment would destroy the sanctity of the home. Appropriations for the Women's Bureau and Children's Bureau were cut, and a two-year extension of the Sheppard-Towner Act was secured only by inserting into the new measure a written statement that the act would permanently expire on June 30, 1929. Congressmen seemed as intent on rebuffing the requests of female reformers in the second half of the decade as they had been in granting them during the first half.[26]

Thus as the 1930s began, much of the energy that had gone into achieving suffrage and into pressuring legislators for reform had dissipated. Most white middle-class women's clubs had become relatively apolitical. The reform generation was not being replaced by young women with a similar dedication to social change. The most fervently feminist organization, the National Woman's Party, was elitist and remote from the concerns of millions of American women whose lives were less privileged than those of Alice Paul and her colleagues. Two groups of white women who were exceptions to this pattern, who had the potential for creating a significant impact on public womanhood, can be singled out.[27] One, composed of leftists, will be discussed in the next chapter. The other was composed of the veterans of the settlement house movement. As of March 1933 one of their own was in the White House, and Eleanor Roosevelt would prove a friend indeed to public women.

It is typical of the era that Belle Moskowitz, the most powerful woman of the 1920s, operated behind the scene, while Eleanor Roosevelt, the most powerful woman in the '30s and '40s—with the possible exception of her friend Frances Perkins, FDR's Secretary of Labor and the first woman to serve in the Cabinet—achieved her power through her marriage. Women politicians were still sufficiently anomalous as to require camouflage. But if many of the women whom fate placed into office to replace deceased husbands were accidental officeholders in these years, with little preparation for public life, this was hardly the case where Eleanor Roosevelt was concerned.[28] Her marriage may have been responsible for her opportunity, but she had assiduously prepared herself for it.

In the years since her death, Roosevelt has been the subject of numerous books, films, and television programs. One of the twentieth century's most admired women, she has become widely known as first a lonely child, then a shy adolescent, and ultimately a wife whose dashing husband engaged in an extramarital affair after she had given birth to six children, one of whom died in infancy. In an age when divorce was less frequent—and fatal to political ambitions—Eleanor and Franklin made their peace, and she poured her very considerable energy into the politics of reform in New York and developed a circle of devoted women friends. Further, she organized women voters for the state Democratic party and became a political leader in her own right. When Americans elected Franklin, then governor of New York, to be President, they little knew how much political experience resided in the person of his wife. They would soon learn that she had no intention of playing a traditional wifely role.

Eleanor Roosevelt's impact on her husband's appointment of unprecedented numbers of women to high office was twofold. In the first place, through her, he had come to know and respect the highly competent women in her circle. In the second place, Eleanor lobbied FDR with respect to specific appointments. In two fine books dealing with women and the New Deal, *Beyond Suffrage* and *Partner and I*,[29] Susan Ware documents the way in which Eleanor operated. Yet she also concludes that another woman was even more consequential in securing the appointment of Frances Perkins to the Cabinet than Eleanor; and that was Molly Dewson, head of the women's division of the Democratic party and the subject of *Partner and I*.

Like so many other of the women in this network, Dewson, born in 1874, had a gender consciousness based on the nineteenth-century model, in her case nourished by her experiences as a member of the class of '97 at Wellesley. In the late nineteenth century Wellesley had an all-female faculty, and the young women who attended it quite naturally formed intense friendships. Some years after graduation, Dewson fell in love with Polly Porter, and together they formed a partnership that lasted for fifty-two years. With so gratifying a personal life, Dewson participated in manifold activities that were quintessentially those of the Progressive woman activist: she was a research assistant at the Women's Educational and Industrial Union in Boston, Superintendent of Probation for the Lancaster State Industrial School for Girls, and executive secretary of the Massachusetts Commission on the Minimum Wage. In 1919 she became Florence Kelley's research secretary at the National Consumers' League. Ware quotes from a letter Frances Perkins wrote to Dewson, in which she spoke of the "loyalty and chivalry between women," and then Ware goes on to state:

> That this "loyalty and chivalry" existed between women is an important part of the story. Women like Dewson and Perkins spent their formative

years in woman-centered institutions, beginning with the women's colleges and moving on to reform groups like the NCL. They were profoundly shaped by their participation in the suffrage campaign. They
learned to work easily and effectively with other women, seeing them
as natural allies and collaborators on the issues they agreed were of
greatest concern to their sex. [30]

Dewson was being loyal to her friend Eleanor when she agreed
to go on the presidential campaign trail in 1928 at Eleanor's behest.
Soon she had demonstrated the political skills that would lead her to
become, in the 1930s, "America's first female political boss." She was
back on the job in the successful campaign of 1932. Employing the
rhetoric of uplift and service as well as specific techniques learned in
the suffrage campaign, she contacted a far-flung network of women
leaders and put together an energetic grass-roots organization designed
to place FDR in the White House. At its height, her women's division
had 80,000 members. Thus when she lobbied for an appointment,
FDR listened. Even before the election of 1932, she had begun to
work on Frances Perkins's behalf, not so much out of personal friendship as out of the conviction that Perkins, with her background as
Industrial Commissioner of New York, would be the person most likely
to convince Congress to pass labor legislation.

The New Deal then represented a benchmark for women in public life in a number of ways. Besides the first woman in the Cabinet,
there were more women in influential positions in this administration
than in any previous one. [31] With so many experienced women in
responsible positions, much of Roosevelt's social welfare legislation bore
their stamp. Ware argues that the women's network influenced the
National Recovery Administration, the Social Security Act, the Fair
Labor Standards Act, and those portions of the Works Progress Administration that dealt with relief programs for women. Moreover, she
quotes Perkins as saying to Dewson, "You and I, Mary, made Roosevelt's labor policy." [32]

In some ways, the female achievement of these years resembled
that of the Civil War period in being linked to the dearth of trained

men—with turf to protect—in a new area. Then the new area had been care of wounded men on a vast scale. In the 1930s it was social welfare policy. By FDR's second term sexist attitudes and barriers began to be manifest as an entrenched bureaucracy of men had begun to take shape.[33]

The New Deal experience also resembled that of the Civil War in that expertise associated with woman's sphere seemed especially salient for dealing with a crisis, the crisis being, of course, the dislocations occasioned by the Great Depression. This also indicates why the progress for public womanhood proved ephemeral: it was not based on a widespread acknowledgment that women had the same right to, and the same general capacity for, public service as men. Therefore, when the crisis ended, the number of women in responsible positions declined precipitously.

When the United States entered the Second World War in 1941, the federal bureaucracy had grown exponentially since the time of the Civil War. The vacuum where there should have been capacity to deal with an important component of war that had existed in 1861 had been filled—though the federal government did have to scramble to mobilize effectively. Therefore, although women were fully as essential to the war effort as they had been eighty years earlier—in this case supplying the womanpower to keep factories producing at top levels—there were fewer of them with the capacity to challenge male authority. Nor did they have the same potent woman's sphere to use as a base of operations, so to speak. In consequence, women were on the periphery of power during the 1940s.

What is more, during the 1940s, FDR, who had announced that social programs would be placed on the back burner for the duration of the war, evolved the method for dealing with women that Presidents would employ for another twenty years or so—token appointments where a few women could be tucked away without real opportunity to have an impact on policy. After substantial pressure from women's organizations, for example, he appointed a Woman's Advisory Commission (WAC) to the War Manpower Commission. But as the situation evolved, the latter body exercised the power and the women's adjunct

performed a rubber-stamp function. According to William Chafe, "Mary
Anderson [Chief of the Women's Bureau] concluded that the WAC
had been created as a calculated device to put women 'off in a corner'
while denying them any real power."[34]

What Chafe calls the "paradox of change" in the 1940s was a
situation whereby there were millions more public women gainfully
employed outside the home, albeit fewer Public Women than in the
'30s. That is to say, more women than ever before were leaving woman's sphere, but fewer of them were genuinely influential. Once again
the social geography of gender was altered fundamentally because so
many women entered the work force; 2 million went to work in offices, almost doubling the clerical work force, and 2.5 million went
to work in factories.

We are now beginning to have a substantial literature on women
and World War II.[35] While scholars debate over the extent to which
postwar change stemmed from the war itself rather than long-term
secular trends, there are a few generally agreed-upon conclusions. In
the first place, during the war not only did the female labor force grow
but it also changed character, in that women workers were older
and likelier to be married than heretofore. As will be discussed more
fully in the next chapter, the numbers of working women belonging to
unions went from 800,000 to 3 million. Many women who were already gainfully employed switched to more remunerative jobs, because
they were able to replace men who had joined the military. For black
women, who had been over-represented in domestic service, this
proved especially beneficial. But when the men returned from war,
they were able to reclaim their old jobs. Therefore, within a short
period after the war had ended, most working women were once again
employed in jobs in the pink-collar ghetto. Yet the wartime accept-
ability of gainful employment for married women persisted, and there
lay the true magnitude of the impact of the Second World War on
women.

Rapid changes during the war where women were concerned pro-
voked a substantial backlash in the late 1940s. Coupled with the general conservatism which had been unleashed by Cold War anxieties—

not to say hysteria—the backlash proved damaging to the cause of public womanhood. Women's magazines glorified the mother of a large family—even nine children were by no means too much of a good thing—and enjoined women to sacrifice their own ambitions for the sake of husband and children.[36]

One area of advance for public womanhood during World War II that should be noted, however, lay in electoral politics: in particular, two members of the small cohort of women elected to national office in the 1940s began to play higher-profile roles than had any of their predecessors—California Democrat Helen Gahagan Douglas and Maine Republican Margaret Chase Smith.

Douglas was a pioneer public woman in many ways, not the least of which was her willingness to risk being glamorous on the campaign trail in an era when most women politicians dressed as "sensibly" as possible so as not to appear frivolous. A former actress, married to the motion-picture star Melvyn Douglas, she began to take an active interest in the plight of California's migrant workers during the 1930s. So effective was she as a speaker that she came to the attention of the Roosevelts, who encouraged her to become active in the state's Democratic party. As a consequence, she ran successfully for Congress in 1944, winning re-election twice before losing to Richard Nixon in a race for the U.S. Senate in 1950, a race that has become notorious for the extent of Nixon's redbaiting. Using Douglas's admitted outspokenness on labor and civil rights issues as well as her liberal voting record against her, he labeled her the "Pink Lady."[37]

As for Margaret Chase Smith, her courage and independence are legendary. Born in 1897, becoming gainfully employed immediately after graduation from high school, Margaret Chase spent many years working for the Skowhegan *Independent-Reporter* before her marriage to Clyde Smith, a politician, in 1930. Moreover, she had been the president of the State Federation of Business and Professional Women's Clubs and active in the Republican party on her own. Thus, although she entered Congress via the widowhood route, she had been publicly active independent of her husband.

Clyde Smith was in the House of Representatives when he suf-

fered a fatal heart attack in April 1940. Because he had been ailing,
Margaret had already committed herself to run for his seat. She then
had to wage four campaigns within seven months: a special primary,
a runoff, an election in May, and an election in November.[38] Having
survived all this, she went on to serve four terms, developing a reputation for voting as a maverick. Relatively liberal on labor, she was
also more of an internationalist than many in her party. In 1948 she
won election to an open seat in the Senate by a landslide.

Of her many accomplishments no doubt the best-known and most
important was her Declaration of Conscience in 1950. Ardently anti-
communist, she was nonetheless appalled by the tactics of her fellow
senator Joseph McCarthy. The only woman in the Senate, she was,
remarkably enough, unafraid of opposing him. She contacted five other
Republican senators and secured their signatures for her Declaration.
Then on June 1 she made a powerful speech to the full Senate in
which she announced that she did not want that body to be "debased
to the level of a forum of hate and character assassination sheltered by
the shield of Congressional immunity" and defended every American's
right to hold unpopular beliefs.[39] Her major crusade where women
were concerned was on behalf of those in the military.

Aside from Douglas and Smith, the prominent political women
of the 1950s largely fell into the "token" category and found themselves circumscribed by that fact and limited in their ability to imple-
ment any kind of woman's agenda. (Whether they even wanted to
accomplish this is another matter.) In On Account of Sex, Cynthia
Harrison delineates the nature of the problem for such women. A
President tended to welcome the opportunity to make a few token
appointments of women because it offered him the chance to score
easy points with women's organizations. "But welcomed as they were
by women's organizations, the appointments had an unanticipated
consequence that worked badly for women seeking substantive measures. By acceding to the request for more women appointees, the
chief executive could evade much more significant policy questions."[40] He could say that in all fairness he could not be expected to
grant every request, especially without a grass-roots movement exerting

pressure. Moreover, the onus on the female appointee was to prove
that she was no different than a male appointee would have been.[41]

Senator Smith's willingness to take on Joe McCarthy placed her
at odds with the surviving remnant of the Woman's Party, led by Alice
Paul. Still single-issue in its orientation, the NWP was as keen for the
passage of the ERA as ever. On its part, the labor movement remained
equally adamant in its opposition to the amendment. Anger at labor
then led Paul and the Woman's Party to militant anti-communism
and to the support of McCarthy.[42] In a book about feminism in the
'50s tellingly entitled *Survival in the Doldrums*, Leila Rupp and Verta
Taylor have this to say about the NWP:

> The story of the National Woman's Party after 1945 is a story of decline
> and survival, since the group failed to achieve its single goal, passage of
> the ERA. It lost membership and failed to attract new and young mem-
> bers, suffered serious internal conflicts that hampered its effectiveness,
> and developed a reputation as a collection of amusingly eccentric and
> anachronistic old feminists, but it sustained a feminist community . . .
> that made continuing activity in a hostile environment possible.[43]

With the leading group of white middle-class feminists having
adopted so reactionary a posture and having been rendered largely ir-
relevant in a chillingly conservative political climate, public womanhood might well be seen as "in the doldrums." Yet if one looks to
other segments of the society besides the white middle class, one can
detect evidence of progress. Indeed, it may be appropriate to see the
years 1920–60 as a staging ground among racial ethnic women for the
social change of the 1960s. Needless to say, we still need much more
research on this subject, but it is possible to reach at least tentative
conclusions. Most important of all, while gender solidarity had been
undermined among white middle-class women, with the concomitant
depoliticization of many organizations, it is clear that organizations
among racial ethnic women could not afford the luxury of being apolitical—although their solidarity was undergirded by race or ethnic
consciousness as well as by gender solidarity.[44]

As we have seen, there had been associational activity among black women beginning in the eighteenth century. Moreover, the church had provided black women with an arena for public activism, as it had for white women. Most of the outstanding black public women of the nineteenth and early twentieth century had been firmly anchored in one or both of these areas. As the twentieth century proceeded, black women's organizations continued to flourish and play an extraordinarily valuable role in the community. We are fortunate enough to have a memoir written by Mamie Garvin Fields, in which she provides an account of her club work in Charleston.[45]

Fields, a teacher born in 1888, recalls her mother's civic work in the late nineteenth century and then, when she herself was a young woman, the encouragement provided by Mary Church Terrell. Terrell came to Charleston and spoke to the women of the Mt. Zion African Methodist Episcopal church, where she invoked the names of Harriet Tubman and Sojourner Truth and challenged her auditors to live up to their standard. Terrell enjoined educated women like Fields to share what they had learned with the less fortunate, and her audience responded enthusiastically. Fields herself subsequently participated in founding a club, the Modern Priscilla, whose first members included teachers, housewives, beauticians, businesswomen, and one domestic worker. Club members drew upon their skills with the needle in order to raise money for community projects.[46] Another inspirational figure for Fields was Mary McLeod Bethune, who founded the National Council of Negro Women to bring together discrete civic clubs. Recalls Fields: "Mrs. Bethune would tell you in no uncertain terms how to do your duty of improving the schools, and how you must build up a citizenship department, never mind if many Negroes couldn't vote yet. And don't sit home and know only what's around the corner from you."[47]

We now have a biography profiling another of the black club women, Lugenia Burns Hope, wife of the president of Atlanta University.[48] Born in Mississippi in 1871, Lugenia Burns came to maturity in Chicago where as a young working woman she was active in social reform and interacted with the women of Hull House. After her marriage to John Hope, a rising young academic, in 1897, she moved back to the South with her husband, who became one of the most prominent educators in the region. Eventually they found themselves in Atlanta, and Lugenia soon launched a social settlement called the Neighborhood Union. The women of the Neighborhood Union fought for improved education for black children, but that was not all.

> As early as the 1908 surveys, the union began confronting the city of Atlanta with urgent needs it was uncovering. Union members petitioned the mayor, the City Council, and the Sanitation and Health Departments to improve facilities. They went to court to ask for better health and housing programs, better streets and more street lights to prevent crimes.[49]

The union also offered classes in nursing, prenatal and infant care, and home hygiene, to say nothing of sponsoring clubs and playgrounds. With her social prominence, Hope made a formidable leader. Another of her accomplishments consisted of a successful campaign to convince the Young Women's Christian Association (YWCA) to accept black members.

It should be remembered that this courageous and dedicated club work was carried on in a climate where the myth of the promiscuous black woman still flourished. In her book about Jessie Daniel Ames, Jacquelyn Hall points out that many southern whites who were Mamie Fields's and Lugenia Burns Hope's contemporaries refused to accord any black woman the title of "Mrs." Indeed, she tells of a black woman who was introduced to a gathering of white church women as "the wife of Mr. Hunt" rather than as "Mrs. Hunt."[50]

In addition to their community involvement, black women joined black men in the important task of validating African-American culture, employing the power of the word to change the nature of public discourse about their people. Indeed, it seems appropriate to compare the relationship between the Harlem Renaissance and the later civil rights movement with that between the domestic novel and the emergence of a woman's movement one hundred years earlier. In both cases, the cultural transformation which created a new power of positive self-representation was essential to the later, more overtly political, phenomenon.[51]

Decades of such activity prepared black women to play leadership roles in the civil rights movement at a time when white middle-class women were only beginning to make an assault on renewed public activism. As for women in other racial ethnic groups during the period in question, they too were emerging into public roles of one sort or another. As we shall be learning in the next chapter, the labor movement proved to be an important vehicle for Chicanas. Nisei women played a significant role in a literary flowering on the West Coast, a flowering brutally ended by internment. Valerie Matsumoto has written about one of the most interesting of the Japanese-American literati, Mary Oyama.[52]

Born in 1907 in Fairfield, California, Oyama graduated from Sacramento High School in 1925 and went on to study journalism at the University of Southern California. Between the mid-'30s and 1941, she wrote for a number of Japanese-American newspapers in Los Angeles—where she lived—and in San Francisco. Matsumoto focuses particular attention on the advice column Oyama wrote for the San Francisco-based *New World Sun* under the pen name of "Deirdre." Deirdre gave advice to the lovelorn, but in so doing she also thought deeply and creatively about what it meant to be a Nisei—a second-generation immigrant—about inter-, as well as intra-, ethnic relations, and about the extent of assimilation that would be desirable. Says Matsumoto:

> While the Nisei writers maintained a critique of American racism, they also believed that part of the answer to the "Nisei problem" lay in their hands. As the *Hokubei Asahi* editor concluded, "Something new must be created by the Nisei—and by only them." Somewhat like the writers of the Harlem Renaissance of the 1920s, the Japanese American literati sought to shape and promote their own culture, exhorting each other to "find a way of their own." Mary Oyama was one of the co-founders of the League of Nisei Artists and Writers, a group that met weekly at her house to foster this creative effort, organizing themselves like the League of American Writers.[53]

Matsumoto found an article profiling the Nisei literati, which listed the names of fifteen men and nine women.

As more of such research is conducted, we will have a clearer picture of public womanhood among racial ethnic women and we will be better able to understand the dynamics of gender solidarity versus racial/ethnic solidarity. In any event, whatever motivated these women, whether loyalty to other women or to their communities, they succeeded in valorizing the worth of the women of their group—as domestic novelists had one hundred years earlier—while playing roles with a degree of public visibility that would have been unthinkable a generation earlier.[54] In effect, this period saw a "Great Awakening" among many women outside the white middle class.

Thus the depiction of depoliticization and feminist declension post-suffrage and into the 1950s, a picture that seems most lifelike if we focus attention on the suburban middle class of Parent–Teacher Associations and "Father Knows Best," ignores vital transformations in other segments of American life. And indeed, even for the suburban middle class, somnolence and conservatism were only part of the picture. Millions of married women were gainfully employed and learning to be at least slightly more autonomous than their mothers. Moreover, the postwar baby boom proved to be a transitory phenomenon, a blip in the long-term trend toward smaller families that began in the early nineteenth century. With more women, in a variety of social settings, learning to be more independent than ever before—and learning how to control their own biology—the "doldrums" could not long survive.

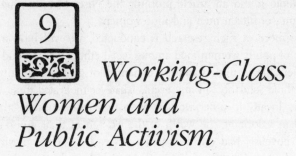

9
Working-Class Women and Public Activism

In the sweep of history women outside the middle and upper reaches of society have been generally freer to leave the domestic sphere than others of their sex. Hence, when we talk about working-class women after the emergence of an industrial proletariat, we are talking about a group that is central to the subject of this book, the slow accretion of possibilities for public womanhood. Yet there are few easy generalizations to be made about working-class women, because we must confront contradictory evidence. On the one hand, there are abundant examples of female courage—including physical courage—in organizing or sustaining a strike, for example. We also find abundant examples of female leadership in many other areas besides strikes. But at the level of the leadership of unions themselves we encounter an overwhelmingly male population. Working-class women have simultaneously been the agents of their own history to a surprising extent, given their economic vulnerability, as well as marginalized by male-led unions. In the long run, the most important generalization to be made is that the strong emergence of public womanhood in the 1960s would have been inconceivable without them, because working-class women, less bound by decorous norms of appropriate female behavior than middle-class women, have been the pioneers of public demonstrations.

By the end of the Civil War, when the American economy was beginning its shift into industrial overdrive, there were two discrete strands of public activism for working-class women, one with a venerable history reaching centuries into the past before there was an industrial working class and one unique to the nineteenth century. Both proved consequential for shaping the way working-class women dealt with the dislocations of a rapidly industrializing United States in the late nineteenth century, and both have been important influences on events of the twentieth century.

In the first place, there was the tradition of "disorderly women." Natalie Davis has written memorably about the theme of female disorderliness in early modern Europe. Adducing much evidence to substantiate the point that a woman was seen as guided by the body more than a man, who was guided by the intellect, Davis says: "Her disorderliness led her into the evil arts of witchcraft, so ecclesiastical authorities claimed; and when she was embarked on some behavior for which her allegedly weak intellect disqualified her, such as theological speculation or preaching, that was blamed on her disorderliness, too."[1] Not surprisingly, a wife's too great enthusiasm for nagging her husband was prima facie evidence of disorderliness.

In the New World, too, there were unruly women, as Laurel Thatcher Ulrich demonstrates in *Good Wives*. Studying women in northern New England between 1650 and 1750, Ulrich encountered court records documenting both what she calls "disorderly violence" and "demonstrative violence" by women. As an instance of the latter, she recounts the story of a widow named Joane Furson, who took three of her married daughters and two of her grandchildren into a cornfield belonging to someone else and began uprooting the shoots to protest a property settlement.[2] Ulrich argues that such conduct by women was seen as especially alarming because it seemed to threaten sexual anarchy more than similar acts by men.

The presence of women in crowds in the eighteenth and nineteenth centuries, including crowds that wreaked substantial violence, such as during the anti-draft riots in New York in 1863, has already been noted. In a few instances, "disorderly" women even led such crowds. Moreover, we are already acquainted with the Bowery Gal of the antebellum period and the dance-hall darling who flourished some decades later. Both of these archetypes represented the flaunting of female sexuality in a way that echoed the behavior of certain of the earlier disorderly women.

Yet there was also an alternative archetype, "Labor's True Woman," to use Susan Levine's phrase.[3] Such women used their moral authority in the home to justify their activism in the world in ways that were parallel to, but not imitative of, their middle-class sisters. For example, thousands of women from the homes of artisans, laborers, shopkeepers, and clerks joined a temperance group called the Martha Washington society in the 1840s. Says their historian, Ruth Alexander:

> The women who joined the Washingtonian movement during its first phase from approximately 1840 to 1843, dedicated themselves to four principal tasks in aid of the cause. Their temperance benevolent societies sought to provide material aid to those in want and to persuade both hardened and moderate drinkers to sign the pledge of total abstinence. They offered instruction to mothers to prevent them from leading their offspring to intemperate habits. Finally, the Martha Washingtonians took messages of inspiration and moral fortitude to recently reformed groups of young men. In each task Washingtonian women revealed their deep absorption in the affairs of the home and the conviction that the use of alcohol was inimical to family happiness.[4]

In pursuit of these goals Washingtonians necessarily became public women, because they left the confines of their own homes in order to visit others and inculcate the proper attitudes and behavior.

Working-class domesticity enjoyed another flowering during the heyday of the Knights of Labor. Throughout the nineteenth century the ideology of domesticity had frequently partaken of a political character, from its incarnation as republican motherhood to the epic style advocated by Stowe in *Uncle Tom's Cabin* to the "Home Protection Ballot" of Frances Willard and the Women's Christian Temperance Union.[5] The Knights of Labor, founded in 1869, had a brief but spectacular life—spectacular because of the organization's outreach to women and other less advantaged groups—that included a type of political domesticity. At a time when many Americans were imagining a "cooperative commonwealth," members of this Gilded Age labor movement saw the domestic ideal as an important component of their social vision. So strongly did they adhere to this belief that "[t]he domestic ideal fundamentally motivated industrial reform and collective action," according to Susan Levine.[6] The Knights were advocates of woman suffrage and temperance, and the women in the group insisted upon equal treatment. Moreover, many of the outstanding public women of the Gilded Age, such as the Populist orator Mary Elizabeth Lease, first came to prominence in the Knights. The Knights' first female master workman was Elizabeth Rodgers, the Irish-born wife of an iron molder and the mother of ten children.[7]

The Gilded Age's best-known female labor activist, Mother Jones, incorporated both of these traditions in her persona. Mary Harris Jones was born in Ireland in 1830 and immigrated to this country as a child. Supporting herself as a teacher and also as a dressmaker, she married an iron molder in 1861 and gave birth to four children. In 1867 her entire family died in a yellow-fever epidemic, and she moved from Memphis, where she had been living with them, back to Chicago where she lived earlier in her life. She then became active in the Knights of Labor. By the 1890s she had found her métier working for the United Mine Workers of America and traveling to trouble spots throughout the country. Her boys could count on her to turn up whenever they needed her in the course of a strike or other struggle. In 1904 a writer said of her: " 'Mother' is the cry when overawed by corporate hirelings and scabs they join hands in a common struggle, and 'Mother' again when the troops reinforced by hunger are beating them to death."[8] She lived to be one hundred years old, and she

carried on her work of organizing and agitating till nearly the end of
her life.

Known as "Mother" for reasons similar to those which made the
troops call Mary Ann Bickerdyke "Mother"—because they both embodied a heroic version of embattled maternity in the eyes of the men
on whose behalf they worked—Mother Jones nonetheless represented
an unusual style of motherhood. Indeed, she was a "disorderly woman"
as well as a saintly mother. For example, in her autobiography, she
recounts an episode that took place in the coal fields of Pennsylvania
in the late nineteenth century. A strike had been going on for four or
five months with no end in sight. Because the men seemed so dis-
couraged, she decided to appeal to their wives to drive the scabs from
the mines. She organized an "army of women housekeepers," saw to
it that they armed themselves with mops, brooms, and pails of water,
and selected a ringleader, inasmuch as she knew that she would immediately be arrested if she tried to lead the army herself. "I said, 'You
lead the army up to the Drip Mouth. Take that tin dishpan you have
with you and your hammer, and when the scabs and mules come up,
begin to hammer and howl. Then all of you hammer and howl and
be ready to chase the scabs with your mops and brooms. Don't be
afraid of anyone.' "[9] The women were successful in driving the scabs
away and then mounted a watch to ensure that they did not return.
Of course, this behavior is reminiscent of the "rough music" of European peasants.

On another occasion, Mother Jones announced her opinion of
woman suffrage to a group of suffragists in no uncertain terms:

> I told the women I did not believe in women's rights nor in men's rights
> but in human rights. "No matter what your fight," I said, "don't be
> ladylike! God almighty made women and the Rockefeller gang of thieves
> made the ladies. I have just fought through sixteen months of bitter
> warfare in Colorado. I have been up against armed mercenaries but this
> old woman, without a vote and with nothing but a hatpin has scared
> them."[10]

Although Mother Jones, who would not endorse woman suffrage and who dedicated her life to helping male workers, makes an unlikely feminist saint, her capacity to unite these disparate images with such success is an indication of the kind of potency that a woman could muster under such conditions, hence should qualify her for the pantheon. Moreover, Mother Jones also became an important public woman as an orator. For example, in the early twentieth century, Socialists in Oklahoma staged encampments, patterned after religious camp meetings, to which as many as 10,000 people came.[11] Mother Jones was a star attraction on these occasions, so influential that in 1906 she spoke to a farmer-labor convention in Shawnee, where delegates were discussing a proposed state constitution. Her fiery speech convinced the delegates to adopt certain Socialist proposals.[12]

If Mother Jones's persona combined elements of domesticity with elements of disorderliness, and her activities included both the direct action of leading strikes and also speeches to political delegates, it is important to point out that her autobiography was a breakthrough, too, because it was one of the first by an American woman of the working class. In 1901 she began to write articles for the *United Mine Workers Journal*, signing them "Mother Jones," and in 1925 the autobiography appeared.[13] It should be noted that in this narrative, her role in public events receives the overwhelming preponderance of attention relative to her private life. Indeed, after the death of her entire family she appears not to have had a private life in the usual sense. When she died in 1930, her funeral was virtually a state occasion. In 1936, 50,000 miners attended a ceremony in Illinois dedicating a monument to their intrepid champion.

We have already discussed the developments during the Gilded Age that made a Mother Jones—or an Emma Goldman—possible: millions of immigrants from southern and eastern Europe, hundreds of thousands more gainfully employed women, thousands of gainfully employed women in cities who were living outside of conventional families. One other factor to recall is the farmer's revolt that resulted in the phenomenon of Populism. Women on the left flourished as public women in those parts of the country where farm families were angriest, for example, Oklahoma. Mother Jones was not the only woman orator of note in the Sooner State. Even more beloved was the Socialist Kate Richards O'Hare, who like Jones spoke both to miners and to embattled farmers.

Born in Kansas in 1876, Kate Richards became a machinist while she was still in her mid-teens in a shop co-owned by her father. At seventeen she joined the International Association of Machinists, its first woman member. Hearing a speech by Mother Jones, after having read a number of contemporary social critiques, she became a Socialist. In 1902 she married Frank O'Hare, a fellow Socialist, and moved with him to Oklahoma Territory. Although they soon moved back to Kansas City, Kate O'Hare had a special affinity for those who flocked to the encampments in Oklahoma, and she became enormously popular as a speaker on such occasions, rivaling the great Gene Debs himself. "I loved the Midwest and Southwest crowds and my work there because I am one of them: I know what pioneering means," she later explained.[14] So successful was she in reaching a broad spectrum of the population in this part of the country that her fame reached France. In consequence, Jean Jaurès, the French Socialist leader, asked her advice about organizing the French peasantry.[15] Unlike Mother Jones, she was mainly a woman of words rather than direct action. The words were, however, strong enough in opposition to American involvement in the First World War that she spent fourteen months in federal prison for violating the Espionage Act—merely for giving an antiwar speech.

As Mari Jo Buhle demonstrates in her splendid *Women and American Socialism*,[16] the Socialist party in the late nineteenth and early twentieth century fostered public activism on the part of a diverse group of women from the native-born and middle-class like Mary Livermore of Civil War fame to recent immigrants. Yet Kate Richards O'Hare notwithstanding, few of the women who were prominent in the Socialist party had themselves been workers. Rather they tended to be housewives or professional women.[17]

Moreover, Socialist women encountered a recurrent difficulty in reconciling women's rights with the class struggle. For example, in 1907 a meeting of the Second International in Stuttgart issued the following directive:

> The Socialist women shall not carry on this struggle for complete equality of right of vote in alliance with the middle class women suffragists, but in common with the Socialist parties, which insist upon woman suffrage as one of the fundamental and most important reforms for the full democratization of political franchise in general.[18]

In other words, Socialist women throughout the world were being enjoined to eschew gender solidarity and trust their male comrades to take their cause seriously.

This highlights a central difficulty for working-class women themselves. Frequently forced to work outside the home, even after marriage, they had a tough time keeping up with the double burden of domestic responsibility and the job. Organizing to improve their lot required resources of time and energy—to say nothing of money—that were already in short supply. Yet when they turned to the Socialist party, they encountered not only a plethora of women with less overburdened lives than their own but also control by males whose sympathies where women's issues were concerned ebbed and flowed over time. To make matters worse, the Knights of Labor had rapidly lost strength after 1886, and the American Federation of Labor (AFL), which replaced the Knights, notoriously lacked a genuine commitment to organizing women workers.

Thus when we survey the situation of working-class women at the turn of the century, we encounter a few dazzling leaders, but little in the way of helpful organizations for the rank and file. The latter's advance into public womanhood had come more from their growing economic independence, the new patterns of leisure, and the new social geography of gender than from union organization per se or from other types of political involvement such as afforded by the Socialist party.

In the early twentieth century, there was a flowering of cross-class gender solidarity which mitigated this situation. In 1903 a group of working-class women and settlement house workers joined forces to form the Women's Trade Union League (WTUL), an organization which flourished throughout the Progressive period. Jane Addams was the vice president (a Boston philanthropist was the president), but several working-class women were also on the board. Although not without tensions among its very divergent constituent parts, the WTUL at its height played a significant role in helping working women sustain strikes, strikes which helped produce much stronger trade unions for women. From the beginning, Samuel Gompers and the AFL endorsed the WTUL, but the AFL retained a certain suspicion about those women in the group who were not workers. Moreover, the AFL was more generous with rhetorical support than with money.[19] Nonetheless, the early twentieth century saw substantial progress, not least because the middle-class women of the WTUL insisted that the working women learn to chair meetings so that they would not automatically defer to male co-unionists.[20]

Let us examine the events in two cities, New York and Chicago. The best-known triumph of the WTUL lay in helping sustain the great shirtwaist strike in New York. In the words of Nancy Schrom Dye, a leading student of the WTUL: "The shirtwaist strike heralded a revolution in the women's clothing industry and in the history of women's unionism. From late 1909 through 1913 nearly one hundred thousand New York City garment workers participated in a series of general strikes [i.e., industry-wide strikes]. . . ."[21] Young women workers risked harm to their persons when they walked the picket line, because employers had hired thugs to intimidate them. That they were joined on the line by their WTUL allies was a material help, especially when those arrested on the picket line included well-known women. The strike ended with nearly 72,000 New York City women in unions, 63,000 of whom were in the needle trades; as of 1913 the International Ladies Garment Workers Union (ILGWU), founded by a relative handful of people in 1900, had become a major union.[22]

Although the union leadership itself was male—and remained so for many years—the strike of women who were predominantly but not

exclusively of Jewish background led many to extraordinary public activism. One legendary episode took place at Cooper Union on the
night of November 22, 1909. Garment workers had been summoned
to hear speeches by Samuel Gompers of the AFL, Mary Dreier of the
WTUL, and others and to deliberate about a proposed general strike.
Suddenly a young woman still in her teens, Clara Lemlich, who was
recovering from a beating sustained on an earlier picket line, rose to
her feet and asked for the floor:

> Making her way to the platform she delivered a "philippic in Yiddish."
> "I am a working girl, one of those who are on strike against intolerable
> conditions. I am tired of listening to speakers who talk in general terms.
> What we are here for is to decide whether we shall or shall not strike.
> I offer a resolution that a general strike be declared—now." [23]

This strike was the largest uprising of working-class women up to
that point in American history. Although the help from the WTUL
proved valuable, it alone cannot explain so massive a mobilization of
women. In *Daughters of the Shtetl*, Susan Glenn explains the uprising
as follows: "A complex of immediate industrial abuses, women's evolv-
ing concerns about their dignity as females and as workers, the influence of a cadre of Jewish radicals within and outside the workplace,
and a sentiment within the Jewish immigrant community sympathetic
to the right and necessity of labor organization contributed to the rising tide of militance." [24]

The WTUL was strong in Chicago, too. There, the League's
leader, Margaret Dreier Robins, a middle-class woman, forged a close
alliance with the men in the Chicago Federation of Labor (CFL). In
1908 Robins supported a proposal for the WTUL to switch its meeting
place from Hull House to the CFL, a move that found favor with the
latter group. As a consequence, Robins herself was elected to the board
of the CFL, a highly unusual development. Shortly thereafter, 40,000
garment workers went on strike in Chicago. The WTUL raised $70,000
to help sustain the strikers and then participated in the collective bargaining that ended the strike, another pioneering development. Out of

this settlement was born the Amalgamated Clothing Workers of America. In the years immediately following, the Chicago WTUL helped organize dressmakers, waitresses, bookbinders, glove makers, Pullman-car cleaners, broom makers, state hospital workers, and stockyard workers.[25]

Especially relevant to this discussion is the resemblance the WTUL bore to the Knights of Labor in its validation of female values and nurture, in essence, in its use of politicized domesticity. Says Robins's biographer: "Although Robins recognized that men dominated the political arena, her conception of motherhood implied that women more fully embodied the public because they alone understood the social consequence of private acts."[26] Thus, like Mother Jones, some WTUL leaders embraced the image and rhetoric of militant maternity—while also endorsing the use of the tactics of direct action. Once again, we can discern that this was a potent combination.

The second decade of the twentieth century thus proved favorable for the organization of working-class women, relative, at least, to anything that had gone before. Although fewer than 10 percent of wage-earning women belonged to unions nationwide in 1920,[27] in certain cities and in certain trades, predominantly female unions flourished. At a time in which the reigning ideology of mainstream labor emphasized the organization of skilled workers by craft—and most women workers were not considered as skilled—this was a substantial achievement. The coalition with middle-class women, however problematic, proved enormously beneficial.

Another arena for cross-class cooperation in these years lay in the drive to achieve woman suffrage. An important article by Ellen DuBois describes the formation of a cross-class suffrage organization in New York in 1907, the Equality League of Self-Supporting Women, under the leadership of Harriet Stanton Blatch. Composed of college-educated professional women—Blatch insisted that they participate as opposed to the usual "club women"—and trade-union women, the Equality League made an immediate impact because some of its trade-union members testified on behalf of suffrage before the New York state legislature a month after the League's formation. According to DuBois, "The unique class character of the Equality League encouraged the development of a new style of agitation, more radical than anything practiced in the suffrage movement since . . . since Elizabeth Stanton's prime."[28]

Such cross-class suffrage alliances flourished in other locales as well. In California, for example, the Wage Earners Suffrage Leagues played a significant role in the attainment of woman suffrage in 1911. The Bay Area League was organized by Maud Younger, the daughter of a wealthy San Francisco family who worked for a while as a waitress and then participated in organizing a Waitress' Union in 1908. In Los Angeles the Socialist and trade unionist Frances Noel organized a separate League. These groups of working-class women then joined a broad-based coalition in a suffrage campaign unprecedented in scope. Women canvassed door to door, spoke on street corners, rented billboards and electric signs, staged plays, and sponsored high-school essay contests. When it was all over, woman suffrage had won by 3,587 votes, an average of one per precinct.[29] With so narrow a suffrage victory, it is clear that all elements of the coalition, including wage-earning women, were necessary to achieve it.

During the Gilded Age, working-class women flocked into gainful employment, became more economically independent than ever before, and transformed urban geography. A few of them also became outstanding public leaders. In the early twentieth century, in alliance with middle-class women, a small percentage began to achieve union organization, albeit in male-led unions. Related to these developments and in effect ratifying them, working-class women also began to employ the power of the word by writing about their lives—as witness, Mother Jones's autobiography. This development represented a major breakthrough for these daughters of immigrants, the group that had constituted the bulk of the working class since the 1850s.

In the main, the written discourse about women's lives in the nineteenth century, both novels and advice literature, had valorized genteel—and Protestant—domesticity. Where a heroine worked with her hands in any capacity other than as a housewife, this circumstance was typically depicted as a bitter necessity, as for example, Frado in *Our Nig*, forced to be a servant under cruel conditions. Another heroine, Ruth Hall in Fanny Fern's novel by the same name, is reduced to working as a laundress for a short period of time, by which the author indicates the depths of inhumanity characterizing those family members who allow this to happen to her.[30] In short, the written discourse of womanhood did little to valorize the subjectivity of an immigrant, non-Protestant, working-class woman.

In the late nineteenth century there began to be advice literature specifically directed to the woman who was gainfully employed. Yet as Sarah Eisenstein demonstrates in an insightful essay, such literature, especially in its early stages, took for granted that its readers were striving to be "ladies" and that being forced to work outside the home threatened that status. Advice-givers cautioned young women to "avoid manual labor, personal service and deference, publicity and familiar contact with strange men" in order to protect their self-definition as ladies. Says Eisenstein, "Working women were, then, excluded from the acceptable image of womanhood and respectability shaped by the dominant values of the period."[31]

Clearly, the daughters of immigrants from southern and eastern Europe had little to do with such literary traditions. Further serving to marginalize them, many came from cultures in which a woman's access to literacy was less than a man's—or from peasant societies in which neither sex had easy access to literacy.[32] Therefore, they were, initially at least, unlikely candidates for the job of inscribing a positive depiction of a working-class woman's identity onto mainstream culture.

Indeed, the earliest autobiography to depict a female factory operative's life in a positive way, Harriet Hanson Robinson's *Loom and Spindle*, came from one who was native-born and by no means a member of the industrial proletariat—although she had worked in a textile mill as a child. Born in Boston in 1825, Harriet Hanson experienced the loss of her father, a carpenter, while still a young child. Mrs. Hanson then moved the family to Lowell, where she kept a boarding-house for mill workers in order to support herself and her children. Not surprisingly, young Harriet was eager to work in a mill herself so as to contribute to the household economy, and she secured employment when she was ten. In *Loom and Spindle* she describes various jobs she performed, as a doffer and a drawing-in girl, for example. When she was twenty-three, she married a newspaper editor and became active in reform causes, including suffrage, for the rest of her life. Thus, during her adulthood, she had a niche in the middle class, although her journalist husband by no means provided an affluent life for his family.[33]

To read *Loom and Spindle*, written by a woman of seventy-three about her girlhood, is undoubtedly to encounter an idealized version of the mill-girl experience. Robinson describes her fellow workers as so literate and so keen for self-improvement as to virtually defy belief. Yet mixed in with the reminiscences of this nature is an account of one of the first strikes in American history and certainly the first by women. It took place when Robinson was eleven:

> My own recollection of this first strike (or "turn-out" as it was called) is very vivid. I worked in a lower room, where I had heard the proposed strike fully, if not vehemently discussed; I had been an ardent listener to what was said against this attempt at "oppression" on the part of the corporation, and naturally I took sides with the strikers.

She then recounts the irresolution of other workers when the day actually came for action and her own "childlike bravado" in leading them out:

> As I looked back at the long line that followed me, I was more proud than I have ever been since at any success I may have achieved, and more proud than I shall ever be again until my own beloved State gives to its woman citizens the right of suffrage.[34]

Without trying to resolve the important but difficult problem of the relationship between the Yankee, Protestant mill girls and the later

and much more proletarianized women workers from Catholic or Jewish immigrant backgrounds, we can nonetheless conclude that so positive a depiction of worker militancy was favorable to the latter's interests.

In the early twentieth century there began to be a written discourse of immigrant, working-class womanhood that could articulate
the experiences of those who had been much written about by others,
but at best written about with patronizing sympathy.[35] The labor press
was publishing fiction that may have had a sentimental quality but
also depicted stalwart working-class heroines.[36] Further, there was a
vibrant left-wing press in these years, one in which women's issues
received substantial attention.[37] Among the more mainstream press,
the *New York Call* opened its pages to women on the left, such as the
Socialist Theresa Malkiel, to write about the shirtwaist strike, for example.

In 1910 Malkiel published a fictionalized account of these events,
The Diary of a Shirtwaist Striker, that, while didactic in tone, is telling about the lives of the women involved. Malkiel depicts the growing politicization of the heroine, Mary, a Gentile, her admiration for
her Jewish comrades, her success in converting her fiancé to the cause,
and her observation of the suffering of other strikers. One episode in
particular is especially illuminating about public womanhood. Mary
is walking around the city wearing a sandwich board advertising an
upcoming meeting when she encounters hostile reactions from those
who believe she is acting in an undignified fashion: "I do wish the
people would stop sending us to homes which we ain't got. What if
we do make ourselves notorious? If we can't gain the people's attention
any other way, then let it be through notoriety. There wasn't a person
that passed me this morning but stopped long enough to read the
poster and that's just what I wanted."[38] It should be noted that the
novella gains in projecting an air of authenticity because the heroine
frequently mentions real people like Clara Lemlich and Mother Jones.

In 1912 the *Atlantic Monthly* published a series of articles by
Mary Antin, a Russian Jew, that became *The Promised Land* and sold
85,000 copies. A fulsome testament to the liberating nature of Amer-

ican society, the autobiography by a young woman of thirty also contains much detail about life in the town of Polotsk, where she had been born and had lived till the age of thirteen. In it, Antin pays tribute to both her parents and their determination to educate their children. Describing the day her father enrolled her and her sister and brother in school in Boston, she characterizes him as "this foreigner, who brought his children to school as if it were an act of consecration, who regarded the teacher of the primer class with reverence . . ."[39] Thus the reader is led to understand the family circumstances that conduced to turn his daughter into a writer.

These two books had little in common in terms of political perspective—one was a harsh condemnation of the exploitation in the United States and the other a lyrical celebration of its opportunity. What they shared was that they both introduced a new type of subjectivity into American letters: heroines who are not genteel Protestants, but who are nevertheless spunkily determined. That is, neither narrator plays the role of passive victim, a role frequently projected onto such women, even by sympathetic observers. One can also compare these heroines with Theodore Dreiser's Carrie Meeber, heroine of *Sister Carrie*, which came out in 1900. Carrie goes to Chicago as a single woman and does very well for herself, but her modus operandi involves the cold-blooded treatment of several male characters.

Another important literary milestone was Anzia Yezierska's *Bread Givers*, which came out in 1925, the same year as Mother Jones's autobiography.[40] A *bildungsroman*, *Bread Givers* presents the story of Polish-born Sara Smolinsky, the daughter of an unworldly Talmudic scholar whose single-minded devotion to his learning condemns his family to poverty in Poland and in America, too, after their immigration. Young Sara is the only one of four daughters to rebel against the tyrannical father. At seventeen, she leaves home, supports herself as an ironer, and attends night school so as to prepare herself to attend college. After attaining her treasured education, she is able to appreciate what has been positive about the legacy from her father, to forgive him and to be reconciled with him. It should be noted that in this work Yezierska makes it obvious that she is critical of the pleasure-loving, Coney Island-visiting young women who are Sara's coworkers in the laundry. In other words, Yezierska's valorization of a working-woman's identity stops short of embracing the display of that hedonistic, sexualized energy pioneered by "New Women" in these years. Indeed, Sara is so austere as to be almost Protestant in her character.[41]

The working-class flapper, not yet enshrined in literature, was beginning to write her name into the history books, however. In a decade with so much activism and cross-class cooperation, thousands of telephone operators briefly sustained a militant, woman-led union, whose members participated in the liberating new consumer culture. At its height, the Telephone Operators Union seemed to signal a promising development, the possibility that women workers could be ensconced in the heart of the labor movement. But in the conservative 1920s cross-class cooperation dwindled as gender solidarity dwindled, and then the workers lost an important strike in 1923. Their historian Stephen Norwood makes clear in *Labor's Flaming Youth* how much the new public access for women had had to do with the appearance of a union at all: "The consumer culture greatly expanded the public space women could enter, bringing them into downtown sections previously the domain of men. It allowed women the opportunity for greater sensual gratification and experience. Operators' promenading the streets in fashionable dress was an assertion that they were deserving of the 'better things' enjoyed by the middle class and reflected a heightened self-esteem. The desire to consume led many operators to organize, since the union could increase their purchasing power and offered the prospect of self-support, an end to dependency and oppressive family ties."[42] After the collapse of the strike in 1923, though, it would be many years before the operators were once again within the fold of the AFL.

As of the mid-'20s, then, there had been an advance of working-class women into public womanhood on many fronts. Still barely organized into unions, still lacking a vehicle for expressing their political will, they had marched, picketed, built bridges to other groups, been arrested and/or beaten, stood on street corners, given fiery speeches in many languages and accents, and a few had begun to write about their lives. The 1920s proved difficult for workers in many respects, however. There were few if any new unions, many unfavorable judicial decisions, and the actual disappearance of established unions.[43] Moreover, their middle-class sisters ceased to take much interest in women workers.

Yet there was one development, born of a cross-class alliance in 1921, that flourished throughout the '20s and into the mid-'30s with important results: the Summer School for Women Workers at Bryn Mawr. M. Carey Thomas, president of Bryn Mawr, endorsed the suggestion put forward by a number of trade union women that the college sponsor an annual training session for working-class women. For fifteen years, dozens of women took unpaid breaks from their jobs every summer and came to two months of classes in history, economics, and labor law, all aimed at preparing them for union leadership. By the time the program had ended, many hundreds had participated—at a time when college training was much less accessible than it is today. Unquestionably, the program had a beneficial impact. Perhaps the best-known Bryn Mawr "graduate" was Rose Pesotta, who went on to become a vice president of the ILGWU.[44]

By the late '20s there were beginning to be signs of the labor unrest that would break out so massively during the Great Depression. Nowhere were these signs more manifest than in the textile mills of North Carolina, mills with a substantial female work force. During a strike in 1929, women workers played a highly significant role, revealing a new boldness of public demeanor that had not been seen in strikes by women workers heretofore. In a recent article, Jacquelyn Hall suggests that male strikers played a role behind the scenes in "rough stuff," but that women "held center stage" in public demonstrations:

> At the outset "hundreds of girls" had ridden down main street "in buses and taxis, shouting and laughing at people who watched them from windows and doorsteps." Now they blocked the road at Gap Creek and refused soldiers' orders that they walk twelve miles to jail in town. "And there was one girl that was awful tough . . . in the bunch. . . . She

said, 'No, by God. We didn't walk out here, and we're not walking back!' And she sat her hind end down in the middle of the road, and we all sat down with her. And the law used tear gas on us! . . . And it nearly put our eyes out, but we still wouldn't walk back to town." At Valley Forge women teased the guardsmen and shamed the strikebreakers. In Elizabethton after picket duty, women marched down the "Bemberg Highway . . . draped in the American flag and carrying the colors"—thereby forcing the guardsmen to present arms each time they passed. Inventive, playful, and shrewd, the women's tactics encouraged a holiday spirit. They may also have deflected violence and garnered community support.[45]

With the high spirits of the Bowery Gals wedded to intense political purpose, these women made a mockery—literally—of the sexually loaded negative stereotypes of public womanhood. Hall describes two especially flamboyant characters, Texas Bill and Trixie Perry. Texas Bill allegedly called a guardsman a "God-damned yellow son-of-a-bitch," and Trixie Perry showed up to testify in court decked out in red, white, and blue and sporting a cap made of an American flag. Moreover, they were known to have led unconventional personal lives. Yet rather than disavowing them as an embarrassment, the other strikers cheered them on:

> What is impressive here is how Trixie Perry and Texas Bill handled the dichotomy between ladyhood and lewdness. Using words that, for women in particular, were ordinarily taboo, they refused deference and signaled disrespect. Making no secret of their sexual experience, they combined flirtation with fierceness on the picket line and adopted a provocative courtroom style. And yet with the language of dress . . . they claimed their place in the female community.[46]

The strike itself may not have been a success—the South has been hostile terrain for trade unions—but these women of the North Carolina Piedmont added a new dimension to public womanhood by being fearless about the taboo that had been most successful in either driving women from the public arena or in circumscribing their options once there.

Thus as the Great Depression began, working-class women were poised to respond to the economic downturn in ways that few other women in the country could. To their long tradition of participation in crowds and in episodes of labor militancy had been added a new public validation of their life experiences. Moreover, there were promising indications of the existence of "New Women" who could successfully defy ancient, and demoralizing, taboos. Finally, a highly successful program designed to produce female trade union leaders was in place.

It is impossible in the context of this study to give more than the sketchiest overview of the experiences of working-class women during the 1930s. We can point to the further development of a working-class woman's literary tradition whose most prominent member was Meridel Le Sueur.[47] Of course, the mainstream culture possessed an unparalleled populist character during the Great Depression, from the films of Frank Capra to the novels of John Steinbeck to the great photographs by Walker Evans, Dorothea Lange, and others. Within this cultural context, the spunky working-class woman began to receive even more attention. We can note further that in addition to their activities on behalf of unions to which they themselves belonged, women in the industrial Midwest played a crucial role in the sit-down strikes by their menfolk. We can acknowledge that women on the left were instrumental in building unions in many locales.[48] All these, however, were extensions, albeit important extensions, of what had gone before.

What was new about the developments of the 1930s was, in the first place, the geographic range and racial ethnic diversity involved in the episodes of female militancy. Although the labor turbulence of the depression decade has been well established, it has typically been depicted in terms of men in mass-production industries, a stereotype so firmly established that the scope of women's public activism has still not been fully appreciated. In every part of the country, women were protesting injustice, such as the immigrant textile workers in Rhode

Island, the subjects of a book by Louise Lamphere.[49] Led by a young woman named Ann Burlak, also known as the "Red Flame," these workers struck in 1931. African-American domestic workers, specifically excluded from the purview of the Wagner Act of 1935, the most important labor legislation to be passed by Congress during the '30s, nonetheless attempted to organize unions in several cities during the decade.[50] Women were staunch allies for their male coworkers in the creation of the United Electrical, Radio and Machine Workers of America (UE).[51] And so on.

To bring up the UE is to be reminded of the second major innovation during the Depression, the birth of the Congress of Industrial Organizations (CIO) with its philosophy of industrial unionism, in mid-decade. Prior to this, only the most skilled workers in a plant typically belonged to a union—a craft union—and they were almost invariably male. After the CIO appeared on the scene, tens of thousands of women workers achieved the benefits of union membership. Nationally, the figure went from 250,000 women in unions at the beginning of the decade to 800,000 at its close.[52]

The case of California's cannery workers, predominantly female and the largest single category of women workers in the state, affords a particularly vivid example of working-class women's activism during the Great Depression. What is remarkable about the cannery workers is that they were not only female but also immigrant, seasonally employed, and deemed to be unskilled—all qualities thought to make them difficult if not impossible to organize—and yet they ended the 1930s as union members.

In southern California, cannery workers were most frequently Chicana, although the work force also contained a sprinkling of Russian Jews. In *Cannery Women, Cannery Lives* Vicki Ruiz describes the woman's culture that made it possible for these disparate groups to join forces in the late '30s in order to create the United Cannery, Agricultural, Packing, and Allied Workers of America (UCAPAWA), a CIO affiliate. For example, a woman named Maria Rodriguez had a Jewish work buddy, and the two girls, as they then were, liked talking about Clark Gable and *True Stories* magazine. Says Ruiz, "Gossiping about real celebrities or fictitious heroines entertained women as they performed rote assembly tasks and, in the process, nurtured important cross-cultural networks. Teenagers began to discuss with one another their problems and concerns, finding common ground not only in their status as cannery workers but as second-generation ethnic women coming of age during the depression." [53]

Women on the left, most notably Luisa Moreno, were key organizers in this effort, and after UCAPAWA came into being, women also served as shop stewards and union officers to a remarkable extent, especially given the prior history of unions composed of 50 percent or more women members but led by men. [54] Moreover, in the mid-'40s, the Food, Tobacco, Agricultural, and Allied Workers of America (FTA) (as UCAPAWA was renamed) fought for, and achieved, "equal pay for equal work" clauses in its contracts. In other words, the prominence of women in the union's leadership translated into results for women workers in contract negotiations. In the climate of hysterical anti-communism of the early 1950s, the Teamsters were able to carry out a successful takeover of this union—which then became less willing to defend the interests of women workers.

In northern California, the story played itself out differently. There, the work force was larger, 20,000 people in the San Jose area alone, and predominantly Italian. [55] The CIO effort to organize the canneries fell victim to an alliance between growers and the AFL's California Federation of Labor, a group which had shown no interest whatsoever in organizing the canneries until the CIO came along. Nonetheless, this alliance did produce a union in 1937, albeit a company union. So militant did the workers then prove themselves to be, and so clever their leadership, that within a few years of the company union's appearance, it had been transformed into an organization prepared to fight for its members. In 1941 the AFL cannery union struck, and workers won important gains. [56]

When the San Jose cannery local, the largest in the state, took shape in the late '30s, there was only one woman among its leadership, Myra Eaton. This disguises the true importance of female leadership to the organization of cannery workers, however, because from 1931 on, women in the Communist party played consequential roles.

In the summer of 1931, workers struck three San Jose canneries to protest a wage cut. That Party members had been organizing in the canneries for months doubtless helped precipitate this strike. One Party organizer was Dorothy Ray Healey, then a sixteen-year-old who had dropped out of Berkeley High School to go to work in the Santa Clara Valley. (With the San Jose strike as her debut, Healey went on to become one of the Party's most high-profile women until her resignation in 1973.) Although the strike was unsuccessful in the short run, it served to mobilize workers and to make them more receptive to organizers, not least because of the amount of violence directed against the strikers.[57]

Another Communist party woman who played a highly visible role in the Santa Clara Valley was Caroline Decker. In the spring of 1933, having chosen the area as state headquarters, the Party sent Decker to San Jose with the mandate to organize all of California's agriculture. Although she did not accomplish this task, she did help organize strikes in many parts of the state; indeed, there were more than 30 agricultural strikes in California in 1933 alone. Decker's work in San Jose ended after a lynching convinced the Party to move its headquarters elsewhere.[58] Her work in the state ended after she was arrested and convicted on criminal syndicalism charges and sent to Tehachapi State Prison for two years.

Elizabeth Nicholas was one of eight or nine Party members who were permanent residents of the area during the '30s. Active in the 1931 strike, Nicholas was subsequently blacklisted and unable to obtain cannery employment. Nonetheless, she spent the entire decade tirelessly visiting those who worked in the food industry in one capacity or another and urging them to join a union. The emergence of a CIO local in the fruit packing industry in the late '30s owed much to her efforts.[59]

The contributions made by these three young women make clear the way the Party recruited and trained women for leadership. Perhaps more than any other mixed-sex institution in American society at the time, the Communist party was willing to give women prominent, possibly dangerous, positions. Hence it played a consequential role in encouraging public women. Unfortunately for such women, in establishing its priorities, the Party routinely subordinated gender to class as the source of exploitation—as the Socialist party had done in the early twentieth century. Moreover, women in the Party had to deal with sexism on the part of male colleagues.[60]

The groundswell of female activism first generated in the 1930s and the growing strength of the CIO combined to help bring millions more women into unions during the 1940s, when so many women were employed in factories. Women constituted 9.4 percent of unionized workers at the beginning of the war, and 22 percent—3 million in absolute numbers—in 1944.[61] Nonetheless, work-based gender discrimination persisted in the 1940s, even in industries organized by the CIO. For example, Ruth Milkman documents this phenomenon in *Gender at Work*, a study of women in the UE and the United Auto Workers, each of which had a quarter of a million female members in 1945.[62] A brilliant analysis of the survival of highly segregated work patterns, despite strong economic incentives to employers to hire women for as many jobs as possible, *Gender at Work* offers disquieting evidence that even the more enlightened male unionists—like male Communists—were far from taking gender equity seriously as an issue.

Persisting inequality in the face of rapid growth in levels of unionization propelled many union women into public activism in the 1940s. In the first place, there was a wave of strikes by women workers after the war ended. The biggest was a walkout by 230,000 telephone operators in 1947, a strike that secured the position of collective bargaining in this industry.[63] In some ways the most dramatic was the walkout by women department store workers in Oakland in 1946 that precipitated a city-wide general strike involving 120,000 workers.[64]

In addition to these episodes of worker militancy, the other significant component of the '40s-era public activism by women workers lay in the first major effort to reform public policy governing their work lives since the Progressive period with its protective labor legislation. The Women's Bureau of the U.S. Department of Labor, which had principally played an investigative role up to this point, began in the '40s to serve a different function, sponsoring meetings of trade union women to discuss pay equity, meetings that eventually led to the Equal Pay Act of 1963.[65] All this has convinced the labor historian Dorothy Sue Cobble to conclude: "For working women, the 1940s was an era of mass mobilization, intense activity, and even advancement."[66] Cobble points out that some of the growth in the '40s came in female-dominated unions and that the women leaders of such unions were especially likely to have a feminist agenda.

No account of the immense contribution made by working-class women to public womanhood can ignore the unhappy subject of racism. More has been written about the racism of male workers than about female.[67] Fortunately, we are beginning to see studies of the latter, such as Dolores Janiewski's work on black and white tobacco workers in Virginia, North Carolina, and Kentucky. Janiewski describes a polarized environment in which women had little public access.[68] Circumscribed as they were, white female tobacco workers were nonetheless unable to make common cause with black women on a basis of gender solidarity for any great length of time.

What, then, can be said about working-class women and public womanhood in conclusion? As we look back we see that in the opening centuries of the American experience, before there was an industrial working class, women, especially Quakers and Puritans, had first explored, then valorized, and ultimately celebrated female subjectivity. As this Protestant culture evolved into the middle-class mainstream of the nineteenth century, later generations of women were both empowered by the gender solidarity it fostered and limited by the narrow definition of appropriate female behavior it required. Another stream of female experience running along with that of literate and genteel Protestantism had encompassed women who were bolder in their public demeanor, from scolds to strumpets to a great variety of unruly, disorderly women, most of whom had little to lose by their flamboyant behavior. Predecessors of the industrial working class that emerged in the nineteenth century, these women had the power to make trouble, but, even less than their men, they had little ability to translate their interests into a political will.

For most of the nineteenth century public womanhood was diminished by the dichotomy between these two categories of women. There was a vast gulf between well-behaved literate women, who had a growing influence on the polity, and working-class women, who grew in numbers as the economy became increasingly industrial and corporate but who suffered from various types of economic and cultural marginalization that continued to hamper their ability to protect their interests. Between 1880 and 1930 the numbers of working-class women grew exponentially, they gained a measure of economic independence, and they began both to gain access to education and to be able to valorize a new kind of female subjectivity. During the Great Depression and World War II such women mobilized to improve their lives as did no other components of the female population. What must be understood is the extent to which they brought new dimensions of physical courage and boldness—in some instances boldness about sexuality—to public womanhood. The possibilities for all would-be public women were thus immeasurably enhanced.

10

The Rebirth of Feminism

Baby boom-era men and women bought suburban homes by the millions, retreated to them, and procreated, while worrying about nuclear annihilation.[1] The families they produced reversed a long-term American trend toward smaller numbers of children, a pattern that had been developing since the early nineteenth century. Yet even in this period of the celebration of "traditional" family values—when the stay-at-home television mom June Cleaver invariably yielded to her husband Ward's superior wisdom and when Lucy Ricardo made a woman's desire for a career seem preposterous—millions of women continued to be gainfully employed outside the home. Few women ran for electoral office, however—as late as 1969 only 4 percent of state legislators were female, for example. Clubs for middle-class white women were largely apolitical, which is not surprising given that their members were receiving messages from the culture to the effect that their experiences were valueless where the conduct of public business was concerned.[2] Yet at the same time black women were joining clubs that aimed to transform American society. Moreover, in certain unions working-class women were able to gain at least a taste of playing a leadership role. Out of such contradictions came the social change of the 1960s and the rebirth of feminism. And the "second wave" of feminism brought more women into public roles than ever before.

In order to understand the sudden reappearance of feminism, it is important to grasp how aberrant the '50s really were in the long sweep of American history. For more than a century, sexuality had been gradually escaping from the bonds of matrimony, and people had come increasingly to focus on recreation in addition to procreation as the reason for engaging in sexual activity.[3] Family size had been steadily declining. Cold War anxieties then made Americans "homeword bound" in the 1950s. In her book with this title, Elaine Tyler May uses the term "domestic containment" to characterize a dominant theme of family life during the Eisenhower years. For a while, it almost seemed as if the genie might go back into the bottle, the genie, that is, that had been for generations inducing certain men and women to want self-fulfillment as well as, perhaps more than, family stability.

Yet while women's magazines, pop psychologists, and other gurus were enjoining togetherness—and female self-sacrifice in order to achieve family stability—the economy was busily churning out a plethora of consumer items that encouraged even the most devoted wives and mothers to dream hedonistic dreams of personal fulfillment.[4] The dreams might not yet encompass being a physician or a CEO, but they may well have entailed gainful employment: in 1950, some 16.5 million women were employed outside the home, and in 1960 the number had reached 22.5 million. What is more, most of the growth took place among married women, 8.5 million of whom were employed in 1950 and 13.5 million of whom were employed in 1960. No doubt, many gainfully employed married women thought of themselves as doing something for their families, but inescapably they were also being led away from their families as the sole focus of their lives.

If 13.5 million married women worked outside the home in 1960, there were even more who were staying home and suffering from the effects of seeing themselves as "just a housewife." After Betty Friedan "named the problem" of the middle-class housewife reduced to feelings of purposelessness and uselessness in her best-selling polemic *The Feminine Mystique*,[5] the flood of letters she received bears witness to the accuracy of her analysis for many women.[6]

One further factor that must be considered in looking at the context for the rebirth of feminism is the change circa 1960 in both the attitude toward and the technology for birth control. The pill began to be widely available about this time, and for the first time in human history women began to anticipate complete control of their reproductive lives.[7] This, in turn, made premenopausal women potentially as free as men to engage in both sexual activity and public activity during the same period of their lives, because they could prevent pregnancy.

The devaluation of female activities, from negative stereotypes of "women drivers" to the oft-seen derisive cartoons of club women, coupled with the growing importance and independence of women as wage-earners—to say nothing of their increasing control of their biological destiny—such was the rather schizoid state of affairs for the white middle class. At the same time, among African-American women the long commitment to public activism was about to bear spectacular fruit.

In 1946 a young black woman named Mary Fair Burks, newly returned from graduate study in Ann Arbor, was teaching English at the Alabama State Laboratory High School in Montgomery when she was arrested on a preposterous charge. Driving alone, she had stopped for a red light and had then proceeded through the intersection after the light had turned green. A white woman who had not yet stepped onto the curb began to curse her, and Burks soon found herself in the custody of a police officer. Happily for her, a lawyer quickly succeeded in having the charges dismissed. Nonetheless and not surprisingly, the incident infuriated her. Shortly thereafter, she heard a rousing sermon by the Reverend Vernon Johns, pastor of the Dexter Avenue Baptist Church immediately before the tenure of Martin Luther King, Jr. Already pondering what could be done about racial injustice, Burks was further inspired by the sermon, and she contacted about fifty other women, inviting them to form what became the Women's Political

Council (WPC) of Montgomery. "We finally agreed on a three-tier approach: first, political action, including voter registration and interviewing candidates for office; second, protest about abuses on city buses and use of taxpayers' money to operate segregated parks . . . and third, education. . . ."[8]

Another black Montgomery teacher, Jo Ann Robinson, suffered a similarly humiliating episode in 1949 when a driver asked her to vacate a seat in the fifth row of a nearly empty bus. Once again, the memory rankled and helped prompt her, as president of the college branch of the WPC some years later, to write a letter to the mayor of Montgomery asking for improved conditions for black bus riders and threatening a boycott should this not take place. Dated May 21, 1954, the letter followed only four days after the Supreme Court handed down its decision in *Brown* v. *Board of Education*.[9] Thus well before Rosa Parks's historic refusal to surrender her seat on a Montgomery bus on December 1, 1955, the Women's Political Council had begun to think in terms of a boycott.

Rosa Parks, the third member of a triumvirate of African-American women who helped launch a revolution, was a seamstress and not a teacher like the other two. But unlike the white community, where cross-class alliances among women have been a sometime thing, the black community has a long tradition of cross-class cooperation, as we have seen. Therefore, the faithful churchgoer and community worker Parks was well known and highly respected by the middle-class blacks of Montgomery, who were willing to work together to protest her arrest.

As of December 1955, Rosa Parks was active not only in the Methodist Church but also in the local branch of the National Association for the Advancement of Colored People (NAACP), for which she served as secretary. It was the latter connection which had led her to spend a week at the Highlander Folk School in Tennessee, where since the 1930s founder Myles Horton and his staff had been training interracial groups in the techniques of non-violent social activism. When a tired Rosa Parks declined to give up her seat on the bus that Decem-

ber day, this was no random act. Rather, it represented the deliberate—and courageous—choice of one who was determined to bring
change to the region and who had prepared herself for that role.

In her memoir Jo Ann Robinson has described the Women's Political Council's response to Parks's arrest: "I informed him [Fred Gray,
a young lawyer working on the case] that I already was thinking that
the WPC should distribute thousands of notices calling for all bus
riders to stay off the buses on Monday, the day of Mrs. Parks' trial."[10]
With the cooperation of a colleague in the business department at
Alabama State, Robinson and two of her most trusted students met at
the college in the middle of the night and ran off 52,500 notices.
Officers of the WPC had already discussed how best to disseminate
such notices, so Robinson was able to follow a preconceived plan. The
rest of the story, of course, has become the stuff of legend. The boycott was more successful than anyone could have dreamed; it united
the black community behind the leadership of the twenty-six-year-old
Martin Luther King, who then became a figure of world-wide importance; and the civil rights movement was launched on a period of both
intense suffering and also many triumphs.

Until recently, the role of the women in the movement had received little attention. Now, we have memoirs by key participants such
as Jo Ann Robinson as well as an anthology of scholarly work on the
subject.[11] Perhaps the most remarkable woman to emerge in the civil
rights movement was Fannie Lou Hamer, remarkable not only for her
considerable achievements on behalf of the Mississippi Freedom
Democratic party but also because she had been one of twenty children in a family of sharecroppers. Then there was Ella Baker, founding mother of the Student Nonviolent Coordinating Committee
(SNCC), Septima Clark, founder of an adult literacy program, and
Unita Blackwell, a grass-roots activist in Mississippi in the '60s who
became her state's first black woman mayor. The list is long.

Trying to account for the relatively greater participation by women
than by men in the Mississippi Delta in the early '60s, Charles Payne
first sets forth this claim: "Women took civil rights workers into their
homes . . . but women also canvassed more than men, showed up

more often at mass meetings and demonstrations and more frequently attempted to register to vote."[12] He then goes on to speculate that the greater spirituality and religiosity of women made it possible for them to join a movement whose chances for success were far from assured in the early days. Moreover, women derived a sense of efficacy from their religion which they then carried over into their civil rights activism.

As another instance in point, an African-American woman whose achievement is still too little-known, Clara Luper, led a children's crusade that desegregated the public accommodations of Oklahoma City in the late '50s. A high school teacher, Luper was inspired by the Montgomery bus boycott and wrote a pageant about it, which her students performed. In the summer of 1957 they took the pageant to New York City, traveling the northern route in one direction and the southern route in the other. When they came home, having had so vivid a lesson in the difference between the two systems, the students were ready to join their teacher in acts of civil disobedience. Luper herself was arrested sixteen times in an escalating series of protests. Aid quickly came from the clergy and the black press; also, many state officials were sympathetic. It is important to recognize that the original leadership for this highly successful undertaking had come from Luper, however.[13]

Besides the heroic example of courageous women in the civil rights movement, another major catalyst for the rebirth of feminism was the work of the Kennedy Commission on the Status of Women. In order to understand the importance of this commission, we have to return to the topic of the Equal Rights Amendment (ERA) and the strange politics it engendered over the course of many decades.

Originally pushed by the National Woman's Party, the ERA became, during the 1920s, the source of a schism in the women's movement, as we have already seen. The Woman's Party shrank in size so that in the '50s it represented a tiny group of eccentrics in the eyes of most other people—to the extent that it had any visibility at all. The good news, insofar as the chances of the ERA being incorporated into the Constitution were concerned, is that gradually other groups began to endorse the ERA, too, and some prominent opponents, the most prominent being Eleanor Roosevelt, began to soft-pedal their opposition. All this presented John F. Kennedy with a dilemma after he came into office. Part of his liberal constituency, labor, had traditionally opposed the ERA, but other parts were beginning to see the necessity for better public policy for women, a necessity that might include the ERA. Appointing a strong leader, Esther Peterson, to head the Women's Bureau, Kennedy took the unusual step of indicating to her that the Women's Bureau could play a role in policy formation, a real departure from the stance of his predecessors.[14] And when she suggested to him the idea of a Presidential Commission on the Status of Women, he proved willing to cooperate. To everyone's considerable delight, Eleanor Roosevelt agreed to serve as chair of the commission. The underlying objective was to resolve the issue of the ERA once and for all.

Esther Peterson had the experience and the contacts to make the most of the opportunity Kennedy gave her. In the '30s she had taught at the Bryn Mawr Summer Schools. She had then gone on to organize teachers' unions in Massachusetts and to work for the Amalgamated Clothing Workers of America. In 1944 she became the union's lobbyist in Washington, where in 1947 she met freshman congressman John F. Kennedy. By the time of her appointment to head the Women's Bureau she had the support of a broad range of women leaders for her work, and Kennedy elevated her position to just below cabinet rank.

Well supported by the President, funded adequately so that a staff headed by Peterson could engage in valuable research, graced with the presence of Eleanor Roosevelt as chair, the commission was composed of twenty-six outstanding men and women, including "members of both houses of Congress, the secretaries of labor, commerce, and HEW, the attorney general, the chairman of the Civil Service Commission, as well as prominent representatives of industry, labor, education, and women's organizations."[15] Without going into elaborate detail on all the recommendations and results after the commission had completed its work and submitted its report, we can safely conclude that there was, in the first place, a substantial ripple effect just from all the women who had been mobilized to participate in one way or another. Peterson explains, for example, that as the work progressed, commission members from women's groups "communicated the work of the commission to millions of women through their respective organizational systems." In the second place, the commission found a way of placating both sides on the ERA, holding back from a full endorsement of it, yet "agreeing that women needed to be considered 'equal under the law.' "[16] Summarizing the importance of the Kennedy Commission, its leading student, Cynthia Harrison, says the following:

> As Peterson intended, the Presidential Commission on the Status of Women had important implications for the politics of women's issues in the 1960s. It drew opposing interest groups together, narrowing the gap between the Women's Bureau coalition and ERA advocates; it enunciated a federal policy against sex discrimination, affirming that women like men, had a right to paid employment; it presented a cogent set of proposals to begin the amelioration of the difficulties women faced; it built up networks of support among women's organizations and served as the model for analogous institutions on the state level. . . .[17]

For all these reasons, Harrison contends that the commission indirectly helped generate the women's movement.

Perhaps the commission's most direct influence on the rebirth of feminism lay in its role in the founding of the National Organization for Women (NOW). Out of the commission on the national level had been born state commissions, members of which had a series of meetings in Washington in the late '60s. In 1966 a rump group of leaders, dissatisfied with the rejection of two resolutions, one of which endorsed the ERA, met and decided to form a new advocacy group to be called NOW. In December 1966 the group officially came into being, with Betty Friedan as the first president. According to Marguerite Rawalt, first chair of NOW's legal committee, "The purpose of NOW was to provide a mechanism with which women could pressure the government."[18]

Thus as we reflect upon the rebirth of feminism in the 1960s, we can identify both long-term causes—the cultural validation going on among various racial ethnic groups, the contradictions between increasing levels of female economic independence and the devaluation of female contributions to society—and proximate causes like the civil rights movement and the Kennedy Commission. Another important ingredient was, of course, the student movement, which mobilized young white men and women to fight for the rights of others and for peace. Repeatedly consigned to subsidiary or auxiliary roles in the movement, young women soon began to apply the current New Left analysis to their own situation.[19]

It is instructive to read the Port Huron statement of 1962, a key document of the '60s and usually taken as the founding statement of the New Left. Eloquent on the subject of the need for participatory democracy, the statement identifies a number of ills in American society—such as racial bigotry, the nuclear arms race, and hysterical anti-communism—yet is utterly oblivious to discrimination against women. A few short years later, young women were beginning to teach their male comrades that they would no longer tolerate this kind of oversight. Moreover, after hundreds of young white students had gone South to work for civil rights and saw the example of women such as Ella Baker and Fannie Lou Hamer, they no longer saw it as "natural" for women to take a back seat in a movement for social change.

It should be further mentioned that even before a broad-based grass-roots women's movement had taken shape, Congress had begun to enact significant new public policy for women. Beginning in the late '40s, women labor leaders in coalition with the Women's Bureau had been pressing for a law mandating equal pay for equal work, and in 1963 Congress obliged them by passing the Equal Pay Act. Again quoting Cynthia Harrison:

> In its final form, the equal pay law guaranteed equal pay for "equal" rather than "comparable" work; it excluded employees not covered by the Fair Labor Standards Act; it contained no provision for administrative enforcement. Yet future amendments to the Fair Labor Standards Act extended coverage, and the procedures established by the Wage and

Hour Division of the Department of Labor ultimately offered good results. Court decisions construed the meaning of "equal pay" liberally, declining to apply the law solely to identical jobs: in the first ten years of its enforcement 171,000 employees had been awarded $84 million in back pay alone under the provisions of the law.[20]

In 1964 Congress passed a landmark Civil Rights Act, which as it had first been drafted, prohibited discrimination based on race in public accommodations and in employment. By the time it eventually became law, it also prohibited discrimination based on sex.[21] Out of this law came the Equal Employment Opportunity Commission (EEOC), and pressure from women's groups began to mount to force the EEOC to take women's issues seriously. Both Title VII of the Civil Rights Act and the Equal Pay Act thus helped to heighten women's level of consciousness about discrimination by making legal redress possible.

The subject of the rebirth of feminism has already inspired several books, and more are sure to come about so important a topic, so this chapter can provide only a preliminary assessment.[22] What seems most remarkable, despite the preceding recitation of abundant long-term and proximate causes for a movement, is the speed with which the public discourse about women's issues underwent a transformation in the late '60s and early '70s. No sooner had the word "sexism" been coined, for example, than it had entered common parlance, so pressing was the need for language with which to write about—and think about—discrimination.[23] Every news magazine had its cover story about the stirrings among women. In cities and towns across the country, groups came together for consciousness-raising sessions. While feminism no doubt made its most numerous converts in metropolitan areas, no section was unaffected.[24] Perhaps the only comparable phenomenon in American history was the birth of the Republican party in the summer of 1854 after Congress had passed the Kansas-Nebraska Act, thereby undermining the Missouri Compromise. In the mid-1850s, as in the late 1960s, groups of ordinary people mobilized politically with stunning speed.

Besides the speed with which women began to apply a feminist analysis to their own lives and to take appropriate action—such as filing a suit, joining a consciousness-raising group, or applying to professional school—it is also noteworthy how broad a range of women mobilized to improve their situations. Feminism has all too often been seen exclusively as a middle-class phenomenon, and it is true that certain phases of the movement were overwhelmingly white and middle-class. But the movement encompassed more issues and more women than either the liberal mainstream of NOW or the more left-wing orientation but largely middle-class composition of radical feminism would suggest.[25] For example, in 1974 women in the trade union movement came together to form the Coalition of Labor Union Women (CLUW). Open only to union members, CLUW acts as a pressure group on male-dominated unions in the AFL-CIO. In 1979 Joyce Miller, the president of CLUW, joined the executive council of the AFL-CIO as its first woman member, and organized labor also began to demonstrate an interest in issues such as child care and sexual harassment.[26]

One of the best indications of the far-reaching nature of the change during these years is the role played by women—including those who were recent immigrants and/or spoke little English—in the United Farm Workers (UFW). Dolores Huerta, vice president of the union, has long been known as one of the most prominent and most respected women in the labor movement, a tough negotiator and a forceful advocate of better treatment for the men and women who toil in California's fields. Less well known have been the activities of a whole host of other women who played a role in the success of the boycotts the UFW staged in the 1970s. Women ran union offices in many parts of the San Joaquin Valley, and women, sometimes in partnership with their husbands and sometimes alone, organized boycott operations in major cities throughout the country. Specifically excluded from the purview of the Wagner Act of 1935, vulnerable in strikes because illegal immigrants, desperate for work, have provided growers with a pool of strikebreakers, the UFW led by Cesar Chavez mobilized entire families for political action. In 1973 Dolores Huerta offered these reflections to two interviewers:

I really believe what the feminists stand for. There is an undercurrent of discrimination against women in our own organization, even though Cesar goes out of his way to see that women have leadership positions. . . . Cesar's stricter with the women, he demands more of us. But the more I think of it, the more I'm convinced that the women have gotten stronger because he expects so much of us. You could even say it's gotten lopsided. . . . women are stronger than the men. . . . Excluding women, protecting them, keeping women at home, that's the middle-class way. Poor people's movements have always had whole families on the line, ready to move at a moment's notice, with more courage because that's all we had.[27]

Thus among the public women to be activated during the '60s and '70s were these Mexican-Americans from a sector of society which had been seen as especially marginal and powerless up to that time.

Women also became publicly active as lesbians in a hitherto unprecedented way. Both feminism and gay liberation influenced lesbians to come out of the closet to defend their interests and to proclaim their pride in their sexual orientation.[28] Moreover, scholars uncovered and wrote about a significant lesbian past, in which loving female partnerships had undergirded public activism for settlement house workers and early academic women.[29] Lesbian writers published theoretical works on the relationship between lesbianism and feminism, and novelists garnering mainstream attention began to explore lesbian themes.[30] All of this meant a change in the public discourse about women's sexuality, which began much more to be discussed for its own sake and less in relationship to male partners. In other words, in addition to advancing their own interests with their public activism, lesbians performed a service for all women by rescuing discussions of female sexuality from a nearly exclusive focus on those male-generated therapeutic categories which had carried the day for most of the twentieth century.[31]

Fannie Lou Hamer, the daughter of sharecroppers, appeared on national television during the 1964 Democratic Convention to talk about the Mississippi Freedom Democratic party. At about this same time Dolores Huerta began to develop her reputation as a formidable negotiator. Within a few years the range of women functioning as public figures in one guise or another and the range of female experiences receiving mainstream attention had exploded beyond all prior imaginings. For example, in that bastion of cultural conservatism, country music, Tammy Wynette's exhortation to "Stand by Your Man" gave way to Loretta Lynn's "Don't Come Home a Drinkin' with Lovin' on Your Mind." Maxine Hong Kingston invented a new literary form, part novel, part memoir, to illuminate growing up female in a Chinese-American household in *The Woman Warrior*.[32] The literary flowering among black women can only be described as dazzling, with Toni Morrison and Alice Walker as perhaps the most distinguished exemplars. In the 1980s Wilma Mankiller won election as chief of the Cherokees. And so on.

If the range of women seeking public access and public influence had grown beyond recognition so too had the range of issues feminists brought into the public arena and the range of problems for which they sought remedies from the state. Because the United States still lags so far behind most of the world's industrial democracies with respect to issues such as family leave and publicly supported child care, it is easy to underestimate the substantial accomplishments of the rebirth of feminism.

Going into the late '60s with the Equal Pay Act and Title VII, women soon articulated the need for battered women's shelters, for the liberalization of laws on abortion, for policies on sexual harassment at the workplace, for better access to credit, for affirmative action in both admission to graduate and professional schools and in hiring, and for the ERA, among other items. Some of these represented the extension to women of rights or benefits already accorded to men, but others represented the pioneering of entirely new areas of policy, as, for example, sexual harassment. In their consciousness-raising groups, women were pondering the meaning of the phrase "The personal is political," which had come out of the student movement, and coming to take it so seriously that they were inventing a new kind of politics.

Sexual harassment is an especially good example of the transformation effected by modern feminism. The problem itself was scarcely a new one. To talk to women of a certain age is to encounter only too frequently the following type of comment: "All of us tellers knew better than to be in the vault at the same time as Mr. ——. He was impossible."[33] The speaker was recalling one of the hazards of working at a bank in Los Angeles during the Great Depression. Needing her job badly, she could not afford to take the chance of complaining about Mr. ——, no doubt the position of her coworkers, too. Therefore, it was up to all of them to be constantly on the alert so as to avoid the indignity of being pawed by a male superordinate. The problem was a personal one, to be handled at an individual level. After millions of women flooded into the workplace in the late '60s and the 1970s, many into workplaces which had hitherto been male preserves, they were at risk to be greeted with unwelcome sexual innuendo or worse, and they were no longer disposed to take it. Filing suit on the basis of the Equal Protection clause of the Fourteenth Amendment, women forced employers to develop rules governing such conduct so as to protect themselves against litigation.[34]

Lesbians talking about their sexual orientation, women employees insisting that their workplaces be free of sexual innuendo—such women were claiming the role of sexual subject, as opposed to accepting the role of mere object of male desire. And as sexual subjects women can—potentially at least—enter the public arena on the same terms as men, whose public activity has never been linked to their sexuality. Earlier public women, most notably Emma Goldman, had anticipated this breakthrough, but modern feminists have made more of it.

It is beyond the scope of this study to provide a full account of the achievements of feminism. Rather we shall take note of one spectacular event that took place on August 26, 1970, the fiftieth anniversary of suffrage, and then go on to examine the four categories of public womanhood with which we began—the legal, the political, the social geographical, and the cultural—to see where women stood in the wake of that event.

When NOW called a demonstration to mark the suffrage anniversary, the organizers could scarcely have anticipated just how successful it would prove to be. Ethel Klein begins her *Gender Politics* with an account of what was called the Women's Strike for Equality, because she believes the event was meaningful to politicians throughout the country:

> On August 26, 1970, the fiftieth anniversary of passage of the Nineteenth Amendment granting women the suffrage, women from all over the country joined in support of the Women's Strike for Equality. The participants in the nationwide demonstration expressed their solidarity by marching, holding teach-ins, and picketing in support of equal employment and educational opportunities, abortion, and child care. Housewives, secretaries, lawyers, mothers, grandmothers, and students were drawn together out of a sense of injustice, personal frustration, and the need to change inequities in the treatment of women. Many of these women had no prior organizational commitment to women's rights. They came with a specific agenda of activities and policies aimed at gaining for women economic and social independence. The golden anniversary of the woman suffrage amendment was thus celebrated with the largest demonstration for women's rights in United States history.[35]

Needless to say, this was a signal moment for public womanhood, because more women claimed the right to demonstrate publicly in more locales than ever before. Not surprisingly, the strike had a major impact on feminist mobilizing for years to come.[36]

As of 1970, women's capacity to protect their interests in the courts—that is, the legal dimension of public womanhood—was not significantly different from what it had been in the 1920s. Married women had emerged from coverture in that they could hold property in their own names, but many other remnants of the past clung to them, such as the laws governing domicile or those governing access to credit. The awareness of these multiple inequities in the law then fueled the renewed—and much broader—movement to ratify the Equal Rights Amendment that emerged in the late 1960s.

Moreover, beginning in 1972, about the time that Congress passed the ERA and while the country waited to see if it would be ratified, the Supreme Court began to apply the Fourteenth Amendment to cases where women alleged discrimination on the basis of sex. The Court then struck down a number of laws that were deemed to be unfair to women.[37] A whole specialty of feminist law developed, with firms such as Equal Rights Advocates of San Francisco coming into being to pursue these cases.

When it comes to the political dimension of public womanhood as of 1970, here too we find remarkably little movement since the achievement of suffrage, except for the role played by female New Dealers. There had been a few prominent women officeholders such as Senator Margaret Chase Smith of Maine, Representative Helen Gahagan Douglas of California, and Representative Martha Griffiths of Michigan. Then, too, Congress had passed the two important laws in the early '60s, the Equal Pay Act and Title VII of the Civil Rights Act. The early '70s, on the other hand, became a time of extraordinary change, with Congress passing a veritable cornucopia of important legislation. Says Klein:

> During the 1960s Congress considered 884 bills concerned with women's issues but only 10 were passed. Only after the Strike for Equality in 1970, which established the presence of a social movement committed to sex equality, did Congress act on women's behalf. Women's activism, which had involved 26 events in 1968, increased to 165 events in 1970 and reached a high of 256 events in 1975; it then sustained an average of 116 events per year for the rest of the decade. Women's influence over public policy increased markedly with their increased activism. During the 1970s Congress passed 71 pieces of legislation concerned with a broad spectrum of women's rights and needs. . . .[38]

It could be argued that of the bills Congress passed, none was more important for public womanhood than the ERA, even though this amendment fell three states short of ratification. This is because the fight for ratification mobilized so many women, in so many parts of the country, to become politically active.[39] Moreover, the AFL-CIO eventually endorsed the ERA, thus ending many decades of internecine strife about how to approach women's issues within progressive circles. Finally, of the women who mobilized to fight for ratification, the evidence indicates that many subsequently went on to run for public office themselves.

As for those women officeholders, quintessential public women, there was a similar pattern of significant change around 1970. Although in the 1990s women still constitute less than 10 percent of Congress, they did begin to run for office at many other levels in the 1970s. From 4 percent of state legislators in 1969, they have gone to 18 percent in 1990. The percentage of women in municipal office tripled between 1975 and 1985, going from 4 to 14 percent.[40]

In 1971 a number of prominent women formed the National Women's Political Caucus, which aimed both to encourage women to run for office and to fight for feminist issues. That development helped spur the organization of similar groups at the local level. For example, in 1971 in Boulder, Colorado, several women formed an organization called Public Office for Women (POW!). They then sought to encourage women to run in an upcoming municipal election. In a city which had seen only six female candidacies for city council since 1917 there were, that year, four women running for the council, one of whom was elected. When POW! had come into being there had been one woman serving on the Board of Education and no other female officeholders serving in any capacity.[41] In 1974 San Jose voters elected Janet Gray Hayes as mayor, the first woman to head a city with a population of more than 500,000 people. Within the decade, Jane Byrne became mayor of Chicago, and women began to serve as mayors of major cities throughout the country. A particularly important milestone for public women came in 1984, when Geraldine Ferraro of New York took her place on a national ticket as the Democratic nominee for vice president. (That this happened owed to the discovery of a "gender gap" in support for Ronald Reagan, that is, a marked difference in the voting behavior of male and female voters, a difference that feminist leaders forcefully called to the attention of Democratic men.) In short, while there was far from perfect parity for women politicians, public womanhood in this arena took a gigantic leap forward circa 1970.

There was change, too, in the social geography of gender, because many spaces which had been off-limits to women were sexually integrated in the 1970s. A host of elite private universities opened their doors to women, for example. Women began to go into blue-collar trades—albeit in small numbers—so that such venues as construction sites were no longer routinely all-male. In certain instances, women successfully sued to gain entrance to bars and private clubs which had been male preserves.

In the realm of culture, the arena for public access where women had enjoyed their earliest triumphs, there was less ground to make up, so the change was perhaps less dramatic than in other arenas. There were, however, two highly significant developments. In the first place, racial ethnic women who had been writing—or performing—for their own communities began to receive mainstream visibility. In the second place, women began to be editors as well as writers, producers and directors as well as actresses. This meant that women were achieving the opportunity to be more influential on the content of the culture than they had hitherto been.

When we look ahead to the decade of the '90s, it is clear that gender-based politics will play an increasingly visible role in American public life, and that this situation will draw ever more women into the public arena. As of this writing, three women occupy gubernatorial office, one of whom, Ann Richards, won a bitterly contested race in the major state of Texas in 1990. Richards's first appointment was that of a young Chicana, Lena Guerrero, to the powerful Railroad Commission, which regulates not only transportation but also energy resources. As of this writing, 16 of the 50 state treasurers are women. As of this writing, the legality of access to abortion constitutes the most volatile domestic issue in the nation. As of this writing—in the wake of the Clarence Thomas hearings—angry women are mobilizing to elect more of their sex to Congress.

After seeing the way male politicians treated Anita Hill, a young law professor who testified to her personal experience of being sexually harassed by Supreme Court nominee Thomas, women throughout the country are demanding change. It should be noted that in the summer of 1991 a distinguished woman surgeon at Stanford Medical School announced that she was quitting because she had had enough sexual harassment from a male colleague. In other words, more women and more prominent women are going public with such charges, and that is bound to change the nature of American politics.

By no means does the change so far and the change realistically in prospect add up to perfect symmetry for "public man" and "public woman." Yet it is important to recognize how much legitimacy women have gained, relatively speaking. At the beginning of our story, we encountered Anne Hutchinson, banished into the wilderness for holding prayer meetings. Anne Bradstreet's brother-in-law felt compelled to explain in the preface to her book that her poems had been written in hours "curtailed from sleep," so unusual and suspect was the act of female authorship. Generations of pious women had to contend with the Pauline injunction to women to keep silent in church. Women had no independent legal identity, except under special circumstances; they could play no active role in the polity. And the woman who rebelled against this fate might well find herself labeled as "Jezebel." The double standard has not yet been entirely vanquished, but "Jezebel" has been retired as an epithet.

Moreover, what is clear to an observer in the early '90s is the fact that public women are increasingly willing to seek power in order to effect their ends. For much of the twentieth century the efficacy of women voters and of women officeholders was limited by the constraints of needing to represent virtue and disinterestedness, a legacy of the means by which generations of public women had legitimated their "trespass" into a hitherto male arena. The new gender-based politics of the '90s—with choice as a central motif—has not only legitimated a quest for power but also required women to think in terms of power politics in order to protect their interests.

Afterword

As we take stock of where would-be public women stand in the 1990s, it must be immediately acknowledged that the quality of American public life itself seems to be in a state of deterioration and degradation. Political debate has devolved into the staging of sound bites for a television camera. The decade of the '80s saw the unleashing of so much greed as to make a mockery of the very concept of the public good. Draconian reductions in spending on social programs have turned our cities into dangerous terrain to the extent that everyone's public access has suffered. In other words, it is increasingly hazardous to move freely around a metropolis.

Yet many of the critiques of what is wrong with American public life now—for which there is abundant material, to put it mildly— imply a golden age of public life that existed at some point in the past. It is certainly true that, in the nineteenth century for example, Americans flocked to attend lengthy political debates and that lectures by brilliant men and women formed a much-loved part of popular entertainment. Yet there has never been a time in human history when the richness of public life for some portion of the population did not rest on the exclusion and exploitation of another—usually women. Therefore, if there is to be a golden age of public life, it is up to those of us who are alive now to create it.

The challenge is to rethink the connection between private and public life. Definitions of "the public" that undervalue the contribution made by a decent private life enhance the likelihood that some component of the population will be relegated to perform despised tasks for others—whether this means illegal immigrants taking care of other people's children or wives and mothers carrying a disproportionate share of the responsibility for housework. Most of the reigning political theories—there are beginning to be exceptions, but not many— are based on male categories and male experience and assume that private life is not worth much attention because somebody else will provide for it.

Would-be public women need more than just the removal of barriers to their access. They need imaginative new social arrangements so that they do not have to choose between the welfare of their loved ones and their public responsibilities. Moreover, men will increasingly require such arrangements, too, as more of them turn fatherhood into a role co-equal to motherhood.

Would-be public women need respect from others for female experience, for the wisdom of grandmothers, to use Stowe's phrase. No matter what their success might be, if once they achieve, say, elected office, they must immediately deny their own female identity, they will be less than public men.

Would-be public women need to cultivate respect for differences among women. In the recent past we have seen all too many instances of women assuming that their particular experiences can be universalized. We have seen women with relatively good access to education and opportunity imply contempt for others, especially housewives, whose lives are more circumscribed than their own. In my judgment, if we are ever to have a chance of better public policy on family and child-care issues, this will require a broad-based coalition of women, as well as men of good will. Such a coalition can come about only by dint of assiduous bridge-building among women who have, unfortunately, learned to fear and distrust one another at the current moment.

Finally, we all need to recognize that women who stand up in public are still subject to scrutiny of their personal lives to an extent that often goes beyond what men experience. A woman candidate may have to contend with sexual innuendo, for example. If she is married, her spouse may rue the day when he agreed to go along with her candidacy, as hordes of journalists pore over records of every business transaction in his past. If the child of a male politician gets into trouble, no one says that this proves he should have stayed home more. A woman politician knows how vulnerable she is on this score. Public woman will take her place alongside of public man only after the last residue of such unequal treatment has been obliterated.

Notes

Introduction

1. Lisa Duggan, "Sexual Secrets Revealed!": Sex, Scandal, and Tragedy in the Popular Press, 1890–1900," paper given at the Organization of American Historians annual meeting, New York City, April 1986.

2. See chaps. 16–21 of Kings.

3. Joan B. Landes, *Women and the Public Sphere in the Age of the French Revolution* (Ithaca: Cornell Univ. Press, 1988), 3.

4. See Jean Bethke Elshtain, *Public Man, Private Woman: Women in Social and Political Thought* (Princeton: Princeton Univ. Press, 1981); Landes, *Women and the Public Sphere*; Susan Moller Okin, *Women in Western Political Thought* (Princeton: Princeton Univ. Press, 1979); Carole Pateman, *The Sexual Contract* (Cambridge: Polity Press, 1988).

5. I Corinthians 14:34, 35.

6. Gerda Lerner, *The Creation of Patriarchy* (New York: Oxford Univ. Press, 1986), 9.

7. Ibid., 135.

8. See Sara M. Evans, *Born for Liberty: A History of Women in America* (New York: Free Press, 1989), chap. 1.

9. See Marylynn Salmon, *Women and the Law of Property in Early America* (Chapel Hill: Univ. of North Carolina Press, 1986).

10. Linda K. Kerber, "Property: The Case of the Confiscated Farm," First Jefferson Memorial Lecture, Oct. 24, 1989, University of California, Berkeley.

11. Ellen Carol DuBois, "Working Women, Class Relations, and Suffrage Militance: Harriet Stanton Blatch and the New York Woman Suffrage Movement, 1894–1909," *Journal of American History* 74 (June 1987): 34–58, p. 50. It may well be that the nineteenth century saw a worsening trend, relative to earlier centuries, before the situation for women improved.

12. Claudia D. Johnson, *American Actress: Perspective on the Nineteenth Century* (Chicago: Nelson-Hall, 1984), 12.

13. Eleanor Flexner, *Century of Struggle: The Woman's Rights Movement in the United States*, rev. ed. (Cambridge, Mass.: Harvard Univ. Press, 1975), 75, 76.

14. Amy Schrager Lang, *Prophetic Woman: Anne Hutchinson and the Problem of Dissent in the Literature of New England* (Berkeley: Univ. of California Press, 1987), 2.

15. Mary P. Ryan, *Women in Public: Between Banners and Ballots, 1825–1880* (Baltimore: Johns Hopkins Univ. Press, 1990).

16. Nancy F. Cott, *The Grounding of Modern Feminism* (New Haven: Yale Univ. Press, 1987), 185.

17. Linda K. Kerber, *Women of the Republic: Intellect and Ideology in Revolutionary America* (Chapel Hill: Univ. of North Carolina Press, 1980); Mary Beth Norton, *Liberty's Daughters: The Revolutionary Experience of American Women, 1750–1800* (Boston: Little, Brown, 1980).

18. See Hazel Carby, *Reconstructing Womanhood: The Emergence of the Afro-American Woman Novelist* (New York: Oxford Univ. Press, 1987).

19. Anne Firor Scott, "Most Invisible of All: Black Women's Voluntary Associations," *Journal of Southern History* 56 (Feb. 1990): 3–22.

20. See Kathryn Kish Sklar, *Catharine Beecher: A Study in American Domesticity* (New Haven: Yale Univ. Press, 1973); Nancy F. Cott, *The Bonds of Womanhood: "Woman's Sphere" in New England, 1780–1835* (New Haven: Yale Univ. Press, 1977).

21. See Joanne J. Meyerowitz, *Women Adrift: Independent Wage Earners in Chicago, 1880–1930* (Chicago: Univ. of Chicago Press, 1988).

22. Candace Falk, *Love, Anarchy, and Emma Goldman* (New York: Holt, Rinehart, and Winston, 1984); Alice Wexler, *Emma Goldman in America* (Boston: Beacon Press, 1989); Wexler, *Emma Goldman in Exile* (Boston: Beacon Press, 1989). Although both Fanny Wright and Victoria Woodhull spoke

out publicly before Goldman, neither of them enjoyed her longevity as a public figure.

23. See Ethel Klein, *Gender Politics: From Consciousness to Mass Politics* (Cambridge, Mass.: Harvard Univ. Press, 1984), for an account of the importance of the Women's Strike for Equality.

24. Nancy F. Cott, "What's in a Name? The Limits of Social Feminism; or, Expanding the Vocabulary of Women's History," *Journal of American History* 76 (Dec. 1989): 809–29, p. 826.

25. Matthews, *"Just a Housewife": The Rise and Fall of Domesticity in America* (New York: Oxford Univ. Press, 1987).

Chapter 1. Woman's Power and Woman's Place in Seventeenth-Century America

1. Gary Nash, *Red, White, and Black: The Peoples of Early America*, 2d. ed. (Englewood Cliffs, N.J.: Prentice-Hall, 1982), 20.

2. Ibid., 21.

3. As quoted in Judith K. Brown, "Economic Organization and the Position of Women Among the Iroquois," *Ethnohistory* 17 (Summer/Fall 1970): 151–67, p. 153.

4. Theda Perdue, "Cherokee Women and the Trail of Tears," *Journal of Women's History* I (Spring 1989): 14–30.

5. Ibid., 15.

6. My sources for the Puritans include Philip J. Greven, Jr., *Four Generations: Population, Land, and Family in Colonial Andover, Massachusetts* (Ithaca: Cornell Univ. Press, 1970); Lyle Koehler, *A Search for Power: The "Weaker Sex" in Seventeenth-Century New England* (Urbana: Univ. of Illinois Press, 1980); Steven Mintz and Susan Kellogg, *Domestic Revolutions: A Social History of American Family Life* (New York: Free Press, 1988); Edmund S. Morgan, *The Puritan Family: Religion and Domestic Relations in Seventeenth-Century New England* (New York: Harper and Row, 1956).

7. Morgan, *The Puritan Family*.

8. Mintz and Kellogg, *Domestic Revolutions*, 6.

9. My understanding of such matters is based on Edmund Morgan, *Visible Saints: The History of the Puritan Idea* (New York: New York Univ. Press, 1963). But see also Charles Lloyd Cohen, *God's Caress: The Psychology of Puritan Religious Experience* (New York: Oxford Univ. Press, 1986), and Philip F. Gura, *A Glimpse of Sion's Glory: Puritan Radicalism in New England* (Middletown, Conn.: Wesleyan Univ. Press, 1984).

10. Mintz and Kellogg, *Domestic Revolutions*, 9.

11. Marylynn Salmon, *Women and the Law of Property in Early America* (Chapel Hill: Univ. of North Carolina Press, 1986), 6.

12. Ibid., 8.

13. Laurel Thatcher Ulrich, *Good Wives: Image and Reality in the Lives of Women in Northern New England, 1650–1750* (New York: Alfred A. Knopf, 1982), chap. 2.

14. Carol F. Karlsen, *The Devil in the Shape of a Woman: Witchcraft in Colonial New England* (New York: W. W. Norton, 1987), 116.

15. Ibid., 213.

16. Barry Levy, *Quakers and the American Family: British Settlement in the Delaware Valley* (New York: Oxford Univ. Press, 1988), 71–79.

17. John Bevan in *A Collection of Memorials Concerning Divers Deceased Ministers and Others of the People Called Quakers* (Philadelphia: Joseph Cruikshank, 1787); John and Barbara Bevan are my eight times great-grandparents. My aunt Virginia Haradon called this document to my attention.

18. Margaret Hope Bacon, *Mothers of Feminism: The Story of Quaker Women in America* (San Francisco: Harper and Row, 1986), 55.

19. Phyllis Mack, "Gender and Spirituality in Early English Quakerism," in Elizabeth Potts Brown and Susan Mosher Stuard, eds., *Witnesses for Change: Quaker Women Over Three Centuries* (New Brunswick, N.J.: Rutgers Univ. Press, 1989), 54f. Of course, the best-known Quaker woman martyr was Mary Dyer, who was hanged in Boston in the mid-seventeenth century.

20. Mary Maples Dunn, "Women of Light," in Carol Ruth Berkin and Mary Beth Norton, eds., *Women of America* (Boston: Houghton Mifflin, 1979), 120.

21. Ibid., 121–23.

22. Salmon, *Women and the Law of Property in Early America*, 9.

23. Ibid., 44–49.

24. Edmund S. Morgan, *American Slavery, American Freedom: The Ordeal of Colonial Virginia* (New York: W. W. Norton, 1975), chap. 8.

25. Julia Cherry Spruill, *Women's Life and Work in the Southern Colonies* (New York: W. W. Norton, 1938, 1972), 233f.

26. Ibid., 236–40. For a more recent discussion of social patterns in the Chesapeake, see Allan Kulikoff, *Tobacco and Slaves: The Development of Southern Culture in the Chesapeake, 1680–1800* (Chapel Hill: Univ. of North Carolina Press, 1986).

27. Salmon, *Women and the Law of Property in Early America*, 9.

28. Daniel Blake Smith, *Inside the Great House: Planter Family Life in*

Eighteenth-Century Chesapeake Society (Ithaca: Cornell Univ. Press, 1980), 285.

29. Rhys Isaac, *The Transformation of Virginia, 1740–1790* (Chapel Hill: Univ. of North Carolina Press, 1982), 61.

30. Laurel Thatcher Ulrich, "Of Pens and Needles: Sources in Early American Women's History," *Journal of American History* 77 (June 1990): 200–207, p. 201.

31. According to Mintz and Kellogg in *Domestic Revolutions*, p. 6, wives could vote at town meetings in the absence of their husbands.

32. See, for example, the account in Robert V. Remini, *Andrew Jackson* (New York: Harper and Row, 1969), 111–16.

33. Mary Beth Norton, "Gender and Defamation in Seventeenth-Century Maryland," *William and Mary Quarterly* 44 (Jan. 1987): 3–39, p. 6.

34. Ibid. See also Robert St. George, " 'Heated' Speech and Literacy in Seventeenth-Century New England," in David D. Hall and David Grayson Allen, eds, *Seventeenth-Century New England* (Boston: Colonial Society of Massachusetts, 1984), for a discussion of the way in which "heated speech" in seventeenth-century New England possessed "a reality that we no longer acknowledge." It should be noted that St. George's data, unlike Norton's, reveal far fewer women than men involved in "speech transgressions" that wound up in court—either as plaintiffs or as defendants.

35. Patricia Caldwell, *The Puritan Conversion Narrative: The Beginnings of American Expression* (Cambridge, Eng.: Cambridge Univ. Press, 1983), 41. See also Cohen, *God's Caress*. I have myself read some of these narratives from the eighteenth century and will discuss them in Chapter 2.

36. Caldwell, *The Puritan Conversion Narrative*, 46–50.

37. I am indebted to Keith Thomas for this summary of the history of private life. See Thomas, "Review of Roger Chartier, ed., *A History of Private Life*, vol. III, *Passions of the Renaissance*," *New York Review of Books*, Nov. 9, 1989.

38. David D. Hall, *Worlds of Wonder, Days of Judgment: Popular Religious Belief in Early New England* (New York: Alfred A. Knopf, 1989), 32. For a recent discussion of women and literacy, with data dealing with women in the eighteenth century, see Joel Perlmann and Dennis Shirley, "When Did New England Women Acquire Literacy?," *William and Mary Quarterly* 48 (Jan. 1991): 50–67.

39. Hall, *Worlds of Wonder*, 29. Roger Chartier has this to say about Puritan reading: "In America's Puritan culture we find the most radical privatization of reading. The book became the center of family life. People read

for themselves and for others. They memorized passages, which by dint of frequent repetition became part of their everyday language." See Chartier, "The Practical Impact of Writing," in Philippe Ariès and Georges Duby, eds., *A History of Private Life*, vol. III, *Passions of the Renaissance* (Cambridge, Mass.: Belknap Press of Harvard Univ. Press, 1989), 134.

40. Ibid., 34, 35.

41. Koehler, *A Search for Power*, 219f.

42. Gerda Lerner provides excerpts of the transcripts in her *The Female Experience: An American Documentary* (Indianapolis: Bobbs-Merrill, 1977), 465–71. See also Koehler, *A Search for Power*, 222f. The most comprehensive collection of documents pertaining to the Antinomian controversy is David D. Hall, *The Antinomian Controversy, 1636–1638: A Documentary History*, 2d. ed. (Durham, N.C.: Duke Univ. Press, 1990).

43. As quoted in Caldwell, *The Puritan Conversion Narrative*, 144.

44. Lerner, *The Female Experience*, 470f.

45. Amy Schrager Lang, *Prophetic Woman: Anne Hutchinson and the Problem of Dissent in the Literature of New England* (Berkeley: Univ. of California Press, 1987), 93, 96. Lang's book deals with the uses made of Anne Hutchinson.

46. Ibid., 1–3.

47. Elizabeth Wade White, *Anne Bradstreet: "The Tenth Muse"* (New York: Oxford Univ. Press, 1971), 125. Lyle Koehler stresses the dearth of women writers in the early period. See Koehler, *A Search for Power*, 54.

48. As quoted in Sandra M. Gilbert and Susan Gubar, eds., *The Norton Anthology of Literature by Women: The Tradition in English* (New York: W. W. Norton, 1985), 67.

49. As quoted in Wendy Martin, *An American Triptych: Anne Bradstreet, Emily Dickinson, Adrienne Rich* (Chapel Hill: Univ. of North Carolina Press, 1984), 48.

50. *Norton Anthology*, 63–66.

51. As quoted in Martin, *An American Triptych*, 58. It should be mentioned that there was also a great woman poet in Mexico in the seventeenth century, Sor Juana Inez de la Cruz.

Chapter 2. The Erosion of Patriarchy

1. Richard Bushman, *From Puritan to Yankee: Character and Social Order in Connecticut, 1690–1765* (New York: W. W. Norton, 1967); Jay

Fliegelman, *Prodigals and Pilgrims: The American Revolution against Patriarchal Authority* (Cambridge, Eng.: Cambridge Univ. Press, 1982).

2. On this subject see James Henretta, *The Evolution of American Society, 1700–1815: An Interdisciplinary Analysis* (Lexington, Mass.: D. C. Heath, 1973).

3. Joan M. Jensen, *Loosening the Bonds: Mid-Atlantic Farm Women, 1750–1850* (New Haven: Yale Univ. Press, 1986).

4. Daniel Blake Smith, *Inside the Great House: Planter Family Life in Eighteenth-Century Chesapeake Society* (Ithaca: Cornell Univ. Press, 1980), 219.

5. Lawrence Stone, *The Family, Sex and Marriage in England, 1500–1800* (New York: Harper and Row, 1977), 8.

6. On this subject see Smith, *Inside the Great House*; Jan Lewis, *The Pursuit of Happiness: Family and Values in Jefferson's Virginia* (Cambridge, Eng.: Cambridge Univ. Press, 1983); Steven Mintz and Susan Kellogg, *Domestic Revolutions: A Social History of American Family Life* (New York: Free Press, 1988).

7. Stone himself attributes the development of affective individualism to economic factors—the growth of a market in England—and to the development of a new personality type among the upper classes based on changed methods of child-rearing. See Lawrence Stone, *The Family, Sex and Marriage in England, 1500–1800* (abr. ed.; New York: Harper and Row, 1979), 179, 180. See also Fliegelman, *Prodigals and Pilgrims*, for the impact of the ideas of John Locke on these developments.

8. See Fliegelman, *Prodigals and Pilgrims*, for a much fuller discussion of this topic. I will deal with the novel myself in Chapter 4.

9. Carl N. Degler, *At Odds: Women and the Family from the Revolution to the Present* (New York: Oxford Univ. Press, 1980), 16–18.

10. Lewis, *The Pursuit of Happiness*, chap. 3.

11. Nancy F. Cott, "Eighteenth-Century Family and Social Life Revealed in Massachusetts Divorce Records," in Nancy F. Cott and Elizabeth H. Pleck, eds., *A Heritage of Her Own: Toward a New Social History of American Women* (New York: Simon and Schuster, 1979), 127.

12. See the classic article by Perry Miller, " 'Preparation for Salvation' in Seventeenth-Century New England," *Journal of the History of Ideas* 3 (1943): 253–86. See also Charles Lloyd Cohen, *God's Caress: The Psychology of Puritan Religious Experience* (New York: Oxford Univ. Press, 1986).

13. See Bushman, *From Puritan to Yankee*, for the argument that growing economic prosperity underlay the Great Awakening.

14. Ibid., 209.

15. Henretta, *Evolution of American Society*, 138. Gary Nash empha-

sizes the radicalism of the Great Awakening. See Nash, *The Urban Crucible: Social Change, Political Consciousness, and the Origins of the American Revolution* (Cambridge, Mass.: Harvard Univ. Press, 1979), chap. 8.

16. John E. Smith, "Edwards' *Religious Affections*," in David Levin, ed., *Jonathan Edwards: A Profile* (New York: Hill and Wang, 1969); Ruth H. Bloch, "The Gendered Meaning of Virtue in Revolutionary America," *Signs* 13 (Autumn 1987): 37–58.

17. The classic article on nineteenth-century sisterhood is by Carroll Smith-Rosenberg, "The Female World of Love and Ritual: Relations Between Women in Nineteenth-Century America," *Signs* 1 (Autumn 1975): 1–29. In her comment at a session entitled "Rethinking Sisterhood," AHA Pacific Coast Branch Meeting, August 1990, Salt Lake City, Jacqueline S. Reinier describes some of the links between the growing female taste for literature in the late eighteenth century and a sisterhood that might be fictive as well as real. Simply stated, because reading required privacy, encouraged introspection, and valorized subjectivity, it promoted the sharing of intimate feelings with a soulmate—to whom a woman might or might not be related. Worth noting is the fact, to be discussed more fully in Chapter 4, that Burr and Prince discussed their opinions of *Pamela* with one another.

I am indebted to Professor Reinier for sharing her comment with me.

18. Carol F. Karlsen and Laurie Crumpacker, eds., *The Journal of Esther Edwards Burr, 1754–1757* (New Haven: Yale Univ. Press, 1984), 257.

19. See, for example, the passage where Burr conjectures about a cozy evening at the Prince home with the men doing all the talking and the women remaining silent until they get by themselves and "tell what [they] think." Ibid., 54.

20. Ibid., 178.

21. Editors Karlsen and Crumpacker note passages where Burr referred to a group of women in Boston as "the sisterhood." They point out that this was one of the earliest American expressions of this theme. Ibid., 34f.

22. The Sarah Prince Gill journal is in the Boston Public Library.

23. Susan Juster, " 'In a Different Voice': Male and Female Narratives of Religious Conversion in Postrevolutionary America," *American Quarterly* 41 (March 1989): 34–62.

24. Samuel Hopkins, *Memoirs of the Life of Sarah Osborn* (Catskill: N. Elliott, 1814); see also Mary Beth Norton, " 'My Resting Reaping Times': Sarah Osborn's Defense of Her 'Unfeminine' Activities, 1767," *Signs* 2 (1976): 515–29.

25. Hopkins, *Memoirs of the Life of Sarah Osborn*, 36.

26. Ibid., 75.

27. Ibid., 151.

28. Ibid., 81, 82.

29. John Cleaveland Papers, Essex Institute, Salem, Massachusetts.

30. Juster, " 'In a Different Voice,' " 53, 57. According to Martha Tom-have Blauwelt and Rosemary Skinner Keller:

> In judging the unregenerate and in taking on clerical roles, women gained public religious functions. Before, their religious roles had been largely private: they gave spiritual advice within the home and experienced conversion "in the closet." But during the Awakening conversion became a dramatic, public event. Women experienced "violent fits" and their cries might be heard far beyond the confines of their homes. As the revival rendered religiosity public and emotional, it drew women into the public sphere.

Blauvelt and Keller, "Women and Revivalism: The Puritan and Wesleyan Traditions," Rosemary Radford Ruether and Rosemary Skinner Keller, eds., *Women and Religion in America*, vol. II, *The Colonial and Revolutionary Periods* (San Francisco: Harper and Row, 1981), 321.

31. Charles Chauncy, *Enthusiasm Described and Caution'd Against* (Boston: S. Eliot, 1742), 13.

32. Jensen, *Loosening the Bonds*, 147.

33. Jean R. Soderlund, "Women's Authority in Pennsylvania and New Jersey Quaker Meetings, 1680–1760," *William and Mary Quarterly* 44 (Oct. 1987): 722–49, p. 734.

34. Ibid., 747.

35. Margaret Hope Bacon, *Mothers of Feminism: The Story of Quaker Women in America* (San Francisco: Harper and Row, 1986), 80.

36. The phrase is used by Mary Maples Dunn in her "Women of Light," Carol Ruth Berkin and Mary Beth Norton, *Women of America: A History* (Boston: Houghton Mifflin, 1979), 131.

37. Jensen, *Loosening the Bonds*, 153.

38. Smith, *Inside the Great House*, conclusion.

39. Julia Cherry Spruill, *Women's Life and Work in the Southern Colonies* (New York: W. W. Norton, 1938, 1972), 243. See also Allan Kulikoff, *Tobacco and Slaves: The Development of Southern Cultures in the Chesapeake, 1680–1800* (Chapel Hill: Univ. of North Carolina Press, 1986), for a more recent discussion of gender roles in this region.

40. Edmund S. Morgan, *Inventing the People: The Rise of Popular Sovereignty in England and America* (New York: W. W. Norton, 1988), 193.

41. Suzanne Lebsock, *The Free Women of Petersburg: Status and Culture in a Southern Town, 1784–1860* (New York: W. W. Norton, 1984), 196.

42. Paul Gilje, *The Road to Mobocracy: Popular Disorder in New York City, 1763–1834* (Chapel Hill: Univ. of North Carolina Press, 1987), 75, 76.

43. Mary P. Ryan, *Women in Public: Between Banners and Ballots, 1825–1860* (Baltimore: Johns Hopkins Univ. Press, 1989), 149, 150.

44. Linda K. Kerber, *Women of the Republic: Intellect and Ideology in Revolutionary America* (Chapel Hill: Univ. of North Carolina Press, 1980); Mary Beth Norton, *Liberty's Daughters: The Revolutionary Experience of American Women, 1750–1800* (Boston: Little, Brown, 1980).

45. Weldon B. Durham, *American Theatre Companies, 1749–1887*, (New York: Greenwood Press, 1986), 548, 549.

46. Laurel Thatcher Ulrich, " 'Daughters of Liberty': Religious Women in Revolutionary New England," in Ronald Hoffman and Peter J. Albert, eds., *Women in the Age of the American Revolution* (Charlottesville: Published for the United States Capitol Historical Society by the Univ. Press of Virginia, 1989); Anne Firor Scott, "Most Invisible of All: Black Women's Voluntary Associations," *Journal of Southern History* 56 (Feb. 1990): 3–22.

47. Laurel Thatcher Ulrich, *A Midwife's Tale: The Life of Martha Ballard, Based on Her Diary, 1785–1812* (New York: Alfred A. Knopf, 1990).

48. Ibid., 343.

49. As quoted in William H. Robinson, ed., *Phillis Wheatley and Her Writings* (New York: Garland, 1984), 22.

50. Ibid., introduction. Just before her own death Susanna Wheatley freed Phillis, whose material circumstances rapidly declined thereafter. See David Grimsted, "Anglo-American Racism and Phillis Wheatley's 'Sable Veil,' 'Lengthened Chain,' and 'Knitted Heart,' " in Hoffman and Albert, *Women in the Age of the American Revolution*, for the suggestion that Mrs. Wheatley belonged to the same circle of female evangelicals as did Sarah Osborn, women who took a special interest in the salvation of African-Americans.

51. As quoted in Sandra M. Gilbert and Susan Gubar, eds., *The Norton Anthology of Literature by Women: The Tradition in English* (New York: W. W. Norton, 1985), 134.

Chapter 3. Women and Republicanism

1. Important books on republicanism include J. G. A. Pocock, *The Machiavellian Moment: Florentine Political Thought and the Atlantic Republican Tradition* (Princeton: Princeton Univ. Press, 1975); Sean Wilentz, *Chants Democratic: New York City and the Rise of the American Working Class, 1788–1850* (New York: Oxford Univ. Press, 1984); Gordon Wood, *The Cre-*

ation of the American Republic (Chapel Hill: Univ. of North Carolina Press, 1969).

2. Linda Kerber has been the pioneer in writing about women and republicanism. See Kerber, *Women of the Republic: Intellect and Ideology in Revolutionary America* (Chapel Hill: Univ. of North Carolina Press, 1980).

3. The classic text is *Patriarcha* by Robert Filmer, written in the reign of Charles I.

4. Pocock, *The Machiavellian Moment*, 75.

5. Jean Bethke Elshtain, *Public Man, Private Woman: Women in Social and Political Thought* (Princeton: Princeton Univ. Press, 1981), 94, 95.

6. Hanna Fenichel Pitkin, *Fortune Is a Woman: Gender and Politics in the Thought of Niccolo Machiavelli* (Berkeley: Univ. of California Press, 1981), 326, 327.

7. A lively discussion of the relative importance of Locke and the Scottish Common Sense school to the drafting of the Declaration of Independence, with the palm going to the latter, can be found in Garry Wills, *Inventing America: Jefferson's Declaration of Independence* (Garden City, N.Y.: Doubleday, 1978).

8. See Jay Fliegelman, *Prodigals and Pilgrims: The American Revolution against Patriarchal Authority, 1750–1800* (Cambridge, Eng.: Cambridge Univ. Press, 1982), on the importance of Locke in this regard. Says Fliegelman (p. 13):

> Locke's educational theory redefined the nature of parental authority in very much the way that the Revolution of 1688, which replaced absolute monarchy with a constitutional one, redefined the rights and duties of the crown. The revolution Locke enthusiastically defended in his political writing declared there was "no king in being."

That is, both fathers and kings were making the transition from reigning to governing.

9. See Barry Levy, *Quakers and the American Family: British Settlement in the Delaware Valley* (New York: Oxford Univ. Press, 1988).

10. Wood, *The Creation of the American Republic*, 24. It should be noted that Wood sees this level of public-spiritedness as rather quickly succumbing to the spirit of capitalism.

11. My understanding of this subject is based on Wood, *The Creation of the American Republic* and also on Bernard Bailyn, *The Ideological Origins of the American Revolution* (Cambridge, Mass.: Belknap Press of the Harvard Univ. Press, 1967).

12. See Kerber, *Women of the Republic*, for an elaboration of this point. See also James T. Kloppenberg, "The Virtues of Liberalism: Christianity, Re-

publicanism, and Ethics in Early American Political Discourse," *Journal of American History* 74 (June 1987): 9–33.

13. Ruth H. Bloch, *Visionary Republic: Millenial Themes in American Thought, 1756–1800* (Cambridge, Eng.: Cambridge Univ. Press, 1985).

14. As quoted in Kerber, *Women of the Republic*, 38.

15. Mary Beth Norton, *Liberty's Daughters: The Revolutionary Experience of American Women, 1750–1800* (Boston: Little, Brown, 1980), 160f; Kerber, *Women of the Republic*, 41. See also Alfred F. Young, "The Women of Boston: 'Persons of Consequence' in the Making of the American Revolution," in Harriet B. Applewhite and Darline G. Levy, eds., *Women and Politics in the Age of the Democratic Revolution* (Ann Arbor: Univ. of Michigan Press, 1990).

16. Kerber, *Women of the Republic*, 99–102.

17. As quoted in William H. Robinson, *Critical Essays on Phillis Wheatley* (Boston: G. K. Hall, 1982), 34.

18. As quoted in ibid., 35.

19. Kerber, *Women of the Republic*, chap. 4.

20. Joan R. Gunderson, "Independence, Citizenship, and the American Revolution," *Signs* 13 (Autumn 1987): 59–77, p. 68.

21. Linda K. Kerber, "The Republican Ideology of the Revolutionary Generation," *American Quarterly* 37 (Fall 1985): 474–95.

22. Ibid.

23. Montesquieu, *The Persian Letters*, George R. Healy, trans. (Indianapolis: Bobbs-Merrill, 1964), 272.

24. Christine Fauré, *La Démocratie sans les Femmes: Essai sur le libéralisme en France* (Paris: Presses Universitaires de France, 1985), 140.

25. As quoted in ibid., 147 (my translation).

26. Ibid., 144–58; see also the discussion of Rousseau in Elshtain, *Public Man, Private Woman*, 196, 197.

27. Fauré, *La Démocratie sans les Femmes*, 158–72.

28. Ibid., chap. 5; see also Karen Offen, "Women's Memory, Women's History, Women's Political Action: The French Revolution in Retrospect, 1789–1889–1989," *Journal of Women's History* 1 (Winter 1990): 211–30.

29. Mary Wollstonecraft, *A Vindication of the Rights of Woman* (London: J. Johnson, 1792), 49.

30. Ibid., 391.

31. Charles Brockden Brown, *Alcuin: A Dialogue* (New Haven: Carl and Margaret Rollins, 1935), 24.

32. Ibid., 51.

33. See Garry Wills, *Inventing America*, for a discussion of the impact of the Scottish Enlightenment on republican ideology.

34. Jacqueline S. Reinier, "Rearing the Republican Child: Attitudes and Practices in Post-Revolutionary Philadelphia," *William and Mary Quarterly* 39 (Jan. 1982): 150–63.

35. Rush, "Of the Mode of Education Proper in a Republic," *The Selected Writings of Benjamin Rush*, Dagobert D. Runes, ed. (New York: Philosophical Library, 1947), 95f.

36. Kerber, *Women of the Republic*, chap. 7.

37. Kerber offered the first formulation of Republican Motherhood. Jan Lewis, on the other hand, contends that it was as wives rather than as mothers that women were crucial to the new Republic. See Lewis, "The Republican Wife: Virtue and Seduction in the Early Republic," *William and Mary Quarterly* 44 (Oct. 1987): 689–721.

38. Mary Beth Norton, "The Evolution of White Women's Experience in Early America," *American Historical Review* 89 (June 1984): 593–619; Paula Baker, "The Domestication of Politics: Women and American Political Society, 1780–1920," *American Historical Review* 89 (June 1984): 620–47.

39. See, for example, the splendid illustrations in Kerber, *Women of the Republic*. See also the subtle discussion of this issue in Mary P. Ryan, *Women in Public: Between Banners and Ballots, 1825–1880* (Baltimore: Johns Hopkins Univ. Press, 1990), 52.

40. Ruth H. Bloch, "The Gendered Meaning of Virtue in Revolutionary America," *Signs* 13 (Autumn 1987): 37–58, p. 40.

41. As quoted in Rosemary Radford Ruether and Rosemary Skinner Keller, eds., *Women and Religion in America*, vol. 2, *The Colonial and Revolutionary Periods* (San Francisco: Harper and Row, 1981), 407.

42. Eleanor Flexner, *Century of Struggle: The Woman's Rights Movement in the United States*, rev. ed. (Cambridge, Mass.: Harvard Univ. Press, 1975), 226.

43. For the Abigail historiography see Edith B. Gelles, "The Abigail Industry," *William and Mary Quarterly* 45 (Oct. 1985): 656–83.

44. Ibid. My generalizations are also based on Charles W. Akers, *Abigail Adams: An American Woman* (Boston: Little, Brown, 1980).

45. Abigail to John, June 17, 1782, as reprinted in Ruether and Keller, *Women and Religion*, 394.

46. As quoted in Kerber, *Women of the Republic*, 84.

47. Mercy Otis Warren to Lady Haselrige, 1773, Mercy Otis Warren Papers, Massachusetts Historical Society.

48. MOW to Catherine Macaulay, Aug. 1787, Warren Papers.

49. MOW to John Adams, March 1776, Warren Papers.

50. MOW to Catherine Macaulay, Aug. 1787, Warren Papers.

51. "Observations on the New Constitution, and on the Federal and

State Conventions." By a Columbian Patriot. (Boston, 1788). See Lester H. Cohen, "Explaining the Revolution: Ideology and Ethics in Mercy Otis Warren's Historical Theory," *William and Mary Quarterly* 38 (April 1980: 200–218, and Cohen, "Mercy Otis Warren: The Politics of Language and the Aesthetics of Self," *American Quarterly* 35 (Winter 1983): 481–98, for a discussion of Warren's political activities during this period.

52. As quoted in entry on Mercy Otis Warren, in *Notable American Women, 1607–1950*, 3 vols., Edward James, Janet James, and Paul S. Boyer, eds. (Cambridge, Mass.: Belknap Press of Harvard Univ. Press, 1971), III, p. 546.

53. Writing about another of the public women of these years, Judith Sargent Murray, Mary Beth Norton asserts: "All the reformers agreed, in other words, that the key to creating—or more accurately, to perpetuating—the republican woman of late eighteenth-century America lay in changing the course of female education." Norton, *Liberty's Daughters*, 255.

54. Claire Curtiss McDonald, from an old Sheffield family, was my informant on the folklore. In 1976 the citizens of Sheffield staged a play about Mumbet as their bicenntenial event, and Ms. McDonald played the role of Mrs. Ashley, the cruel mistress.

55. Catharine Sedgwick, "Slavery in New England," *Bentley's Magazine* 34 (1853): 417–24.

56. Arthur Zilversmit, "Quok Walker, Mumbet, and the Abolition of Slavery in Massachusetts," *William and Mary Quarterly* 25 (Oct. 1968): 614–24.

57. Zilversmit says he thinks the suit was arranged to test the constitutionality of slavery (under the state constitution) in Massachusetts. Ibid.

58. Cohen, "Mercy Otis Warren: The Politics of Language," 485.

59. Ibid., 498.

60. As quoted in Harriet Martineau, *Society in America*, Seymour Martin Lipset, ed. (Gloucester, Mass.: Peter Smith, 1968), 126.

Chapter 4. The Power of the Word

1. Mary Kelley is the pioneer on the subject. See Kelley, *Private Woman, Public Stage: Literary Domesticity in Nineteenth-Century America* (New York: Oxford Univ. Press, 1984). See also Barbara Bardes and Suzanne Gossett, *Declarations of Independence: Women and Political Power in Nineteenth-Century American Fiction* (New Brunswick: Rutgers Univ. Press, 1990).

2. As quoted in Patricia Meyer Spacks, *Gossip* (Chicago: Univ. of Chicago Press, 1985), 10.

3. See the discussion of this theme in ibid., 262.

4. Ian Watt, *The Rise of the Novel: Studies in Defoe, Richardson, and Fielding* (Berkeley: Univ. of California Press, 1957), 138. Recent works on women and the rise of the novel are Nancy Armstrong, *Desire and Domestic Fiction: A Political History of the Novel* (New York: Oxford Univ. Press, 1987), and Jane Spencer, *The Rise of the Woman Novelist: From Aphra Behn to Jane Austen* (Oxford: Basil Blackwell, 1986).

5. Defoe may have some claim to this title. Nonetheless, according to Watt:

> Richardson's deep imaginative commitment to all the problems of the new sexual ideology and his personal devotion to the exploration of the private and subjective aspects of human experience produced a novel where the relationship between the protagonists embodies a universe of moral and social conflicts of a scale and complexity beyond anything in previous fiction.

Watt, *The Rise of the Novel*, 220.

6. Keith Thomas, "Review of Roger Chartier, ed., *A History of Private Life*, vol. III, *Passions of the Renaissance*," *New York Review of Books*, Nov. 9, 1989.

7. Watt, *The Rise of the Novel*, 201.

8. Ibid., 152, 153.

9. Armstrong, *Desire and Domestic Fiction*, 29.

10. See Jay Fliegelman, *Prodigals and Pilgrims: The American Revolution against Patriarchal Authority* (Cambridge, Eng.: Cambridge Univ. Press, 1982), on Richardson's popularity in the United States. He even quotes (p. 89) John Adams as saying, "The people are Clarissa."

11. Carol F. Karlsen and Laurie Crumpacker, eds., *The Journal of Esther Edwards Burr, 1754–1757* (New Haven: Yale Univ. Press, 1984), 98.

12. On this subject see Spencer, *The Rise of the Woman Novelist*.

13. An insightful book on this subject in the nineteenth century is Deirdre David, *Intellectual Women and Victorian Patriarchy: Harriet Martineau, Elizabeth Barrett Browning, and George Eliot* (Ithaca: Cornell Univ. Press, 1987).

14. Jan Lewis, "The Republican Wife: Virtue and Seduction in the Early Republic," *William and Mary Quarterly* 44 (1987): 689–721, p. 716. Rowson lived in the United States as a child and then returned to England. Later on, she moved back to the United States and ran a school. *Charlotte Temple* went into 200 editions.

15. See Cathy N. Davidson, *Revolution and the Word: The Rise of the Novel in America* (New York: Oxford Univ. Press, 1986), 75–78 on the extent to which this novel was loved.

16. Lewis, "The Republican Wife," 698.

17. Susanna Haswell Rowson, *Charlotte Temple*, edited with an introduction by Cathy N. Davidson (New York: Oxford Univ. Press, 1986), 29.

18. Mrs. Hannah W. Foster, *The Coquette*, edited with an introduction by Cathy N. Davidson (New York: Oxford Univ. Press, 1986), 44.

19. On the subject of moralistic attacks on novel reading in the early Republic, see Davidson, *Revolution and the Word*. There is no evidence that either Rowson or Foster was singled out for particular attack, but they must have known the risks.

20. Ibid., 114.

21. Relevant works illuminating the power of domesticity include Nancy Cott, *The Bonds of Womanhood: "Woman's Sphere" in New England, 1780–1835* (New Haven: Yale Univ. Press, 1977), and Kathryn Kish Sklar, *Catharine Beecher: A Study in American Domesticity* (New Haven: Yale Univ. Press, 1973). See also Nina Baym, *Woman's Fiction: A Guide to Novels by and about Women in America, 1820–1870* (Ithaca: Cornell Univ. Press, 1978); Mary Kelley, *Private Woman, Public Stage;* Jane Tompkins, *Sensational Designs: The Cultural Work of American Fiction, 1790–1860* (New York: Oxford Univ. Press, 1985); Matthews, *"Just a Housewife": The Rise and Fall of Domesticity in America* (New York: Oxford Univ. Press, 1987).

22. Catharine Maria Sedgwick, *Hope Leslie; or, Early Times in the Massachusetts*, edited and with an introduction by Mary Kelley (New Brunswick: Rutgers Univ. Press, 1987).

23. Helen Waite Papashvily, *All the Happy Endings: A Study of the Domestic Novel in America, the Woman Who Wrote it, the Women Who Read it, in the Nineteenth Century* (New York: Harper and Brothers, 1956).

24. Ann Douglas, *The Feminization of American Culture* (New York: Alfred A. Knopf, 1978).

25. Kelley, *Private Woman, Public Stage.*

26. Baym, *Woman's Fiction.*

27. Tompkins, *Sensational Designs.*

28. Ibid., 145.

29. Susan K. Harris, *19th-Century American Women's Novels: Interpretative Strategies* (Cambridge: Cambridge Univ. Press, 1990), 210.

30. Bardes and Gossett, *Declarations of Independence*, 184.

31. My point here is that woman has usually been seen as closer to nature than man. She could "unfold" while he needed to learn. On female *Bildungsromans* see Beverly R. Voloshin, "The Limits of Domesticity: The Female *Bildungsromans* in America," *Women's Studies* 10 (1984): 283–302.

32. I regard *The Wide, Wide World* and much of Stowe as being especially noteworthy in this regard. See Matthews, *"Just a Housewife,"* chaps. 1 and 2 for an extended discussion of this subject.

33. Kelley, *Private Woman, Public Stage*, 153.

34. Nina Auerbach, *Communities of Women: An Idea in Fiction* (Cambridge, Mass.: Harvard Univ. Press, 1978); Sarah Elbert, *A Hunger for Home: Louisa May Alcott and Little Women* (Philadelphia: Temple Univ. Press, 1984).

35. On the female Gothic, see Ellen Moers, *Literary Women: The Great Writers* (Garden City, N.Y.: Anchor Books, 1977), chap. 5.

36. Spencer, *The Rise of the Woman Novelist*, 5; see also Nina Baym, *Novels, Readers, and Reviewers: Responses to Fiction in Antebellum America* (Ithaca: Cornell Univ. Press, 1984), for the argument that novels were respectable by the mid-nineteenth century.

37. Kelley, *Private Woman, Public Stage*, 14–16.

38. Elizabeth Fox-Genovese, *Within the Plantation Household: Black and White Women of the Old South* (Chapel Hill: Univ. of North Carolina Press, 1988), 245–47.

39. Harriet E. Wilson, *Our Nig*, introduction by Henry Louis Gates, Jr. (New York: Random House, 1983), introduction.

40. Ibid.

41. Ibid.

42. Harriet A. Jacobs, *Incidents in the Life of a Slave Girl*, Jean Fagan Yellin, ed. (Cambridge, Mass.: Harvard Univ. Press, 1987), 36.

43. Slaves "married," but if their masters chose to separate a married couple by selling one away from the other, they had no recourse. Moreover, a slave might fall in love with someone on a neighboring plantation and be denied permission to spend time with the loved one. Finally, as with the case of "Linda Brent," a jealous master might arrogate a slave woman only to himself.

44. See the discussion of this subject in Fox-Genovese, *Within the Plantation Household*, 375–96.

45. It seems to me that this is true irrespective of whether every word of the narrative is factually accurate.

46. Rebecca Harding Davis, *Life in the Iron Mills*, Tillie Olsen, ed. (New York: Feminist Press, 1975).

47. See Kelley, *Private Woman, Public Stage*, on the psychic cost to women of publishing.

48. Henry F. May, *Coming to Terms: A Study in Memory and History* (Berkeley: Univ. of California Press, 1987), 63.

49. Stowe, *Oldtown Folks*, edited with an introduction by Dorothy Berkson (New Brunswick: Rutgers Univ. Press, 1987), 283.

50. I am indebted to a women's studies class at Irvine for much valuable

insight on this subject. We read *Oldtown Folks* in conjunction with George Eliot's *Adam Bede*, and all of us were struck by how much more generous Stowe is to Emily than is Eliot to Hetty Sorrel, her seduced heroine. I might also say that I assigned the Stowe novel after having read and loved it some years earlier. Upon rereading it just before the class, I was filled with trepidation, because it contains so much technical detail about Calvinism. To my delight, my students loved it, too, because there are so many strong and admirable women characters in it.

51. Barbara Sicherman, "Sense and Sensibility: A Case Study of Women's Reading in Late-Victorian America," Cathy N. Davidson, ed., *Reading in America: Literature and Social History* (Baltimore: Johns Hopkins Univ. Press, 1989), 214.

Chapter 5. "Woman's Place" and Public Space, 1800–1860

1. Sarah Josepha Hale, "Editor's Table," *Godey's* (July 1853), 84f.

2. Hale, "Editor's Table," *Godey's* (March 1852), 228f.

3. Mary Kelley, *Private Woman, Public Stage: Literary Domesticity in Nineteenth-Century America* (New York: Oxford Univ. Press, 1984), vii.

4. As cited in Nancy Cott, *The Bonds of Womanhood: "Woman's Sphere" in New England, 1780–1835* (New Haven: Yale Univ. Press, 1977), 35 n. 21.

5. On this topic see Lawrence Cremin, *American Education: The National Experience, 1783–1876* (New York: Harper and Row, 1980); Anne Firor Scott, "The Ever-Widening Circle: The Diffusion of Feminist Values from the Troy Female Seminary, 1822–1872," *History of Education Quarterly* (Spring 1979): 3–25; Kathryn Kish Sklar, *Catharine Beecher: A Study in American Domesticity* (New Haven: Yale Univ. Press, 1973).

6. Polly Welts Kaufman, *Women Teachers on the Frontier* (New Haven: Yale Univ. Press, 1984), 23f.

7. As quoted in ibid., 120.

8. Ibid., 159.

9. Ibid., 34.

10. My account of the Lowell women is based on Thomas Dublin, *Women at Work: The Transformation of Work and Community in Lowell, Massachusetts, 1826–1860* (New York: Columbia Univ. Press, 1979). I'll deal with other groups of women factory operatives more substantively when the focus is on working-class women in Chapter 9. The quote is from Harriet Hanson Robinson, *Loom and Spindle or Life Among the Early Mill Girls*, intro. by Jane Wilkins Pultz (Kailua, Hawaii: Press Pacifica, 1976), 53.

11. As quoted in Dublin, *Women at Work*, 91.

12. Ibid., 93.

13. Linda K. Kerber, " 'I Have Don . . . Much to Carrey on the Warr': Women and the Shaping of Republican Ideology after the American Revolution," Harriet B. Applewhite and Darline G. Levy, eds., *Women and Politics in the Age of the Democratic Revolution* (Ann Arbor: Univ. of Michigan Press, 1990), 229.

14. See John Mack Faragher, *Women and Men on the Overland Trail* (New Haven: Yale Univ. Press, 1979), and Julie Roy Jeffrey, *Frontier Women* (New York: Hill & Wang, 1979), for a discussion of the way in which westering women clung to familiar patterns. See Matthews, *"Just a Housewife": The Rise and Fall of Domesticity in America* (New York: Oxford Univ. Press, 1987), for a discussion of the ways in which domesticity empowered women. As I did the research for *"Just a Housewife"*, I was repeatedly struck by how political the domestic advice treatises were; that is, the writers of such treatises frequently intermingled technical advice with the language of republicanism.

15. Professor Patricia Cline Cohen of the University of California at Santa Barbara is engaged in researching this topic in depth.

16. Elizabeth Fox-Genovese, *Within the Plantation Household: Black and White Women of the Old South* (Chapel Hill: Univ. of North Carolina Press, 1989), 195.

17. Rebecca Harding Davis, *Life in the Iron Mills and Other Stories*, Tillie Olsen, ed. (New York: Feminist Press, 1985), as quoted in introduction, p. 101.

18. The word "promiscuous" repeatedly shows up to characterize an audience or other assemblage composed of both men and women.

19. Frances Trollope, *Domestic Manners of the Americans*, Herbert Van Thal, ed. (London: Folio Society, 1974), 33–37.

20. Ibid., 140.

21. Frederika Bremer, *The Homes of the New World, Impressions of America*, Mary Howitt, trans., vol. I (New York: Harper & Brothers, 1853), 37.

22. Ibid., vol. II (London: Arthur Hall, Virtue, 1853), 235.

23. Ibid., 256.

24. Louisa May Alcott, *Hospital Sketches* (Boston: James Redpath, 1863), 17.

25. Ibid., 22–27.

26. It is important to point out that free black women did not receive the same courtesies while traveling as did white women. I will discuss this subject in the next chapter.

27. Nathan D. Hatch, *The Democratization of American Christianity* (New Haven: Yale Univ. Press, 1989), 3–5. Donald G. Mathews says about

the Second Great Awakening: "Indeed, it may have been the greatest organization and mobilization of women in American history." See Mathews, "The Second Great Awakening as an Organizing Process, 1780–1830: An Hypothesis," *American Quarterly* 21 (Spring 1969): 23–42, p. 42.

28. Hatch, *The Democratization of American Christianity*, 56.

29. For a discussion of church architecture in this vein see Rhys Isaac, *The Transformation of Virginia, 1740–1790* (Chapel Hill: Univ. of North Carolina Press, 1982), 58–63.

30. Trollope, *Domestic Manners of the Americans*, 75.

31. Hatch, *The Democratization of American Christianity*, 78f.

32. Jarena Lee's autobiography has been reprinted in William L. Andrews, *Sisters of the Spirit: Three Black Women's Autobiographies of the Nineteenth Century* (Bloomington: Indiana Univ. Press, 1986). My account is drawn from Andrews's introduction as well as from the autobiography itself.

33. Cott, *Bonds of Womanhood*, 135.

34. Mary P. Ryan, *Cradle of the Middle Class: The Family in Oneida County, New York, 1790–1865* (Cambridge, Eng.: Cambridge Univ. Press, 1981), 83f.

35. Joanna Bowen Gillespie, " 'The Clear Leadings of Providence': Memoirs and the Problems of Self-Realization for Women in the Early Nineteenth Century," *Journal of the Early Republic* 5 (Summer 1985): 197–221, p. 199f.

36. Ibid., 211.

37. For an excellent assessment of the strengths and limitations of domesticity see Jeanne Boydston, Mary Kelley, and Anne Margolis, *The Limits of Sisterhood: The Beecher Sisters on Women's Rights and Woman's Sphere* (Chapel Hill: Univ. of North Carolina Press, 1988).

38. Sue Bridwell Beckham suggests that the front porch was a quintessentially American architectural development, and that it came into its own during the high-water period of domesticity. See Beckham, "The American Front Porch: Women's Liminal Space," in Marilyn Motz and Pat Browne, eds., *Making the American Home: Middle-Class Women and Domestic Material Culture, 1840–1940* (Bowling Green, Ohio: Bowling Green State Univ. Popular Press, 1988).

39. Although he does not pay much heed to gender, Paul Boyer is insightful on the anxiety engendered by this change. See Boyer, *Urban Masses and Moral Order in America, 1820–1920* (Cambridge, Mass.: Harvard Univ. Press, 1978).

40. Christine Stansell, *City of Women: Sex and Class in New York, 1789–1860* (Urbana: Univ. of Illinois Press, 1987), 27.

41. Ibid., 93.

42. Paul A. Gilje, *The Road to Mobocracy: Popular Disorder in New*

York City, 1763–1834 (Chapel Hill: Univ. of North Carolina Press, 1987), 213.

43. Mary P. Ryan, *Women in Public: Between Banners and Ballots, 1825–1880* (Baltimore: Johns Hopkins Univ. Press, 1990), 139.

44. Elizabeth Cady Stanton, Susan B. Anthony, and Matilda Joslyn Gage, eds., *History of Woman Suffrage*, vol. I (Salem, N.H.: Ayer Company, 1985), 465.

45. Carroll Smith-Rosenberg, "Beauty, the Beast, and the Militant Woman: A Case Study in Sex Roles and Social Stress in Jacksonian America," in Smith-Rosenberg, *Disorderly Conduct: Visions of Gender in Victorian America* (New York: Oxford Univ. Press, 1986).

46. Claudia D. Johnson, *American Actress: Perspective on the Nineteenth Century* (Chicago: Nelson-Hall, 1984), 3.

47. Ibid. See also the following: James H. Dormon, Jr., *Theater in the Ante Bellum South, 1805–1861* (Chapel Hill: Univ. of North Carolina Press, 1967); Weldon B. Durham, *American Theatre Companies, 1749–1887* (New York: Greenwood Press, 1986); Joanne Lafler, "The Profession of Actress," unpublished paper; Lawrence W. Levine, *Highbrow, Lowbrow: The Emergence of Cultural Hierarchy in America* (Cambridge, Mass.: Harvard Univ. Press, 1988); Mary Ryan, *Women in Public*.

48. My account is principally based on the superb biography by Celia Morris. See Morris, *Fanny Wright: Rebel in America* (Urbana, Ill.: Univ. of Illinois Press, 1992).

49. Ibid., 80–82.

50. Ibid., 156.

51. Ibid., 171f.

52. Trollope, *Domestic Manners*, 68–70.

53. As quoted in Sean Wilentz, *Chants Democratic: New York City and the Rise of the American Working Class, 1788–1850* (New York: Oxford Univ. Press, 1984), 177.

54. Ibid., 176–83.

55. John D'Emilio and Estelle Freedman, *Intimate Matters: A History of Sexuality in America* (New York: Harper & Row, 1988), 114.

56. Anne Firor Scott, "Most Invisible of All: Black Women's Voluntary Associations," *Journal of Southern History* 56 (Feb. 1990): 3–22. See also Gary B. Nash, *Forging Freedom: The Formation of Philadelphia's Black Community, 1720–1840* (Cambridge, Mass.: Harvard Univ. Press, 1988), for an account of the black community in Philadelphia, the largest in the country.

57. Marilyn Richardson, ed., *Maria W. Stewart: America's First Black Woman Political Writer: Essays and Speeches* (Bloomington: Indiana Univ. Press, 1987), 24, 25.

58. Ibid., 19, 20.

266

NOTES

59. Stanton et al., *History of Woman Suffrage*, 473.

60. *The Boston Morning Post*, Aug. 25, 1837, as quoted in Gerda Lerner, *The Grimké Sisters from South Carolina: Pioneers for Woman's Rights and Abolition* (New York: Schocken, 1971), 205.

61. Sarah M. Grimké, *Letters on the Equality of the Sexes and the Condition of Women* (New York: Burt Franklin, 1970), 118.

62. Stanton et al., *History of Woman Suffrage*, 476.

63. Elizabeth Cazden, *Antoinette Brown Blackwell: A Biography* (Old Westbury, N.Y.: Feminist Press, 1983), 27–40.

64. Ibid., 41–57.

65. Olive Gilbert, *Narrative of Sojourner Truth: A Bondswoman of Olden Times* (Boston: published for the author, 1875).

66. Stanton et al., *History of Woman Suffrage*, 473.

67. Elizabeth Brown Pryor, *Clara Barton: Professional Angel* (Philadelphia: Univ. of Pennsylvania Press, 1987), 48.

68. Kaufman, *Women Teachers on the Frontier*, 33.

69. Much current scholarship suggests that even working-class women, with rare exceptions, saw themselves as "true women." See, for example, Mary H. Blewett, *Men, Women, and Work: Class, Gender, and Protest in the New England Shoe Industry, 1780–1910* (Urbana: Univ. of Illinois Press, 1988).

70. Anne Firor Scott, "Women's Voluntary Associations: From Charity to Reform," in Kathleen McCarthy, ed., *Lady Bountiful Revisited: Women, Philanthropy and Power* (New Brunswick, N.J.: Rutgers Univ. Press, 1990).

71. Nancy A. Hewitt, *Women's Activism and Social Change: Rochester, New York, 1822–1872* (Ithaca: Cornell Univ. Press, 1984), 246–49. See also Lori D. Ginzberg, *Women and the Work of Benevolence: Morality, Politics, and Class in the Nineteenth-Century United States* (New Haven: Yale Univ. Press, 1990), 65, for the argument that the women in Hewitt's "benevolent" category were also serving their own class interests.

72. On Seneca Falls see Ellen Carol DuBois, *Feminism and Suffrage: The Emergence of an Independent Women's Movement in America, 1848–1869* (Ithaca: Cornell Univ. Press, 1978), and Eleanor Flexner, *Century of Struggle: The Woman's Rights Movement in the United States*, rev. ed. (Cambridge, Mass.: Belknap Press of Harvard Univ. Press, 1975).

73. As quoted in Flexner, *Century of Struggle*, 76.

74. As reprinted in Aileen S. Kraditor, ed., *Up from the Pedestal: Selected Writings in the History of American Feminism* (Chicago: Quadrangle Books, 1970).

75. Blanche Glassman Hersh, *The Slavery of Sex: Feminist-Abolitionists in America* (Urbana: Univ. of Illinois Press, 1978), 62.

76. See Linda Gordon, *Woman's Body, Woman's Right: A Social His-

tory of Birth Control in America (New York: Penguin Books, 1977), chap. 5 for a discussion of voluntary motherhood, by which Gordon means a married woman's right to say no to her husband's sexual advances. This marked the limits of what it was possible to discuss at all openly in the nineteenth century. It should be noted that the public culture was sufficiently reticent about sex that men were not encouraged to be particularly forthcoming either, by modern standards at least.

77. John Mack Faragher, *Sugar Creek: Life on the Illinois Prairie* (New Haven: Yale Univ. Press, 1986), 151, 214. See also Ryan, *Women in Public* on women and public rituals. She argues the following: "Between 1825 and the outbreak of the Civil War, gender made a progressively more distinct and consequential impression on a remodeled public life. The female gender stood out in sharpest relief on ceremonial occasions . . . but as a symbol of newly feminine civic values—chastity, sobriety, passivity, domesticity" (p. 173).

78. Ryan, *Women in Public*, 76f.

79. As quoted in Pryor, *Clara Barton*, 55–58.

80. Ibid., 61f.

81. Hersh, *The Slavery of Sex*, 42, 43.

Chapter 6. Northern Women and the Crisis of the Union

1. Mary P. Ryan, *Women in Public: Between Banners and Ballots, 1825–1880* (Baltimore: Johns Hopkins Univ. Press, 1990), 142–46.

2. The word "feminism" was not coined until much later. On its popularization in the United States (it originated in France) see Nancy F. Cott, *The Grounding of Modern Feminism* (New Haven: Yale Univ. Press, 1987), 14, 15.

3. Georgianna Woolsey Bacon and Eliza Woolsey Howland, *Letters of a Family During the War for the Union, 1861–1865* (printed for private distribution, 1899), 142–44.

4. Anne Firor Scott, *The Southern Lady: From Pedestal to Politics, 1830–1930* (Chicago: Univ. of Chicago Press, 1970).

5. Suzanne Lebsock, *The Free Women of Petersburg: Status and Culture in a Southern Town, 1784–1860* (New York: W. W. Norton, 1984).

6. Jacqueline Jones, *Labor of Love, Labor of Sorrow: Black Women, Work, and the Family from Slavery to the Present* (New York: Vintage, 1985), 51.

7. George C. Rable, *Civil Wars: Women and the Crisis of Southern Nationalism* (Urbana: Univ. of Illinois Press, 1989), 39. It should be pointed out

that Rable provides details of many incidents in which southern women were quite critical of male authority, especially late in the war.

8. Drew Gilpin Faust, "Altars of Sacrifice: Confederate Women and the Narratives of War," *Journal of American History* 76 (March 1990): 1200–1228, p. 1228.

9. L. P. Brockett, M.D., and Miss Mary C. Vaughan, *Woman's Work in the Civil War: A Record of Heroism, Patriotism and Patience,* intro. by Henry Bellows (Philadelphia: Zeigler, McCurdy, 1867), 279–83.

10. A letter from Bellows and others to Simon Cameron, May 18, 1861, USSC Documents, vol. I, no. 1, detailed the three participating associations: Woman's Central, Advisory Commission of the Boards of Physicians and Surgeons of the Hospitals of New York, and the New York Medical Association for Furnishing Hospital Supplies in Aid of the Army.

11. This report is USSC Documents, vol. I, no. 32. It should also be mentioned that there was another commission, the Christian Commission, originally designed to provide spiritual comfort to the men, which eventually provided supplies, too.

12. Charles J. Stillé, *History of the United States Sanitary Commission* (Philadelphia: J. B. Lippincott, 1866), 44.

13. George M. Fredrickson, *The Inner Civil War: Northern Intellectuals and the Crisis of the Union* (New York: Harper & Row, 1965), chap. 7.

14. Brockett and Vaughan, *Woman's Work in the Civil War,* 83–85.

15. Elizabeth Brown Pryor, *Clara Barton: Professional Angel* (Philadelphia: Univ. of Pennsylvania Press, 1987), 83.

16. Ibid., 96–99.

17. Stillé, *History of the United States Sanitary Commission,* 169–79. Brockett and Vaughan provide the estimate of 50 million individual gifts. Brockett and Vaughan, *Woman's Work in the Civil War,* 66.

18. Mary A. Livermore, *My Story of the War: A Woman's Narrative of Four Years Personal Experience* (Hartford, Conn.: A. D. Worthington, 1889), 513.

19. Ibid., 157.

20. James M. McPherson, *Ordeal by Fire: The Civil War and Reconstruction* (New York: Alfred A. Knopf, 1982), 383f.

21. Ibid., 385. Nina Bennett Smith gives the figure of 9000 women who nursed for the Union Army. See Smith, "The Women Who Went to the War: The Union Army Nurse in the Civil War" (Ph.D. dissertation, Northwestern University, 1981), 3.

22. Both Hoge and Livermore wrote about this incident in their memoirs. The quote is from Hoge, *The Boys in Blue* (E. B. Treat, 1867), 91.

23. This was no doubt the first time the federal government had called

so directly on the country's women for help. By the time of the world wars in the twentieth century, the federal bureaucracy was considerably larger and more complex. While the government needed cooperation from its women in the twentieth century, too, I believe there was less play in the system in the later period.

24. On Howe see Deborah Pickman Clifford, *Mine Eyes Have Seen the Glory* (Boston: Little, Brown, 1979).

25. Ryan, *Women in Public*, 42.

26. This correspondence can be found in the Sarah Josepha Hale Papers in the Huntington Library, San Marino, California.

27. Anna Dickinson to William Lloyd Garrison, March 16, 1862, Anna Dickinson Papers, Library of Congress.

28. Garrison to Dickinson, March 27, 1862, Dickinson Papers, LC.

29. Elizabeth Cady Stanton, Susan B. Anthony, and Matilda Joslyn Gage, *History of Woman Suffrage*, vol. II, pp. 40–49.

30. Susan B. Anthony to Dickinson, June 19, 1867; J. D. Humphrey to Dickinson, June 19, 1867, Dickinson Papers, LC.

31. Henry Homes to Dickinson, Nov. 28, 1863, Dickinson Papers, LC.

32. Wendy F. Hamand, "The Women's National Loyal League: Feminist Abolitionists and the Civil War," *Civil War History* 35 (March 1989): 39–58.

33. Stanton et al., *History of Woman Suffrage*, vol. II, p. 23.

34. Bacon and Howland, *Letters of a Family*, 27–31.

35. Brockett and Vaughan, *Woman's Work in the Civil War*, Bellows intro., p. 40f.

36. A whole cult seems to have grown up around Anna Ellen Carroll of Maryland, who claimed to have been responsible for suggesting crucial military strategies that were employed by the Union Army. Many women took her seriously in the late nineteenth century. A book which is a brief for Carroll is Sarah Ellen Blackwell, *A Military Genius: Life of Anna Ellen Carroll* (Washington, D.C.: pub. by the *Woman's Journal*, 1891).

37. Bacon and Howland, *Letters of a Family*, 161–64.

38. Annie Wittenmyer, *Under the Guns: A Woman's Reminiscences of the Civil War* (Boston: E. B. Stillings, 1895), 106–14. See also Glenda Riley, "Annie Turner Wittenmyer, Reformer," *Iowa Woman* 6 (Sept. 1986): 26–33.

39. John R. Brumgardt, ed., *Civil War Nurse: The Diary and Letters of Hannah Ropes* (Knoxville: Univ. of Tennessee Press, 1980), 80–89.

40. Livermore, *My Story of the War*, 224. Other sources document this phenomenon, too.

41. Bacon and Howland, *Letters of a Family*, 522f.

42. Livermore, *My Story of the War*, 476f. According to Nina Bennett

Smith, "By 1864 Sherman's troops called her 'General' as often as they did 'Mother'; by the closing days of the War, she had her own horse and rode where she willed, often receiving salutes from the soldiers she passed." Smith, "The Women Who Went to the War," 77.

43. Mary A. Gardner Holland, *Our Army Nurses* (Boston: Lounsbery, Nichols, and Worth, 1897), 532.

44. Livermore devotes several admiring chapters of her memoir to Bickerdyke, but archival material suggests that their wartime working relationship was occasionally strained. See, for example, Bickerdyke to Julia Clark, May 1, 1865, Lincoln Clark Papers, Huntington Library, for a letter in which Bickerdyke complained of the treatment she had received from Livermore. The Huntington Library has several of Bickerdyke's letters, all dictated to an amanuensis.

45. Livermore, *My Story of the War*, 511.

46. Bickerdyke to Mrs. Colt, written by Catherine Lincoln Clark, March 14, 1864; Eliza Porter to Julia Clark, May 23, 1864, Lincoln Clark Papers, Huntington Library.

47. William Quentin Maxwell, *Lincoln's Fifth Wheel: The Political History of the United States Sanitary Commission* (New York: Longman, Green, 1956), 301; Livermore, *My Story of the War*, 516.

48. Brockett and Vaughan, *Woman's Work in the Civil War*, Bellows introduction, pp. 40–42. A recent work with a quite different interpretative framework is Lori D. Ginzberg, *Women and the Work of Benevolence: Morality, Politics, and Class in the Nineteenth-Century United States* (New Haven: Yale Univ. Press, 1990). Says Ginzberg:

> If benevolent women (and a few men) sought in the 1830s and early 1840s to control male passions by infusing the male realm with female virtues, the Civil War gave a new generation an opportunity to reverse completely that rhetoric. Increasingly, male values were viewed as necessary to control and limit a female effusion of emotion, sensibility, or passion; either those sensibilities would submit to law and system or they would become entirely ineffective, even dangerous. The wartime masculinizing of the ideology of benevolence consolidated trends that had been apparent in the 1850s. It pushed women—many of whom continued to accept an ideology of benevolence based on female values—further from the symbolic and real centers of power for social change" (p. 173).

I find this to be provocative, but not entirely convincing: Ginzberg sees the Civil War as, in effect, a time of declension. Moreover, the scale of operation during the war made efficiency a necessity, it seems to me, rather than efficiency representing the triumph of "male" values. Nonetheless, I agree that male values were gaining renewed stature, a trend that would become fully manifest during the Gilded Age.

49. Livermore, *My Story of the War*, 503–5.

50. Ibid., 410–55.

51. Rable, *Civil Wars*, 47.

52. Bacon and Howland, *Letters of a Family*, 219.

53. Brockett and Vaughan, *Woman's Work in the Civil War*, Bellows introduction, p. 39.

54. Henrietta Stratton Jaquette, ed., *South after Gettysburg: Letters of Cornelia Hancock from the Army of the Potomac* (Philadelphia: Univ. of Pennsylvania Press, 1937), 1–47.

55. Ibid., 92.

56. Ibid., 85.

57. Ibid., 97f, 103f, 143.

58. Frederick Law Olmsted, *A Memoir* (Boston: Ticknor and Fields, 1863), 32f.

59. Bacon and Howland, *Letters of a Family*, 594.

60. As quoted by Georgianna Woolsey in ibid., 596.

61. Louisa May Alcott, *Hospital Sketches* (Boston: James Redpath, 1863), 35–37.

62. See Gary B. Nash, *Forging Freedom: The Formation of Philadelphia's Black Community, 1720–1840* (Cambridge, Mass.: Harvard Univ. Press, 1988), for information about the Forten family.

63. Ray Allen Billington, ed., *The Journal of Charlotte L. Forten* (New York: W. W. Norton, 1981), 10.

64. Ibid.

65. See Pryor, *Clara Barton*. There will be more on this in the next chapter.

66. Livermore, *My Story of the War*, 188, 314–18.

67. Ibid., 604.

68. Livermore, *The Story of My Life* (Hartford, Conn.: A. D. Worthington, 1899), 604–8.

69. Billington, *The Journal of Charlotte L. Forten*, 187.

70. [Katherine Prescott Wormeley], *The United States Sanitary Commission* (Boston: Little, Brown, 1863); Wormeley, *The Other Side of War* (Boston: Ticknor, 1889). Wormeley was the daughter of a British rear admiral.

71. Adelaide W. Smith, *Reminiscences of an Army Nurse During the Civil War* (New York: Greaves, 1911), 153f.

72. Wormeley, *The Other Side of War*, introduction, 246.

73. James Phinney Munroe, ed., *Adventures of an Army Nurse in Two Wars* (Boston: Little, Brown, 1904), 164.

74. Elizabeth Keckley, *Behind the Scenes* (New York: G. W. Carleton, 1868), 113.

75. Mary Elizabeth Massey, *Bonnet Brigades* (New York: Alfred A. Knopf, 1966).

76. Marilyn Richardson, ed., *Maria W. Stewart: America's First Black Woman Political Writer: Essays and Speeches* (Bloomington: Indiana Univ. Press, 1987), 84.

77. Olive Gilbert, *Narrative of Sojourner Truth: A Bondswoman of Olden Times* (Boston: published for the author, 1875), 177–90.

78. Rable, *Civil Wars*, 108–11.

79. Ibid., 134.

80. Ryan, *Women in Public*, 149.

81. Bellows to Hoge and Livermore, Oct. 29, 1863, USSC Documents, Vol. II, no. 63. The sheer volume of books about women in the Civil War in the collection of the Huntington Library bears out Bellows's contention.

82. Ibid.

Chapter 7. Public Womanhood and the Incorporation of America

1. Cindy Sondik Aron, *Ladies and Gentlemen of the Civil Service: Middle-Class Workers in Victorian America* (New York: Oxford Univ. Press, 1987), 163.

2. Ibid., 170.

3. My daughter Karen Matthews conducted research on this topic for her senior thesis at Yale. In so doing, she amassed a collection of photocopied articles, from which I was able to draw.

4. *Illustrated Phonographic World*, July 1895, p. 265.

5. *Troy Telegram* as quoted in *The Phonographic Magazine*, May 1890, p. 134.

6. *The Phonographic World*, July 1890, p. 341.

7. Susan Porter Benson, *Counter Cultures: Saleswomen, Managers, and Customers in American Department Stores, 1890–1940* (Urbana: Univ. of Illinois Press, 1986), 20.

8. Ibid., 134, 135.

9. Joanne J. Meyerowitz, *Women Adrift: Independent Wage Earners in Chicago, 1880–1930* (Chicago: Univ. of Chicago Press, 1988), 5. The title

comes from the nomenclature used by contemporaries to describe women living apart from families.

10. Ibid., 17.

11. Mary H. Blewett, *Men, Women, and Work: Class, Gender, and Protest in the New England Shoe Industry, 1780–1910* (Urbana: Univ. of Illinois Press, 1988), 79. I suspect that Stansell's Bowery Gals, harbingers of what was to come, were atypical of the antebellum period. There will be a fuller discussion of this topic in Chapter 9. See Christine Stansell, *City of Women: Sex and Class in New York, 1789–1860* (Urbana: Univ. of Illinois Press, 1987).

12. Blewett, *Men, Women, and Work*, 94.

13. See Elizabeth Israels Perry, *Belle Moskowitz: Feminine Politics and the Exercise of Power in the Age of Alfred E. Smith* (New York: Oxford Univ. Press, 1987).

14. Kathy Peiss, *Cheap Amusements: Working Women and Leisure in Turn-of-the-Century New York* (Philadelphia: Temple Univ. Press, 1986), 184.

15. For a discussion of the impact of Darwinism on woman's culture, see Matthews, *"Just a Housewife": The Rise and Fall of Domesticity in America* (New York: Oxford Univ. Press, 1987), chap. 5. I am not trying to suggest that there was/is a female subjectivity, emerging from the *Zeitgeist* that is trans-racial and trans-class. Nor am I trying to suggest that there is a modal female personality in each distinct historical period. What I do believe to be true is that the possibilities for personal expression change over time, and that every woman alive during a certain period will share to a greater or lesser extent in those possibilities. The ideology of republicanism, for example, made it possible for both Elizabeth Freeman and Mercy Otis Warren to have politicized selves.

16. See Estelle Freedman, "Separatism as Strategy: Female Institution Building and American Feminism, 1870–1930," *Feminist Studies*, 5 (Fall 1979): 512–29, for an insightful discussion of this transition. For a brilliant and broad-ranging critique of woman's culture see Peggy Pascoe, *Relations of Rescue: The Search for Female Moral Authority in the American West, 1874–1934* (New York: Oxford Univ. Press, 1990). Says Pascoe: "But whether the women's culture in question is modern or historical, focusing on the 'female values' at its center draws attention away from the power relations at its boundaries" (p. 210). She thinks that middle-class women "consistently underestimate the differences among groups of women."

17. Elizabeth Cady Stanton, *Eighty Years and More: Reminiscences, 1815–1897* (New York: Schocken, 1971), 253.

18. There is a substantial literature on the relationship between the bearing of arms and citizenship. Linda Kerber is working on this issue.

19. Elizabeth Cady Stanton, Susan B. Anthony, and Matilda Joslyn Gage, eds., *History of Woman Suffrage*, vol. 2 (Salem, N.H.: Ayer Company, 1985).

20. The standard treatment is by Ellen Carol DuBois, *Feminism and Suffrage: The Emergence of an Independent Women's Movement in America, 1848–1864* (Ithaca: Cornell Univ. Press, 1978). See also Eleanor Flexner, *Century of Struggle: The Woman's Rights Movement in the United States*, rev. ed. (Cambridge, Mass.: Harvard Univ. Press, 1975); Carl N. Degler, *At Odds: Women and the Family from the Revolution to the Present* (New York: Oxford Univ. Press, 1980), chap. 14.

21. Ruth Bordin, *Women and Temperance: The Quest for Power and Liberty, 1873–1900* (Philadelphia: Temple Univ. Press, 1981), 17.

22. Ibid., 19.

23. Ibid., 27.

24. In 1939 the WCTU surveyed the number of public buildings, fountains, and other facilities named in honor of Frances Willard: there are dozens, and they exist in many parts of the country.

25. Kathryn Kish Sklar, "Hull House in the 1890s: A Community of Women Reformers," *Signs* 10 (Summer 1985): 658–77, as reprinted in Ellen Carol Dubois and Vicki L. Ruiz, eds., *Unequal Sisters: A Multi-Cultural Reader in U.S. Women's History* (New York: Routledge, 1990), 109.

26. Ibid., 111.

27. Anne Firor Scott, "Most Invisible of All: Black Women's Voluntary Associations," *Journal of Southern History* 56 (Feb. 1990): 3–22, p. 7.

28. Anne Firor Scott, "Women's Voluntary Associations: From Charity to Reform," in Kathleen McCarthy, ed., *Lady Bountiful Revisited: Women, Philanthropy, and Power* (New Brunswick, N.J.: Rutgers Univ. Press, 1990). See also Karen J. Blair, *The Clubwoman as Feminist: True Womanhood Redefined, 1868–1914* (New York: Holmes and Meier, 1980).

29. Elizabeth Brown Pryor, *Clara Barton: Professional Angel* (Philadelphia: Univ. of Pennsylvania Press, 1987), 202–38.

30. See Mari Jo Buhle, *Women and American Socialism, 1870–1920* (Urbana: Univ. of Illinois Press, 1981), chap. 2 on Livermore as a Socialist.

31. See Scott, "Most Invisible of All."

32. Hazel Carby, *Reconstructing Womanhood: The Emergence of the Afro-American Woman Novelist* (New York: Oxford Univ. Press, 1987); Frances E. W. Harper, *Iola Leroy or Shadows Uplifted*, intro. by Hazel Carby (Boston: Beacon Press, 1987).

33. Harper, *Iola Leroy*, 116.

34. On the extent and nature of racist ideologies in the late nineteenth century see George M. Fredrickson, *The Black Image in the White Mind: The*

Debate on Afro-American Character and Destiny, 1817–1914 (New York: Harper & Row, 1971).

35. Ellen Carol DuBois, ed., *Elizabeth Cady Stanton, Susan B. Anthony: Correspondence, Writings, Speeches* (New York: Schocken Books, 1981), 103–4.

36. Ibid., 162.

37. On Stanton and "voluntary motherhood" see Linda Gordon, *Woman's Body, Woman's Right: A Social History of Birth Control in America* (New York: Penguin, 1977), chap. 5.

38. Stanton, *Eighty Years and More*, 452.

39. DuBois, *Stanton and Anthony*, 189.

40. Robert A. Bremner, "Josephine Shaw Lowell," in Edward James, Janet James, and Paul Boyer, eds., *Notable American Women, 1607–1950*, 3 vols. (Cambridge, Mass.: Belknap Press of Harvard Univ. Press, 1971), vol. II, pp. 437–39.

41. George M. Fredrickson, *The Inner Civil War: Northern Intellectuals and the Crisis of the Union* (New York: Harper & Row, 1965), 212–15.

42. For a discussion of the ways in which woman's culture was under attack in these years, see Matthews, *"Just a Housewife"*. I argue that the "bad boy" subgenre of literature, whose most impressive practitioner was Mark Twain, represented an expression of male hostility to domestic feminism and to female attempts to control male drinking behavior.

43. A bottle in the shape of Henry Ward Beecher can be found on display at his sister Harriet's house at Nook Farm in Hartford, Connecticut.

44. Jeanne Boydston, Mary Kelley, and Anne Margolis, eds., *The Limits of Sisterhood: The Beecher Sisters on Women's Rights and Woman's Sphere* (Chapel Hill: Univ. of North Carolina Press, 1988), 295.

45. Stowe's conservatism about sexual morality is revealed in a letter she wrote to Mary Livermore. Undated, it can be presumed from its context to have been written around 1870. She complained because Stanton was praising George Sand in *The Revolution*. Stowe thought that the great Frenchwoman's books were too physical and too animal in their descriptions of love. Letter in the Boston Public Library.

46. Geoffrey Blodgett, "Victoria Woodhull," in *Notable American Women*, vol. III, pp. 652–55.

47. Alice Wexler, *Emma Goldman in America* (Boston: Beacon Press, 1989), xv.

48. Ibid., 75–78.

49. Ibid., 93. In her autobiography Goldman cites the example of the pioneer free-lovers, Moses Harman and Ezra Heywood, among others, from

whom she learned a great deal both about risk-taking and about substantive issues. See Goldman, *Living My Life*, vol. II (New York: Dover, 1970), 553–70. It should also be pointed out that she had heard Sigmund Freud lecture in Vienna in the 1890s.

50. Ibid., chap. 10. See also Candace Falk, *Love, Anarchy, and Emma Goldman* (New York: Holt, Rinehart, and Winston, 1984).

51. Wexler, *Emma Goldman in America*, 165.

52. This, of course, is still one of the major unsolved problems for would-be public women. See Blanche Glassman Hersh, *The Slavery of Sex: Feminist-Abolitionists in America* (Urbana: Univ. of Illinois Press, 1978), for an account of the numerous supportive husbands to be found in nineteenth-century reform circles.

53. As quoted in Alfreda M. Duster, ed., *The Autobiography of Ida B. Wells* (Chicago: Univ. of Chicago Press, 1970), 65f.

54. Ibid., 221.

55. Amy Dru Stanley, "Conjugal Bonds and Wage Labor: Rights of Contract in the Age of Emancipation," *Journal of American History* 75 (Sept. 1988): 471–500, p. 499.

Chapter 8. A Kind of Power: Women and Politics, 1900–1960

1. Michael McGerr, "Political Style and Women's Power, 1830–1930," *Journal of American History* 77 (Dec. 1990): 864–85, p. 878.

2. Ibid., 874.

3. See Ellen Carol DuBois, *Feminism and Suffrage: The Emergence of an Independent Women's Movement in America, 1848–1869* (Ithaca: Cornell Univ. Press, 1978).

4. William H. Chafe, *The American Woman: Her Changing Social, Economic and Political Roles, 1920–1970* (New York: Oxford Univ. Press, 1972), 19.

5. Irwin N. Gertzog, *Congressional Women: Their Recruitment, Treatment, and Behavior* (New York: Praeger, 1984), 3. The figure on women in state legislatures comes from Nancy F. Cott, *The Grounding of Modern Feminism* (New Haven: Yale Univ. Press, 1987), 110.

6. Recent articles include Maureen A. Flanagan, "Gender and Urban Political Reform: The City Club and the Women's City Club of Chicago in the Progressive Era," *American Historical Review* 95 (Oct. 1990): 1032–50; Sonya Michel and Seth Koven, "Womanly Duties: Maternalist Politics and the Origins of Welfare States in France, Germany, Great Britain, and the

United States, 1880–1920," *American Historical Review* 95 (Oct. 1990): 1076–108; S. Sara Monoson, "The Lady and the Tiger: Women's Electoral Activism in New York City Before Suffrage," *Journal of Women's History* 2 (Fall 1990): 100–135. Says Monoson, "The [Woman's Municipal] League was, during the years 1894–1905, an autonomous women's political club. As a separate institution it proved an important source of social and political power for its members . . ." (p. 126).

Having lived in both California and Oklahoma, I have become aware of key figures such as California's Katherine Edson, who pioneered protective labor legislation for women, and Oklahoma's Kate Barnard, who was the state's first Commissioner of Charities and Corrections. Kathryn Kish Sklar's eagerly anticipated biography of Florence Kelley will help us to get a better handle on a subject of enormous importance.

7. Susan Englander, "Right-Minded Women: Clubwomen and the San Francisco Graft Trials," *Journal of History* 1 (June 1989): 11–28. This journal is published by the history department at San Francisco State University.

8. Anne Firor Scott, "Getting to Be a Notable Georgia Woman," in Scott, *Making the Invisible Woman Visible* (Urbana: Univ. of Illinois Press, 1984), 319.

9. Jacquelyn Dowd Hall, *The Revolt against Chivalry: Jessie Daniel Ames and the Women's Campaign Against Lynching* (New York: Columbia Univ. Press, 1979), 65–72. See also Jacqueline Jones, "The Political Implication of Black and White Women's Work in the South, 1890–1965," in Louise A. Tilly and Patricia Gurin, eds., *Women, Politics and Change* (New York: Russell Sage Foundation, 1990).

10. Hall, *The Revolt against Chivalry*, 112.

11. Helen Lefkowitz Horowitz, *Alma Mater: Design and Experience in the Women's Colleges from Their Nineteenth-Century Beginnings to the 1930s* (Boston: Beacon Press, 1984), 282.

12. Paula S. Fass, *The Damned and the Beautiful: American Youth in the 1920's* (New York: Oxford Univ. Press, 1977), chap. 8.

13. Matthews, *"Just a Housewife": The Rise and Fall of Domesticity in America* (New York: Oxford Univ. Press, 1987).

14. On women scientists becoming home economists see Margaret W. Rossiter, *Women Scientists in America: Struggles and Strategies to 1940* (Baltimore: Johns Hopkins Univ. Press, 1982), chap. 7.

15. Susan Ware, *Partner and I: Molly Dewson, Feminism, and New Deal Politics* (New Haven: Yale Univ. Press, 1987), chap. 12.

16. Cott, *The Grounding of Modern Feminism*, 95.

17. Chafe, *The American Woman*, 36.

18. Matthews, *"Just a Housewife"*, chap. 6.

19. Kristi Andersen, "Women and Citizenship in the 1920s," Louise A. Tilly and Patricia Gurin, eds., *Women, Politics, and Change* (New York: Russell Sage Foundation, 1990). On black women's voting behavior see Sandra Baxter and Marjorie Lansing, *Women and Politics: The Invisible Majority* (Ann Arbor: Univ. of Michigan Press, 1980).

20. Cott, *The Grounding of Modern Feminism*, 76. It should be noted that when one is talking about events of 1920 and later, it is no longer anachronistic to use the word "feminist."

21. See ibid. for a further discussion of this subject. See also Chafe, *The American Woman*.

22. The quote furnishes the frontispiece to William L. O'Neill, *Everyone Was Brave: A History of Feminism in America* (Chicago: Quadrangle Books, 1969). On the New York network see Elizabeth Israels Perry, *Belle Moskowitz: Feminine Politics and the Exercise of Power in the Age of Alfred E. Smith* (New York: Oxford Univ. Press, 1987), chap. 8.

23. Robert A. Caro, *The Power Broker: Robert Moses and the Fall of New York* (New York: Vintage, 1975), 91.

24. Perry, *Belle Moskowitz*, xii.

25. Ibid., 161.

26. Chafe, *The American Woman*, 29.

27. Racial ethnic women will be discussed later in the chapter.

28. See Gertzog, *Congressional Women*, chap. 1, on the characteristics of the early congresswomen.

29. Ware, *Beyond Suffrage: Women in the New Deal* (Cambridge, Mass.: Harvard Univ. Press, 1981); Ware, *Partner and I*, 1987.

30. Ware, *Partner and I*, 145.

31. In *Beyond Suffrage* Ware provides a valuable list of all these women. No doubt they exceeded the total in all previous administrations combined.

32. Ware, *Beyond Suffrage*, 87.

33. Ibid., 192.

34. Chafe, *The American Woman*, 152. In his entry on Eleanor Roosevelt in *Notable American Women*, Chafe says that ER and FDR became more distant during the war; indeed, he says that they were frequently adversaries. William H. Chafe, "Anna Eleanor Roosevelt," in Barbara Sicherman and Carol Hurd Green with Ilene Kantrov and Harriette Walker, eds., *Notable American Women: The Modern Period* (Cambridge, Mass.: Belknap Press of Harvard Univ. Press, 1980), 595–601.

35. See in addition to Chafe, Karen Anderson, *Wartime Women: Sex Roles, Family Relations, and the Status of Women During World War II* (Westport, Conn.: Greenwood Press, 1981); D'Ann Campbell, *Women at War*

with America (Cambridge, Mass.: Harvard Univ. Press, 1984). On the impact of the war on housewives, see Matthews, *"Just a Housewife"*, chap. 8.

36. In conducting research for *"Just a Housewife,"* I was struck by the way in which women's magazines glamorized both early marriage and very large families in these years.

37. This account is based on Ingrid Winther Scobie, "Helen Gahagan Douglas: Broadway Star as California Politician," *California History* 66 (Dec. 1987): 242–61.

38. Frank Graham, Jr., *Margaret Chase Smith: Woman of Courage* (New York: John Day, 1964), 33.

39. As quoted in ibid., 75. It should be remembered that Senator McCarthy was for a while quite successful in punishing those who opposed him, as Senator Millard Tydings of Maryland learned to his sorrow, when he was defeated for re-election.

40. Cynthia Harrison, *On Account of Sex: The Politics of Women's Issues, 1945–1968* (Berkeley: Univ. of California Press, 1988), 212.

41. Ibid. It should be acknowledged that Martha Griffiths (D-Michigan), who became essential to the flourishing of woman-centered public policy in the 1960s, was first elected in the '50s.

42. Leila J. Rupp and Verta Taylor, *Survival in the Doldrums: The American Women's Rights Movement, 1945 to the 1960s* (New York: Oxford Univ. Press, 1987), 143.

43. Ibid., 25.

44. Worth noting is this finding by Nancy Cott: "Group consciousness among minority group women was a major source of new organizations. Both Jewish women and Catholic women founded numerous voluntary associations during the 1920s and 1930s." Cott, "Across the Great Divide: Women in Politics Before and After 1920," in Louise A. Tilly and Patricia Gurin, eds., *Women, Politics, and Change* (New York: Russell Sage Foundation, 1990), 164.

45. Mamie Garvin Fields and Karen Fields, *Lemon Swamp and Other Places: A Carolina Memoir* (New York: Free Press, 1983).

46. Ibid., 198.

47. Ibid., 236. Bethune had am important position during the New Deal when she was the head of the Office of Minority Affairs in the National Youth Administration.

48. Jacqueline Anne Rouse, *Lugenia Burns Hope: Black Southern Reformer* (Athens: Univ. of Georgia Press, 1989).

49. Ibid., 71.

50. Hall, *The Revolt Against Chivalry*, 101.

51. Zora Neale Hurston was, of course, the major female figure of the Harlem Renaissance. See Robert E. Hemenway, *Zora Neale Hurston: A Literary Biography* (Urbana: Univ. of Illinois Press, 1980).

52. Valerie Matsumoto, "Desperately Seeking 'Deirdre': Gender Roles, Multicultural Relations and Nisei Writers of the 1930s," *Frontiers* 12 (1991): 19–32. Stan Yogi of Berkeley shared with me a bibliography of Asian-American women writers. The earliest writing to reflect a Chinese American point of view was Sui Sin Far [pseud. for Edith Eaton, a Eurasian], *Mrs. Spring Fragrance* (Chicago: A. C. McClurg, 1912).

53. Matsumoto, "Desperately Seeking 'Deirdre.' "

54. This generalization clearly does not apply to black women, who were playing public roles from the time of Phillis Wheatley on. Women in other racial ethnic groups were more recent immigrants.

Chapter 9. Working-Class Women and Public Activism

1. Natalie Zemon Davis, "Women on Top," in Davis, ed., *Society and Culture in Early Modern France* (Stanford: Stanford Univ. Press, 1975), 124.

2. Laurel Thatcher Ulrich, *Good Wives: Image and Reality in the Lives of Women in Northern New England, 1650–1750* (New York: Oxford Univ. Press, 1983), 192f.

3. Susan Levine, "Labor's True Woman: Domesticity and Equal Rights in the Knights of Labor," *Journal of American History* 70 (Sept. 1983): 323–39.

4. Ruth M. Alexander, " 'We Are Engaged as a Band of Sisters': Class and Domesticity in the Washingtonian Temperance Movement, 1840–1850," *Journal of American History* 75 (Dec. 1988): 763–85, 770.

5. Paula Baker, "The Domestication of Politics: Women and American Political Society, 1780–1920," *American Historical Review* 89 (June 1984): 620–47.

6. Levine, "Labor's True Woman," 338f.

7. Ibid., 331.

8. As quoted in the introduction to Mary Harris Jones, *The Autobiography of Mother Jones*, Mary Field Parton, ed., intro. by Fred Thompson (Chicago: Charles H. Kerr, 1972).

9. Ibid., 35.

10. Ibid., 204.

11. James R. Green, *Grass-Roots Socialism: Radical Movements in the Southwest, 1895–1943* (Baton Rouge: Louisiana State Univ. Press, 1978).

12. Ibid., 57f.

13. We still lack a study that would provide a precise account of the first working-class woman to write an autobiography.

14. As quoted in Green, *Grass-Roots Socialism*, 50. See also Philip S. Foner and Sally M. Miller, eds., *Kate Richards O'Hare: Selected Writings and Speeches* (Baton Rouge: Louisiana State Univ. Press, 1982).

15. Green, *Grass-Roots Socialism*, 52.

16. Mari Jo Buhle, *Women and American Socialism, 1870–1920* (Urbana: Univ. of Illinois Press, 1981).

17. Ibid., 187.

18. As quoted in ibid., 222.

19. This account is based on Barbara Mayer Wertheimer, *We Were There: The Story of Working Women in America* (New York: Pantheon, 1977), 267–70.

20. Nancy Schrom Dye, *As Equals and as Sisters: Feminism, the Labor Movement, and the Women's Trade Union League of New York* (Columbia: Univ. of Missouri Press, 1980), 70.

21. Ibid., 88.

22. Ibid., 101.

23. Wertheimer, *We Were There*, 301.

24. Susan A. Glenn, *Daughters of the Shtetl: Life and Labor in the Immigrant Generation* (Ithaca: Cornell Univ. Press, 1990), 173.

25. This account is based on Elizabeth Anne Payne, *Reform, Labor, and Feminism: Margaret Dreier Robins and the Women's Trade Union League* (Urbana: Univ. of Illinois Press, 1988), 61–99.

26. Ibid., 127.

27. Alice Kessler-Harris suggests that a reasonable estimate would be that 6.6 percent of wage-earning women were in unions in 1920. Kessler-Harris, *Out to Work: A History of Wage-Earning Women in the United States* (New York: Oxford Univ. Press, 1982), 152.

28. Ellen Carol DuBois, "Working Women, Class Relations, and Suffrage Militance: Harriet Stanton Blatch and the New York Woman Suffrage Movement, 1894–1909," *Journal of American History* 74 (June 1987): 34–58.

29. Nancy F. Cott, *The Grounding of Modern Feminism* (New Haven: Yale Univ. Press, 1987), 34. See also Eleanor Flexner, *Century of Struggle: The Woman's Rights Movement in the United States*, rev. ed. (Cambridge, Mass.: Belknap Press of Harvard Univ. Press, 1975), 263–65. On California see Sherry Jeanne Katz, "Dual Commitments: Feminism, Socialism, and Women's Political Activism in California, 1890–1920" (Ph.D. dissertation, UCLA, 1991).

30. On nineteenth-century women's writing see Hazel Carby, *Reconstructing Womanhood: The Emergence of the Afro-American Woman Novelist* (New York: Oxford Univ. Press, 1987), and Mary Kelley, *Private Woman, Public Stage: Literary Domesticity in Nineteenth-Century America* (New York: Oxford Univ. Press, 1984). On the women who wrote for the *Lowell Offering* and *Voices of Industry* see Thomas Dublin, *Women at Work: The Transformation of Work and Community in Lowell, Massachusetts, 1826–1860* (New York: Columbia Univ. Press, 1979).

31. Sarah Eisenstein, *Give Us Bread But Give Us Roses: Working Women's Consciousness in the United States, 1890 to the First World War* (London: Routledge and Kegan Paul, 1983), 112.

32. Discussing this issue, Mari Jo Buhle says, "Here historic Jewish culture made its mark. Women had been by definition profane, denied the sacred Hebrew language, kept ignorant to such an extent that illiteracy among Jewish immigrant women was twice that of their menfolk and nearly 50 percent." Buhle, *Women and American Socialism*, 124.

33. Claudia Bushman, *"A Good Poor Man's Wife": Being a Chronicle of Harriet Hanson Robinson and Her Family in Nineteenth-Century New England* (Hanover, N.H.: Univ. Press of New England, 1981).

34. Harriet Hanson Robinson, *Loom and Spindle or Life Among the Early Mill Girls*, intro. by Jane Williams Pultz (Kailua, Hawaii: Press Pacifica, 1976), 52.

35. As, for example, in Jacob Riis, *How the Other Half Lives*, written in 1890.

36. See Ann Schofield, "From 'Sealskin and Shoddy' to 'The Pig-headed Girl': Patriarchal Fables for Workers," Carol Groneman and Mary Beth Norton, eds., *"To Toil the Livelong Day": America's Women at Work, 1780–1980* (Ithaca: Cornell Univ. Press, 1987).

37. See the account of this press in Buhle, *Women and American Socialism*, and Green, *Grass-Roots Socialism*.

38. Theresa S. Malkiel, *The Diary of a Shirtwaist Striker*, intro. by Francoise Basch (Ithaca: ILR Press, School of Industrial and Labor Relations, Cornell University, 1990), 163.

39. Mary Antin, *The Promised Land* (Princeton: Princeton Univ. Press, 1969), 205.

40. Anzia Yezierska, *Bread Givers*, intro. by Alice Kessler-Harris (New York: Persea, 1975). See also Marie Ganz and Nat J. Ferber, *Rebels: Into Anarchy—and Out Again* (New York: Dodd, Mead, 1920), for another view of New York's Jewish community.

41. All the heroines I encountered in my reading seemed to be remarkably earnest.

42. Stephen H. Norwood, *Labor's Flaming Youth: Telephone Operators and Worker Militancy, 1878–1923* (Urbana: Univ. of Illinois Press, 1990), 311. It should be pointed out that Norwood also sees a less positive impact from the consumer culture in that women workers may have been influenced to care overmuch about their appearance.

43. The standard account of this is Irving Bernstein, *The Lean Years: A History of the American Worker, 1920–1933* (Boston: Houghton Mifflin, 1972).

44. Kessler-Harris, *Out to Work*, 243–45.

45. Jacquelyn Dowd Hall, "Disorderly Women: Gender and Labor Militancy in the Appalachian South," *Journal of American History* 73 (Sept. 1986): 354–82, 366. In *Like a Family* Hall and her co-authors say that "public work" was what the southern farmers called their mill jobs. By and large these jobs provided the first-ever wages for these men and women. Jacquelyn Dowd Hall, James Leloudis, Robert Korstad, Mary Murphy, Lu Ann Jones, and Christopher B. Daly, *Like a Family: The Making of a Southern Cotton Mill World* (Chapel Hill: Univ. of North Carolina Press, 1987), 44.

46. Hall, "Disorderly Women," 375.

47. Novels by Meridel Le Sueur include *North Star Country*, *Women on the Breadlines*, and *Salute to Spring*.

48. See Dorothy Healey and Maurice Isserman, *Dorothy Healey Remembers: A Life in the Communist Party* (New York: Oxford Univ. Press, 1990), and Rose Pesotta, *Bread Upon the Waters*, ed. by John Nicholas Beffel, intro. by Ann Schofield (Ithaca: ILR Press, New York State School of Industrial and Labor Relations, Cornell University, 1987).

49. Louise Lamphere, *From Working Daughters to Working Mothers: Immigrant Women in a New England Industrial Community* (Ithaca: Cornell Univ. Press, 1987).

50. Phyllis Palmer, *Domesticity and Dirt: Housewives and Domestic Servants in the United States, 1920–1945* (Philadelphia: Temple Univ. Press, 1989), 125–27.

51. See Ronald W. Schatz, *The Electrical Workers: A History of Labor at GE and Westinghouse, 1923–60* (Urbana: Univ. of Illinois Press, 1983).

52. Ruth Milkman, *Gender at Work: The Dynamics of Job Segregation by Sex during World War II* (Urbana: Univ. of Illinois Press, 1987), 34.

53. Vicki L. Ruiz, *Cannery Women, Cannery Lives: Mexican Women, Unionization, and the California Food Processing Industry, 1930–1950* (Albuquerque: Univ. of New Mexico Press, 1987), 35.

54. Ibid., 89–91.

55. These workers are the subject of my doctoral dissertation, "A California Middletown: The Social History of San Jose during the Depression" (Stanford University, 1977).

56. For a full account of these events, see Matthews, "The Fruit Workers of the Santa Clara Valley: Alternative Paths to Union Organization during the 1930s," *Pacific Historical Review* 54 (Feb. 1985): 51–70. There is no evidence that this union, absorbed by the Teamsters in 1945, ever took an interest in gender equity.

The canneryworkers' union never achieved the status of being an international within the AFL. Rather, it had the status of being a federal labor union, chartered directly by the AFL and inherently vulnerable to being taken over by another international.

57. Healey and Isserman, *Dorothy Healey Remembers*, 37.

58. The lynching in November 1933 had nothing to do with the labor movement, but it terrified all those who were trying to organize in the area. During the general strike in San Francisco in the summer of 1934, vigilantes visited the homes of all known radicals in the Santa Clara Valley, beat them, and drove them into the adjoining county, where they were unceremoniously dumped. See John Terry, "The Terror in San Jose," *The Nation*, Aug. 8, 1934.

59. See Matthews, "The Fruit Workers of the Santa Clara Valley."

60. See Robert Shaffer, "Women and the Communist Party, USA, 1930–1940," *Socialist Review* 9 (May/June 1979): 73–118.

61. Kessler-Harris, *Out to Work*, 291.

62. Milkman, *Gender at Work*.

63. Dorothy Sue Cobble, "Reassessing the 'Doldrum Years': Working-Class Feminism," talk given to the Eighth Berkshire Conference on the History of Women, Rutgers University, June 1990. Professor Cobble has kindly given me a copy of the paper.

64. Ibid.

65. Ibid. A recent article by Ruth Milkman is helpful in understanding the changing nature of the relationship between unions and their female constituency. She sets forth four distinct waves of unionization, during each of which women were treated differently.

1) Old-line craft unions in the nineteenth century, women excluded from public life in the country, few women members of unions and no leaders.

2) "New unions" of the 1910s—women workers beginning to be organized but male leaders were suspicious of them.

3) "The third cohort, the CIO unions, emerged in a period when women's position in public life was quite different than it had been in the 1910s." Formal equality for women, but still a disproportionately male membership and leadership.

4) Postwar growth in service sector led to unions with an "affirmative action" ideology—lots of local officers who are female.

See Ruth Milkman, "Gender and Trade Unionism in Historical Perspective," in Louise A. Tilly and Patricia Gurin, eds., *Women, Politics, and Change* (New York: Russell Sage Foundation, 1990).

66. Cobble, "Reassessing the 'Doldrum Years.' "

67. See, for example, Alexander Saxton, *The Indispensable Enemy: Labor and the Anti-Chinese Movement in California* (Berkeley: Univ. of California Press, 1971).

68. Dolores Janiewski, "Seeking 'A New Day and a New Way': Black Women and Unions in the Southern Tobacco Industry," in Carol Groneman and Mary Beth Norton, eds., *"To Toil the Live-long Day": America's Women at Work, 1780–1980* (Ithaca: Cornell Univ. Press, 1987).

Chapter 10. The Rebirth of Feminism

1. On this subject see Elaine Tyler May, *Homeward Bound: American Families in the Cold War Era* (New York: Basic Books, 1988).

2. Matthews, *"Just a Housewife": The Rise and Fall of Domesticity in America* (New York: Oxford Univ. Press, 1987), chap. 8.

3. See John D'Emilio and Estelle Freedman, *Intimate Matters: A History of Sexuality in America* (New York: Harper & Row, 1988), for a further elaboration of this theme.

4. On the profusion of material goods in the postwar era see Thomas Hine, *Populuxe* (New York: Alfred A. Knopf, 1987).

5. Betty Friedan, *The Feminine Mystique* (New York: Dell, 1963).

6. The letters are housed at the Schlesinger Library at Radcliffe. I read a sample of them in my research for *"Just a Housewife"*.

7. The best history of birth control is Linda Gordon, *Woman's Body, Woman's Right: A Social History of Birth Control in America* (New York: Penguin, 1977). I would argue that the greater "safety" of the pill in terms of preventing conception (whatever its safety may be with respect to side effects) relative to such riskier methods as the diaphragm made a vast difference in women's attitudes. I do not know of a study that deals with this issue; my opinion is based on my personal observation.

8. Mary Fair Burks, "Trailblazers: Women in the Montgomery Bus Boycott," in Darlene Clark Hine, ed., and Elsa Barklay Brown, Tiffany R. L. Patterson, and Lillian S. Williams, assoc. eds., *Black Women in United States History*, vol. 16, *Women in the Civil Rights Movement* (Brooklyn: Carlson, 1990), 79.

9. David J. Garrow, ed., *The Montgomery Bus Boycott and the Women*

Who Started It: The Memoirs of Jo Ann Gibson Robinson (Knoxville: Univ. of Tennessee Press, 1987). In the foreword Garrow says that his interest in the Women's Political Council was stimulated by the sight of this letter.

10. Ibid., 44.

11. Charles Payne, "Men Led, but Women Organized: Movement Participation of Women in the Mississippi Delta," in Hine et al., *Women in the Civil Rights Movement.*

12. Ibid., 1f.

13. Carl R. Graves, "Oklahoma City's Lunch Counter Sit-Ins, 1958–1964," *Chronicles of Oklahoma* 59 (Summer 1981): 152–66.

14. Cynthia Harrison, *On Account of Sex: The Politics of Women's Issues, 1945–1968* (Berkeley: Univ. of California Press, 1988), 83.

15. Esther Peterson, "The Kennedy Commission," in Irene Tinker, ed., *Women in Washington: Advocates for Public Policy* (Beverly Hills: Sage Publications, 1983), vol. 7 in Sage Yearbooks in Women's Policy Studies, 27.

16. Harrison, *On Account of Sex*, 137.

17. Ibid., 165.

18. Marguerite Rawalt, "The Equal Rights Amendment," in Tinker, *Women in Washington*, 60.

19. The standard work is Sara Evans, *Personal Politics: The Roots of Women's Liberation in the Civil Rights Movement and the New Left* (New York: Vintage, 1979).

20. Harrison, *On Account of Sex*, 105.

21. Ibid., 176–82.

22. One of the earliest accounts was Jo Freeman, *The Politics of Women's Liberation: A Case Study of an Emerging Social Movement and Its Relation to the Policy Process* (New York: David McKay, 1975). A recent account of radical feminism is Alice Echols, *Daring to Be Bad: Radical Feminism in America, 1967–1975* (Minneapolis: Univ. of Minnesota Press, 1989).

23. I well remember the first time that I used the word "sexism." In 1969, I was the host of a weekly League of Women Voters television program on a local channel in San Jose. I was interviewing a San Jose State University sociologist named Gail Fullerton about the dawning women's movement, and I asked her what she thought about sexism as a concept. We both agreed that it seemed to be useful. Worth noting is the fact that Gail Fullerton went on to be the president of San Jose State University for thirteen years.

24. In 1984 I was teaching at Oklahoma State University, and I received an invitation to talk in honor of women's history month in the small town of Woodward, out near the panhandle. To my delight, the town's women leaders had arranged a women's history exhibit in the local museum. They proudly told me about the battered women's shelter they had founded. In a town of

10,000 people, there were several female medical practitioners and the executive director of the Chamber of Commerce was a woman. I call this strong evidence of profound social change.

25. On radical feminism see Echols, *Daring to be Bad*.

26. See Rochelle Gatlin, *American Women Since 1945* (Jackson: Univ. of Mississippi Press, 1987), 118–28, for a discussion of CLUW.

27. Barbara Baer and Glenna Matthews, "The Women of the Boycott," *The Nation*, Feb. 23, 1974, 234.

28. See D'Emilio and Freedman, *Intimate Matters*, for the history of American sexual attitudes.

29. On supportive lesbian networks in the past see, for example, Blanche Wiesen Cook, "Female Support Networks and Political Activism: Lillian Wald, Crystal Eastman, and Emma Goldman," *Chrysalis* 3 (1977): 43–61.

30. I am thinking of the novels of Rita Mae Brown, for example, *Rubyfruit Jungle*.

31. There is now a vast literature on the relationship between lesbianism and feminism. To my mind a good place to start would be with the work of Adrienne Rich.

32. As Stan Yogi of Berkeley points out, "In the past few years the number of Asian American women writers has grown exponentially." Letter to the author.

33. This is the recollection of my mother, Alberta Nicolais Ingles.

34. See Catherine A. MacKinnon, *Sexual Harassment of Working Women: A Case of Sex Discrimination* (New Haven: Yale Univ. Press, 1979).

35. Ethel Klein, *Gender Politics: From Consciousness to Mass Politics* (Cambridge, Mass.: Harvard Univ. Press, 1984), 1.

36. Ibid., 124.

37. For a fuller discussion of this topic, see Jane J. Mansbridge, *Why We Lost the ERA* (Chicago: Univ. of Chicago Press, 1986), chap. 6.

38. Klein, *Gender Politics*, 22.

39. See, for example, Donald G. Mathews and Jane Sherron De Hart, *Sex, Gender, and the Politics of ERA: A State and the Nation* (New York: Oxford Univ. Press, 1990), on the impact of the ERA in North Carolina.

40. These figures come from the Center for the American Woman and Politics, Eagleton Institute, Rutgers University.

41. Karen M. Eggert Paget, "A Woman in Politics: Change in Role Perception" (Ph.D. dissertation, University of Colorado, Boulder, 1975), chap. 4. From 1978 to 1992 Boulder had an unbroken string of women mayors; from 1981 there were always at least four women on a nine-member city council.

Index